# 게임으로 배우는 영어 회화

조기석 지음

ame-based

# English Conversation

임으로 배우는 영어 회화

조기석 지음

130
pressions
Exams
Review

Real Talk of Native Speakers

MP3
음원 제공

HU:iNE

# Foreword

영어 회화를 할 수 있는 능력을 갖추기 위해서는 문법을 공부하고 영어 단어와 표현을 폭넓게 학습할 필요가 있다. 하지만 문법을 알고 영어 단어와 표현을 익히는 것만으로는 영어 회화가 되지 않는다. 영어 회화는 알고 있는 영어 표현을 실전에 사용하는 능력으로서 수동적인 영어 지식을 능동적인 영어 능력으로 바꾸는 훈련을 통해서 가능해진다.

수동적인 영어 지식을 능동적인 영어 능력으로 바꾸기 위해서는 영어 회화에 실제로 참여할 수 있는 강한 동기 부여가 있어야 한다. 대화에 뛰어들지 않으면 영어 단어를 많이 알고 있고 문법 실력이 좋아도 영어 회화 실력은 향상되지 않는다. 즉 영어 회화의 핵심은 알고 있는 표현을 실제 상황에서 사용하도록 동기를 부여하고 영어 회화를 할 수 있는 여건을 만드는 것이다.

본 교재의 특징은 영어 회화에 필요한 130여 개의 핵심 표현을 학습하고 이 표현을 워드 게임을 통해서 실제로 활용하도록 해주는 전략이다. 본 교재에서 다루는 130여 개의 핵심 표현은 영어 회화를 잘하는 데 필요한 전략적 표현들로서 어떤 주제를 영어 회화에서 다루더라도 꼭 알아야 하는 표현들이다. 이러한 핵심 표현을 학습하고 워드 게임에서 실제로 활용하게 되면 핵심 표현을 공부할 뿐만 아니라 핵심 표현의 활용이 동시에 이루어지는 일석이조의 효과를 기대볼 수 있다. 따라서 본 교재는 영어 초보자뿐만 아니라 영어를 오랫동안 공부했지만, 영어 회화에 자신이 없는 분들에게 아주 적합한 교재이다. 본 교재를 통해서 영어 회화의 지경이 크게 넓혀지기를 바란다.

본 교재가 나오기까지 수고와 격려를 아끼지 않은 한국외국어대학교 출판부 신선호 팀장님과 장혜정 편집자께 감사드리며, 원고 완성에 도움을 준 장성이 선생님께도 감사의 마음을 전한다. 오늘날까지 나를 인도하시고 인생의 새로운 길을 열어주신 하나님께 이 교재를 바친다.

Week 0

# Bookmap

| 주차 | 제목 |
|---|---|
| Week 1 | **What are your hopes?** |
| Week 2 | **Follow-up Questions** |
| Week 3 | **Asking for Clarification** |
| Week 4 | **Interrupting** |
| Week 5 | **Accepting a Question or Interruption** |
| Week 6 | **Expressing Opinions** |
| Week 7 | **Agreeing** |
| Week 8 | **Midterm Exam** |
| Week 9 | **Disagreeing** |
| Week 10 | **Mitigation** |
| Week 11 | **Asking for Opinions and Information** |
| Week 12 | **Ending a Topic of Conversation** |
| Week 13 | **Initiating Conversation** |
| Week 14 | **Review** |
| Week 15 | **Final Exam** |

| 주요 학습 내용 |
|---|
| **Rejoinder**를 사용하여 상대방의 말에 반응하는 전략 |
| **Follow up Question**을 사용하여 대화를 이어나가는 전략 |
| 대화 내용을 명확하게 하는 **Clarification** 전략 |
| 상대의 말에 끼어드는 전략 |
| 상대방의 질문이나 인터럽션을 수용하는 전략 |
| 자신의 의견을 표현하는 전략 |
| 상대방의 의견에 동의하는 전략 |
| 중간고사 |
| 상대방의 의견에 반대하는 전략 |
| 대화를 완화하는 전략 |
| 의견이나 정보를 묻는 전략 |
| 대화 주제를 종결시키는 전략 |
| 모르는 사람과 대화를 시작하는 전략 |
| 복습 |
| 기말고사 |

# Contents

Week 1

# What Are Your Hopes?

**Contents**
1. Rejoinders to show agreement
2. Rejoinders to show support
3. Rejoinders to show surprise
4. Rejoinders to show disbelief
5. Rejoinders to show understanding and make time to respond
6. Rejoinders to show sympathy

**Objectives**
1. To understand functions of 6 types of rejoinders
2. To understand how 6 types of rejoinders are used in real talks
   1) What hopes do you have for your life?
   2) How have your hopes changed since you were young?
   3) What in your life would you not change?

## Intro

### Speaking Skills: Rejoinders

**1. Yeah.**

- to show agreement

Example

A: Gina is a nice person, isn't she?

B: Yeah.

**2. That's right.**

- to show a strong agreement

Example

A: The best place to get fast food is Subway.

B: That's right.

**3. That's cool.**

to show support of a good idea or say that you like something

Example

A: Is it ok if I bring a friend to your party?

B: That's cool.

**4. That's great.**

- to show support of a good idea or say that you like something

Example

A: I got a perfect score on the test!

B: That's great!

**5. Wow!**

- to show surprise

Example

A: I have 10 siblings.

B: Wow!

**6. Really?**

- to show surprise

Example

A: I just got a raise.

B: Really?

**7. Seriously?**

- to show surprise or disbelief

Example

A: I saw a UFO last night.

B: Seriously?

**8. Oh!**

- to show understanding and make time to respond

Example

A: I missed the bus.

B: Oh! That's too bad. What will you do?

9. **I am sorry to hear that.**
   - to show sympathy

Example

A: I failed the test.

B: I'm sorry to hear that.

10. **Oh, no!**
   - to show sympathy or shock

Example

A: I lost my wallet.

B: Oh, no!

## Lecture 1

### Conversation Question 1

▶ **What hopes do you have for your life?**

**Q1. Who mentions wanting to be a healthy person?**

a) Cassandra

b) Andrea

c) Branden

**Q2. Which of the following does not relate to Branden's hopes for a simple life?**

a) Good food

b) His own house

c) Learn Korean

d) Make a lot of money

**Q3. How is Andrea learning Korean?**

a) She uses a language learning app.

b) She takes Korean classes.

c) She learns Korean from her Korean friends.

Script

**Intro**

Branden: Hello, everyone. I'm Branden.

Andrea: Hi, I'm Andrea.

Cassandra: Hi, I'm Cassandra.

Branden: Now, we're going to practice some of those rejoinders that you've been learning in class with a game. Ok? Which will probably be won by me, but we'll see.

Andrea: Hey, hey. Games. If we're talking games, I'm here to win.

Branden: Oh. So...

Cassandra: Don't count me out, don't count me out yet.

Branden: Ok, guys, so the object of the game is to use as many rejoinders as possible within the time limit. So we'll have three minutes, and whoever uses the most rejoinders is the winner.

Andrea: This is a real conversation, right?

Branden: Yeah, we'll be having a natural conversation, based on a question. So, you guys ready?

Andrea: I'm ready.

Cassandra: Sure.

Branden: Ok, let's get started. I'll set the timer now, but first I'll ask the question. What hopes do you have for your life? What hopes do you have for your life? So, we're talking about the future. Starting now.

Andrea: Alright, timer's on.

Branden: What do you guys think?

Andrea: Cassandra, what hopes do you have for your life?

Cassandra: Oooh, that's a pretty hard question to answer. I think my biggest hope is just to be a healthy person. I want to live a very long, healthy life.

Andrea: That's great.

Cassandra: Yeah, it is great! Yeah.

Branden: Wow! So how do you plan on being a healthy person? What will you do?

Cassandra: Ok, well, I meditate, I take vitamins, and I'm trying to get in shape.

Andrea: Aha. Uh.

Branden: So, really, so what is your plan for getting in shape?

Cassandra: My plan...well, actually, I want to join a boxing gym.

Andrea: Really?

Cassandra: Yeah, yes.

Andrea: Uh, have you ever tried boxing before?

Cassandra: No, I've never tried it. But I really like boxing. I would always watch it on TV with my father. So, it would be a cool hobby I think.

Andrea: Ok, so I...I really like working out. I do a lot of things at the gym, and I've tried boxing, but I didn't like it.

Cassandra: Really?

Andrea: Yeah, because I want to really punch a person, but I know I can't do that...

Branden: Oh, no! You can't mean that really, right?

Andrea: Well, I mean you have that feeling, right? So you're doing the action, but you can only punch the air?

Cassandra: Yeah.

Andrea: So, it's...I feel awkward, like I'm not punching anything.

Branden: Yeah, I can understand you might feel that way.

Andrea: Have you ever tried boxing classes?

Branden: Oh, no, I'm not a really physical person. I'm kind of out of shape. Which...well...anyway...

Cassandra: I'm sorry to hear that, Branden! I had to sneak that in there.

Branden: Anyway, yeah, I've always...as for my future aspirations, I don't know. I've always just wanted a simple life, you know? Good food, have my own house, uh, no debt. Simple. Maybe learn Korean.

Andrea: Uh, that went...ok, that was one of my hopes that I wanted to talk about. I've lived in Korea for a long time and my Korean skills are terrible.

Branden: I'm sorry to hear that!

Andrea: Yeah, seriously. Um, so these days I am trying a little harder, I'm using a language learning app, and everyday I try some new words, new vocabulary words, so I hope that my Korean skills will be better.

Branden: Oh, that's great!

**Cassandra:** That's great!

**Branden & Cassandra:** AH!

**Andrea:** I think he got it first.

**Cassandra:** I still have my card.

**Branden:** That's good. Yeah, I took classes. I took Korean classes. And, really, the apps are very good for learning a new language, but you also gotta get that communication in there, so...

**Andrea:** Yeah.

**Branden:** So, friends.

**Andrea:** Yeah. I know I have lots of Korean friends, but they all like speaking English. So...

**Branden:** Oh! I understand.

**Cassandra:** Oh, no!

**Branden:** Because they want to learn English too, yeah.

**Andrea:** That's right.

**Branden:** So we have ten seconds, you guys.

**Andrea:** Oh! Ten seconds? Seriously?

**Branden:** Don't worry. That's cool. We're all doing pretty good! Oh, look!

**Cassandra:** I have so many cards...

**Branden:** We're out, we're out. Ok, alright, so, that's it. Time's over. How many cards do we have? I have two.

**Andrea:** Ok, well I though in an 'oh, no' at the end but really I shouldn't have so I have three.

**Cassandra:** I have six.

**Andrea:** Wh- what happened?

**Branden:** Wah wah wah.

**Cassandra:** I don't know!

**Branden:** Ok, well, it's a tie, but don't worry, Cassandra, you're going to have another chance. We have two more rounds to go.

**Andrea:** We believe in you.

**Cassandra:** Thank you. That's great.

**Branden:** So we're gonna see what happens next time. Let's see what happens.

**[Answer]**

**Q1. Who mentions wanting to be a healthy person?**

a) Cassandra

b) Andrea

c) Branden

Cassandra: Oooh, that's a pretty hard question to answer. I think my biggest hope is just to be a healthy person. I want to live a very long, healthy life.

**Q2. Which of the following does not relate to Branden's hopes for a simple life?**

a) Good food

b) His own house

c) Learn Korean

d) Make a lot of money

Branden: Anyway, yeah, I've always...as for my future aspirations, I don't know. I've always just wanted a simple life, you know? Good food, have my own house, uh, no debt. Simple. Maybe learn Korean.

**Q3. How is Andrea learning Korean?**

a) She uses a language learning app.

b) She takes Korean classes.

c) She learns Korean from her Korean friends.

Andrea: I'm using a language learning app, and everyday I try some new words, new vocabulary words, so I hope that my Korean skills will be better.

## Conversation Question 2

▶ **How have your hopes changed since you were young?**

**Q1. What did Branden wish for when he was a child?**

a) He wanted to be a special savior like Luke Skywalker.

b) He wanted to be a dinosaur.

c) He wanted to be a father.

**Q2. What did Cassandra wish for when she was a child?**

a) She wanted to be a mother.

b) She wanted to be a dinosaur.

c) She wanted to have superpowers.

**Q3. What did Andrea wish for as a child?**

a) She wanted to have children.

b) She wanted to be a dinosaur.

c) She wanted to have superpowers.

### Script

Branden: Alright, welcome back for round two. Now, if I remember correctly...I won? The last round?

Andrea: You won the last round.

Branden: Oh, that's what I wanted to hear.

Andrea: It was very close.

Branden: Very close.

Andrea: You squeaked out a win.

Branden: Don't worry. You guys have your own chance. You have another chance to win. So, we're going to give you that. So, just like last time we have three minutes to answer a question. Whoever uses the most rejoinders will be the winner. Probably me, but we'll see what happens.

Andrea: It's gonna be me.

**Branden:** Alright, so the question is "How have your hopes changed since you were young?" So I'll start the timer now. How have your hopes changed since you were young? Who wants to start us off?

**Andrea:** I can jump in, I can jump in. I think lots of things have changed since I was young. What does that even mean? When I was five? When I was a teenager? Lots of things...

**Cassandra:** Yeah.

**Andrea:** Oh, nice one.

**Branden:** Yeah.

**Andrea:** Um, I would say, to go very serious here, I think a big change would be when I was a teenager I hoped to have children. And now as an adult I've decided I don't want to have children anymore.

**Branden:** Oh, wow. So that's a huge change.

**Andrea:** I think so. I think so. And it happened slowly, but you know it's, yeah, I think that's the biggest change. And I'm sorry to start with such a...I feel like that's a serious topic.

**Branden:** Yeah, yeah, I totally understand. Like. People change. I'm the same way. Like when we're younger, when I was younger, children? Maybe. But now? Probably not. We'll see.

**Andrea:** So we have something in common there.

**Branden:** Yeah.

**Cassandra:** I'd like to jump in because I'm the opposite. When I was younger, I thought no I would never want to have children...

**Branden:** Oh, really?

**Cassandra:** And now that I'm getting older, I won't say my age, I'm starting to feel the desire. I would like to have children one day.

**Andrea:** Wow! Really?

**Cassandra:** Yeah! Really, really.

**Branden:** Oh, that's cool. Family's good. What can I say? It's good to have people.

**Andrea:** Yeah, and everybody makes their own decisions. That's interesting that you went the opposite of what we're saying.

**Cassandra:** The opposite, yeah.

**Branden:** Well, I was, I was a little different. Uh, When I...no...when I was young, I looked up to superheroes, like Batman, Superman...

**Cassandra:** Really?

**Branden:** Because I wanted to be like a special savior, like Luke Skywalker.

Andrea: That's great.

Branden: Maybe have a special power. But, alas, I'm older now and I have no superpowers.

Cassandra: I'm sorry to hear that!

Branden: I'm just a normal guy, so what can I say.

Cassandra: Seriously? You're just a normal guy?

Branden: That's right.

Cassandra: I think you're pretty cool.

Branden: Ok.

Andrea: Um, how would you, Cassandra, how have your hopes changed since you were young?

Cassandra: Ok, it's a little bit embarrassing, but um, when I was very young, like um let's say five or six years old? My biggest hope was to be a dinosaur.

Branden: Oh!

Andrea: Wow!

Branden: Oh!

Cassandra: Yeah.

Andrea: I love that.

Cassandra: Uh, yeah, I mean it. Like, I was obsessed with dinosaurs, um I would study about them. I would try to memorize all their names. And, you know, what they did and which ones were, you know, the carnivores, which ones were the herbivores.

Branden: Seriously?

Andrea: That's cool.

Branden: What kind of dinosaur did you want to be?

Cassandra: Um, I guess it changed a lot but I think I wanted to be a brontosaurus, like with the long neck? It was very gentle. So, I liked that dinosaur a lot. But that's when I was super young. Then, of course, I got a little bit older and my hopes changed. Then I think next I wanted to be an actress or something.

Andrea: Oh, no! So you don't still want to be a dinosaur?

Cassandra: Um, where's the "that's right" card? I don't have it.

Branden: Alright, guys, actually stop right there, we're out of time. Three minutes is up. So let's count our points. Hmmm. Three points. I mean, three cards.

Andrea: I have three, too!

Cassandra: I have six.

Branden: Oh, ok.
Andrea: Same as last time!
Branden: Uh, ok, so it's a tie.
Andrea: Oh! No, sorry.
Branden: So, to reiterate...cheating! Cheating! Ok, so, I have one, and then we are tied for the second round, we'll keep it as a tie. Cassandra, I'm sorry to say that you're falling behind. But, don't worry, you'll have one more chance. Ok?
Cassandra: Ok.
Branden: So, we have one more round after this. Let's get ready for that.

**[Answer]**

**Q1. What did Branden wish for when he was a child?**

a) He wanted to be a special savior like Luke Skywalker.
b) He wanted to be a dinosaur.
c) He wanted to be a father.

Branden: Because I wanted to be like a special savior, like Luke Skywalker.

**Q2. What did Cassandra wish for when she was a child?**

a) She wanted to be a mother.
b) She wanted to be a dinosaur.
c) She wanted to have superpowers.

Cassandra: Ok, it's a little bit embarrassing, but um, when I was very young, like um let's say five or six years old? My biggest hope was to be a dinosaur.

**Q3. What did Andrea wish as a child?**

a) She wanted to have children.
b) She wanted to be a dinosaur.
c) She wanted to have superpowers.

Andrea: Um, I would say, to go very serious here, I think a big change would be when I was a teenager I hoped to have children. And now as an adult I've decided I don't want to have children anymore.

## Conversation Question 3

▶ **What in your life would you not change?**

**Q1. What would Branden not change in his life?**

a) His height
b) His job
c) His family

**Q2. Where did Andrea meet her husband?**

a) Korea
b) Canada
c) Switzerland

**Q3. What would Cassandra not change in her life?**

a) Her height
b) Her boyfriend
c) Her family

### Script

**Branden:** Hello, everyone, and welcome back. So now it's time for round three. So, who is winning so far?
**Andrea:** Ugh, I don't remember. I can't remember who's winning. Do you?
**Cassandra:** Well...
**Branden:** I'm winning. I'm winning. I'm the winner.
**Cassandra:** We know. You don't need to rub it in.

Branden: Ok, so just to reiterate, I won round one. And then Andrea and I, we tied for round two. That's correct.

Anrea: Yup. Tied. Same amount.

Branden: And what about Cassandra? How many rounds did she win?

Cassandra: None yet...

Branden: Zero.

Cassandra: But I think I'll win this round.

Branden: Yeah...

Cassandra: There's a chance...

Branden: There's a chance. Because, uh, round three is special. We're going to have four minutes to talk and to use our rejoinders. And round three is worth not one point, but two points. So there is a chance for Cassandra to win, if you win round three. Kind of unlikely, but we're giving her a chance.

Cassandra: Hey, hey.

Branden: Alright, so let's get started. I'll set the timer for four minutes. The question: "what in your life would you not change?" Ok? So, there are some things in our life that are good, that we don't want to change. Let's talk about that. Uh, would any of you like to start us off?

Andrea: I can, I can. Uh...I would say this one is a pretty easy answer for me. So, maybe the biggest decision I've ever made in my life was to move to Korea. I'm from Canada. Oh, yeah, get in the game!

Cassandra: Oh! Me too. I'm Canadian. I'm Canadian as well.

Andrea: And, so, uh, moving to Korea was a big...a big jump and I made the decision very quickly.

Branden: Oh.

Andrea: And I would ne- I'm so glad that I did it. I met my husband here.

Branden: Oh, that's great!

Cassandra: Really?

Andrea: Yes, and, you know, all...like I said in other ones, my life has changed a lot but all for the good. I'm happy. It's a good life.

Cassandra: That's great to hear.

Branden: Yeah, it seems like your decision to move to Korea has turned out for the best.

Andrea: I would say that. Maybe you guys have similar...similar experience? You've...

Branden: Sure, yeah, one thing that I wouldn't change is my family. I have my parents, my brother, what can I say? I had a happy childhood. It's great to have a brother, you know, when you're- there's always somebody to play with, somebody to hang out with, so what can I say? I wouldn't change it for the world.

**Andrea:** That's cool. That's really nice to hear. That's heartwarming.

**Cassandra:** Yeah, that's great.

**Branden:** Thank you. Thank you. Cassandra, what about you? Is there something in your past that you wouldn't change?

**Cassandra:** My past... I was thinking of answering this question a little differently. Because I want to focus on my stature.

**Branden:** Seriously?

**Cassandra:** Yeah, so...

**Branden:** So, stature is how tall or short you are.

**Cassandra:** Yeah, so, like, I know there are some girls who would want to be taller, you know, to look like a model.

**Branden:** That's right.

**Cassandra:** But for me I'm kind of on the shorter side, and, you know what, I wouldn't change it. I like being a shorter person.

**Andrea:** Wow!

**Cassandra:** Yeah.

**Branden:** That's cool.

**Andrea:** I'm pretty tall, and I sometimes...I like being tall, but uh sometimes I would rather be shorter. On an airplane, for example. If you're taller on an airplane, that's terrible. I would love to be short traveling like that.

**Branden:** Yeah, I think I sort of understand what you're saying. I hit my head all the time. The other day, I was leaving my house.

**Andrea:** Oh!

**Cassandra:** I'm sorry to hear that.

**Branden:** Walked...I walked out the door and hit my head because the floor is too short. So...yeah, definitely being tall has its ups and downs.

**Cassandra:** Literally.

**Branden:** Literally.

**Cassandra:** Good pun.

**Andrea:** Was that a joke? Yeah...

**Branden:** Yeah.

**Andrea:** Yeah. Nice one.

**Branden:** Good.

Andrea: Yea, it's hard to think about what we would not change. Because there's so many things...people usually ask what would you change?

Cassandra: Yeah.

Andrea: What would you change? And you have those lists going in your head. But, yeah, it's good to think about what would you not change. What are you happy about?

Branden: I think there's many things to be happy about. I mean, no matter, no matter who we are, we're better off than somebody else. You know. We're.. I think. It's all a matter of perspective.

Andrea: The grass is always greener. If you're an idiom kind of person.

Branden: Yeah.

Andrea: Look it up. This is not an idiom lesson.

Cassandra: That's cool, that's cool.

Branden: Really? Are you sure? Right.

Andrea: Alright, so, anything else?

Branden: Anything else?

Andrea: Hmm...I have, I have two cats, and I would say I would not change that. They are lovely. I have a friend, though, that also has two cats, she rescued two cats, they have disabilities.

Cassandra: Oh, no!

Branden: I'm sorry to hear that.

Andrea: Yeah, but, and she loves them. They're so cute and they're so sweet, but they cause her a lot of problems.

Cassandra: Seriously?

Andrea: Seriously!

Cassandra: Seriously?

Branden: Seriously? Are you done?

Cassandra: Yeah, I just placed it and I want to hear her finish.

Andrea: And she regrets...she's like, she can't give her cats away because she would feel sad but she regrets adopting these cats because she's paying a lot of money. And every day she deals with some problem. So, but, I would not change my cats, so that's mine.

Branden: We're out of time, actually, but I totally understand that with all of the joy that pets bring us, they also bring us some sadness.

Andrea: Yeah. Oh, my goodness.

Branden: Alright, so we are out of time. I am so surprised that I didn't win, Cassandra congratulations I have to hand it to you.

Cassandra: Yeah! The comeback queen. Look at this.
Andrea: And, you were the only one who got rid of...because we never got rid of all of our cards.
Branden: Yeah. You were on fire this time.
Cassandra: Wow. Yeah. Yes. I was saving it until the end.
Andrea: Yeah. Two points for you.
Cassandra: Thank you.
Branden: Alright, so that's all the time we have for now. Um, let's move on to the next part.

**[Answer]**

**Q1. What would Branden not change in his life?**

a) His height
b) His job
c) His family

> Branden: Sure, yeah, one thing that I wouldn't change is my family. I have my parents, my brother, what can I say? I had a happy childhood.

**Q2. Where did Andrea meet her husband?**

a) Korea
b) Canada
c) Switzerland

> Andrea: And, moving to Korea was a big jump and I made the decision very quickly. And I would ne- I'm so glad that I did it. I met my husband here.

**Q3. What would Cassandra not change in her life?**

a) Her height
b) Her boyfriend
c) Her family

Cassandra: I know there are some girls who would want to be taller, you know, to look like a model. But for me I'm kind of on the shorter side, and, you know what, I wouldn't change it. I like being a shorter person.

## Lecture 2

### Rejoinders in Action

**1. Yeah.**

- to show agreement

**Game 2**

Andrea: I think so. I think so. And it happened slowly, but you know it's, yeah, I think that's the biggest change.

Branden: Yeah, yeah, I totally understand. Like. People change. I'm the same way.

Andrea: So we have something in common there.

Branden: Yeah.

**Game 1**

Branden: Ok, guys, so the object of the game is to use as many rejoinders as possible within the time limit. So we'll have three minutes, and whoever uses the most rejoinders is the winner.

Andrea: This is a real conversation, right?

Branden: Yeah, we'll be having a natural conversation, based on a question.

**2. That's right.**

- to show a strong agreement

**Game 2**

Branden: I'm just a normal guy, so what can I say.

Cassandra: You're just a normal guy?

Branden: That's right.

**Game 3**

Cassandra: Yeah, so, like, I know there are some girls who would want to be taller, you know, to look like a model.

Branden: That's right.

**3. That's cool.**

- to show support of a good idea or say that you like something

**Game 3**

Cassandra: But for me I'm kind of on the shorter side, and, you know what, I wouldn't change it. I like being a shorter person.

Branden: That's cool.

**Game 3**

Branden: Sure, yeah, one thing that I wouldn't change is my family. I have my parents, my brother, what can I say? I had a happy childhood. It's great to have a brother, you know, when you're- there's always somebody to play with, somebody to hang out with, so what can I say? I wouldn't change it for the world.

Andrea: That's cool.

**4. That's great.**

- to show support of a good idea or say that you like something

**Game 1**

Cassandra: Oooh, that's a pretty hard question to answer. I think my biggest hope is just to be a healthy person. I want to live a very long, healthy life.

Andrea: That's great.

**Game 2**

Branden: Well, I was, I was a little different. When I was young, I looked up to superheroes, like Batman, Superman... Because I wanted to be like a special savior, like Luke Skywalker.

Andrea: That's great.

5. **Wow!**

- to show surprise

**Game2**

Cassandra: And now that I'm getting older, I won't say my age, I'm starting to feel the desire. I would like to have children one day.

Andrea: Wow!

**Game2**

Cassandra: Ok, it's a little bit embarrassing, but um, when I was very young, like um let's say five or six years old? My biggest hope was to be a dinosaur.

Andrea: Wow!

6. **Really?**

- to show surprise

**Game1**

Branden: So what is your plan for getting in shape?

Cassandra: My plan... well, actually, I want to join a boxing gym.

Andrea: Really?

**Game2**

Cassandra: I'd like to jump in because I'm the opposite. When I was younger, I thought no I would never want to have children...

Branden: Oh, really?

7. **Seriously?**

- to show surprise or disbelief

**Game1**

Branden: So we have ten seconds, you guys.

Andrea: Oh! Ten seconds? Seriously?

**Game3**

Branden: Thank you. Cassandra, what about you? Is there something in your

| | |
|---|---|
| | past that you wouldn't change? |
| **Cassandra:** | My past... I was thinking of answering this question a little differently. Because I want to focus on my stature. |
| **Branden:** | Seriously? |

**8. Oh!**

- to show understanding and make time to respond

**Game1**

| | |
|---|---|
| **Andrea:** | Cassandra, what hopes do you have for your life? |
| **Cassandra:** | Oooh, that's a pretty hard question to answer. I think my biggest hope is just to be a healthy person. I want to live a very long, healthy life. |

**9. I am sorry to hear that.**

- to show sympathy

**Game1**

| | |
|---|---|
| **Andrea:** | Have you ever tried boxing classes? |
| **Branden:** | Oh, no, I'm not a really physical person. I'm kind of out of shape. Which...well...anyway... |
| **Cassandra:** | I'm sorry to hear that, Branden! I had to sneak that in there. |

**Game3**

| | |
|---|---|
| **Branden:** | Yeah, I think I sort of understand what you're saying. I hit my head all the time. The other day, I was leaving my house. |
| **Cassandra:** | I'm sorry to hear that. |

**10. Oh, no!**

- to show sympathy or shock

**Game3**

| | |
|---|---|
| **Andrea:** | Hmm...I have, I have two cats, and I would say I would not change that. They are lovely. I have a friend, though, that also has two cats, she rescued two cats, they have disabilities. |
| **Cassandra:** | Oh, no! |

## Word Power

**1. count out**
- leave out, exclude

| | |
|---|---|
| Branden: | Ok? Which will probably be won by me, but we'll see. |
| Andrea: | Games. If we're talking games, I'm here to win. |
| Cassandra: | Don't count me out, don't count me out yet. |

**2. get in shape**
- be in good physical condition

| | |
|---|---|
| Branden: | Wow! So how do you plan on being a healthy person? What will you do? |
| Cassandra: | Ok, well, I meditate, I take vitamins, and I'm trying to get in shape. |

**3. squeak out**
- achieve something by a small margin

| | |
|---|---|
| Andrea: | You won the last round. |
| Branden: | Oh, that's what I wanted to hear. |
| Andrea: | It was very close. |
| Branden: | Very close. |
| Andrea: | You squeaked out a win. |

**4. be obsessed with**
- keep thinking about something without being able to think about anything else

| | |
|---|---|
| Cassandra: | Uh, yeah, I mean it. Like, I was obsessed with dinosaurs, um I would study about them. I would try to memorize all their names. And, you know, what they did and which ones were, you know, the carnivores, which ones were the herbivores. |

**5.** **tie**

- to be equal in a competition

> Branden: Ok, so just to reiterate, I won round one. And then Andrea and I, we tied for round two. That's correct. .

**6.** **hang out**

- spend time socializing in a particular place or with particular people

> Branden: I had a happy childhood. It's great to have a brother, there's always somebody to play with, somebody to hang out with, so what can I say? I wouldn't change it for the world.

## Outro

### Dialogue

Cassandra: Hey, Branden, how have you been?

Branden: Hi, Cassandra. I'm good. I've been thinking a lot about my future, actually.

Cassandra: Really? Why? Are you not happy with your life?

Branden: Well, my life is fine. I just want to make sure I achieve everything I hoped to achieve in my life.

Cassandra: That's cool. So, what are your hopes for the future? Anything specific?

Branden: Well, I really want to learn how to play the piano. I also hope that I'll become fluent in Korean. And I hope that I'll be able to retire early...

Cassandra: Seriously? You've got some high hopes for your future.

Branden: I thought they were reasonable. Why? What are your aspirations for the future?

Cassandra: Well, let's see. This weekend I am hoping to meet some friends in Apgujeong to go shopping. Then after that I am hoping to try a new restaurant I heard about. Oh, and Sunday I am really hoping to relax and watch Netflix.

Branden: Ha-ha, so, you don't even think about your future? You don't have any plans you want to accomplish?

Cassandra: That's right. I'd rather live in the present and not worry about the future.

Branden: Oh! Well, I guess everyone has different goals. Funnily enough, I can't accomplish anything without my daily cup of coffee. I'm going to run to the café now. Want something?

Cassandra: Sure, a latte sounds good. I'll join you.

Branden: We never really talked about your hopes. What are your hopes for the future? You must have some.

Cassandra: Yeah. You're right I do have some things I want to accomplish. For example, I really like painting, and I'd love to have my own art exhibit someday.

Branden: That's great! What do you paint?

Cassandra: Oh, whatever inspires me. I mostly paint sceneries, but in Korea there's such cool architecture that I've been painting a lot of that. But I haven't been able to paint recently, because I've been quite depressed.

Branden: Oh, no! Why?

Cassandra: Well, my cat recently passed away, so I haven't felt like painting.

Branden: I'm sorry to hear that.

Cassandra: It's ok. He was old and had been sick for a long time. Hey – there's another aspiration of mine! I'd like to get a new pet.

Branden: Wow! I wasn't expecting you to move on so fast, but actually... I think a new pet could help you feel better. So, do you have any other aspirations? There's got to be something else you hope for your future. Something bigger, perhaps?

Cassandra: Hmmm. Ok. I've got one. I hope that one day I will win the lottery.

Branden: That's a terrible hope! It's so unlikely!

## Wrap-up

1. **Yeah.**
   - to show agreement

2. **That's right.**
   - to show strong agreement

3. **That's cool.**
   - to show support of a good idea or say that you like something

4. **That's great.**
   - to show support of a good idea or say that you like something

5. **Wow.**
   - to show surprise

6. **Really?**
   - to show surprise

7. **Seriously?**
   - to show surprise or disbelief

8. **Oh!**
   - to show understanding and make time to respond

9. **I'm sorry to hear that.**
   - to express sympathy

10. **Oh, no!**
    - to show sympathy or shock

## Assignment

**1. Select the expression that best completes the passage.**

A: That movie was so boring!
B: ____________ It was hard to stay awake while watching it.

1) Wow.
2) I'm sorry to hear that.
3) Oh, no!
4) Yeah.

**2. Select the expression that best completes the passage.**

A: To be honest, I'm not feeling well. My girlfriend broke up with me yesterday.
B: ____________ No wonder you look so gloomy.

1) Oh, no!
2) That's cool.
3) That's right.
4) Oh, so.

**3. Select the expression that best completes the passage.**

A: What grade did you get in the math class?
B: I got an A.
A: ____________ I thought you were terrible at math.
B: I know, right? I studied a lot.

1) True.
2) That's too bad.
3) Wow.
4) Oh, no!

**4. Select the expression that best completes the passage.**

> A: Ok, let's move on to the next interview question. What do you think is your biggest strength as an employee?
>
> B: ________ Well, people have said that I am a great team player and a very diligent worker.

1) Seriously?
2) Really?
3) That's great.
4) Oh!

**5. Select the expression that best completes the passage.**

> A: I am sorry to have to tell you this, but we are going to have to let you go.
>
> B: ________ Can I ask why?
>
> A: It's nothing personal. The company has been having a hard time these days. We are being forced to reduce the number of employees.

1) Yeah.
2) That's right.
3) Seriously?
4) Honestly.

**6. Select the expression that best completes the passage.**

> A: Do you think it would be possible for me to take the day off tomorrow? My grandmother just passed away and I need to take care of some family matters.
>
> B: ________ Take all the time you need.

1) I'm sorry to hear that.
2) It's great to hear that.
3) Yes, I mind.
4) That's right.

**7. Select the expression that best completes the passage.**

A: Did you know that Jason finally got a promotion this time?
B: ____________ That's surprising. I thought that he was a mediocre worker.

1) Really?
2) That's right.
3) That's cool.
4) It's great to hear that.

**8. Select the expression that best completes the passage.**

A: I am thinking about hosting a party at my house this weekend.
B: ____________ Can I come?

1) That's cool.
2) That's right.
3) Oh, no!
4) Suddenly.

**9. Select the expression that best completes the passage.**

A: I am thinking about getting married.
B: ____________ It's about time you settled down.

1) I'm sorry to hear that.
2) Oh, no!
3) That's great.
4) That's right.

**10. Select the expression that best completes the passage.**

A: Is it true that you bought a new car?
B: ______________ A bright red sports car.

1) Wow.
2) Really?
3) Seriously?
4) That's right.

Week

2

# Follow-up Questions

**Contents**

1. Follow-up questions to ask about alternative options or opinions
2. Follow-up questions to ask for clarification
3. Follow-up questions to ask for elaboration

**Objectives**

1. To understand 3 types of follow-up questions
2. To understand how 3 types of follow-up questions are used in real conversations
   1) What was the last major change that you made in your life?
   2) Do you think that change is important?
   3) Do you often rearrange the furniture in your house?

## Intro

### Speaking Skills: Follow-up questions

**1. What about...?**

- to ask about an alternative options or opinions

Example

A: I don't really eat sweet food because sugar is unhealthy.

B: What about fruit?

**2. Is that...?**

- to ask for clarification

Example

A: I went to Pattaya last month.

B: Is that in Thailand?

3. **Do you mean...?**
- to ask for clarification

Example

A: The party will be held at the house on University Avenue.

B: Do you mean the yellow one by the river?

4. **Did you...?**
- to ask about facts and opinions

Example

A: Did you have a party for your birthday?

B: Yes. It was a great party.

5. **Do you...?**
- to ask about facts and opinions

Example

A: Do you use an i-phone or an android phone?

B: I use an android phone.

6. **What...?**
- to ask about facts and opinions

Example

A: I would like to make some small changes.

B: What are some changes you'd like to make?

7. **When...?**
- to ask about time

Example

A: I usually clean out my basement once a year.

B: When do you do that?

8. **Where...?**
- to ask about location

Example

A: I love to travel on vacation.

B: Where do you usually go?

**9. Who...?**

- to ask about people

Example

A: I went to the movies last night.

B: Who did you go with?

**10. How...?**

- to ask about explanations and methods

Example

A: I speak Chinese, Russian, Spanish, and German.

B: How did you learn so many languages?

**11. Why...?**

- to ask about reasons

Example

A: I have to bail early.

B: Why?

## Lecture 1

### Conversation Question 1

▶ **What was the last major change that you made in your life?**

**Q1. What was the last major change Caoimhe made in her life?**

a) She moved to Korea.

b) She stopped drinking.

c) She started intermittent fasting.

**Q2. What color did Cassandra want to dye her hair?**

a) Blue

b) Blonde

c) Brown

**Q3. Who has recently stopped drinking?**

a) Branden

b) Cassandra

c) Caoimhe

### Script

**Branden:** Hello, everyone. Welcome back. I'm Branden Noland.

**Caoimhe:** I'm Caoimhe McCotter.

**Cassandra:** I'm Cassandra Nykyforak.

**Branden:** Alright. So, it's time for a game. This time we're going to be using the rejoinders that you learned for asking questions. Ok? So, just like last time, whoever uses the most rejoinders will be the winner. Probably me, just saying. But we'll see what happens.

**Caoimhe:** You'll see.

**Branden:** Ok. So round 1 will last for three minutes guys, right?

**Caoimhe:** Ok.

**Branden:** Ok. Three minutes. And within that time whoever uses the most rejoinders will be the winner. Ok? Are we ready to start? Let's start this thing. Ok. So, the question is "What was the last major change you made in your life?" Ok? What was the last major change you made in your life? Who wants to start?

**Caoimhe:** I guess I'll start.

**Branden:** Ok, I'll start the timer now.

**Caoimhe:** So, I would say the last big change that I made in my life was intermittent fasting. So, I only eat during certain hours of the day.

**Branden:** Oh! When did you start that?

**Caoimhe:** Oh, I started it maybe about two months ago?

**Cassandra:** Why, why did you start that?

**Caoimhe:** For health reasons I guess, so I want to get into better eating habits.

**Branden:** Did you find that difficult?

**Caoimhe:** It was at the beginning, it's getting easier. What about you, Cassandra? What was the last major change that you made in your life?

**Cassandra:** Hmm, major change. That's a hard question. Maybe the decision to stop dying my hair.

**Caoimhe:** Oh, why did you make that decision?

Cassandra: There's a little bit of a story behind it. Um, a year ago, my hair was dyed blue at a salon by mistake. I wanted to become blonde, but I ended up turning blue.

Branden: Oh, is that your natural color?

Cassandra: Blue?

Branden: No, blonde.

Cassandra: Blonde, well a girl has her secrets. But this is my natural color.

Caoimhe: Did you get your money back when you went to the new experience, the hairdresser? What happened?

Cassandra: No, no. I think the stylist was embarrassed. I was embarrassed. So I went home and washed my hair many times.

Branden: What about a different color? Could you see yourself using a different color? Someday?

Cassandra: I think I want to be natural. I want to enjoy my natural hair color for many many years into the future.

Caoimhe: And can I ask where was the hair salon? Bec ause I do not want to go there.

Cassandra: Oh, just a little salon near my house. So, I think you wouldn't go there.

Branden: Ok. I guess I should start next. So, changes I've made in my life, I go hiking when I'm not working, I try to hike whenever possible for my health. And what else? I stopped drinking. Just because for my health, you know to lose weight. If I drink, I eat too much. So I stopped.

Caoimhe: Oh, who do you go hiking with? I'm so competitive, sorry.

Branden: I usually go hiking alone, but sometimes friends will join me.

Cassandra: Where? Where do you go hiking?

Branden: Uh, there are various mountains in Seoul, such as Suraksan, Bukhansan, Dobongsan, places like that.

Cassandra: When? When do you like to go hiking usually?

Branden: Uh, when it's cooler, so either early in the morning or later in the afternoon.

Caoimhe: So, you quit drinking... what is your favorite thing to drink or what do you miss most about drinking?

Branden: Oh, I used to drink everything normally, wine, yeah, I used to be a wine drinker.

Cassandra: What about beer? Do you drink that too?

Branden: Oh, uh, yes I used to drink beer. But, so do you know about various types of alcohol? You guys?

**Caoimhe:** Um, a little bit. So do you know about various types of alcohol Cassandra?

**Cassandra:** I feel like this is a personal question. Um, I mostly know about wine.

**Branden:** Oh, who do you usually drink with?

**Cassandra:** Who do I usually drink with? Well, I don't really know. My friends?

**Branden:** Oh, ok. That is excellent. Well, I'm sorry to say guys we have to stop here. The three minutes is over, so who's the winner? I have four cards remaining. What about you guys?

**Cassandra:** Oh, I have six remaining.

**Caoimhe:** Whoa, I have three cards remaining!

**Branden:** No!

**Caoimhe:** So we have a winner!

**Branden:** Ok, so I have to hand it to Caoimhe. She was the winner this time. However, we have two more rounds, so we will see what happens next.

**[Answer]**

**Q1. What was the last major change Caoimhe made in her life?**

a) She moved to Korea.

b) She stopped drinking.

c) She started intermittent fasting.

**Caoimhe:** So, I would say the last big change that I made in my life was intermittent fasting. So, I only eat during certain hours of the day.

**Q2. What color did Cassandra want to dye her hair?**

a) Blue

b) Blonde

c) Brown

Cassandra: There's a little bit of a story behind it. Um, a year ago, my hair was dyed blue at a salon by mistake. I wanted to become blonde, but I ended up turning blue.

**Q3. Who has recently stopped drinking?**

a) Branden

b) Cassandra

c) Caoimhe

Branden: I stopped drinking! Just because, for my health, you know to lose weight. If I drink, I eat too much. So I stopped.

## Conversation Question 2

**▶ Do you think change is important?**

**Q1. Why does Cassandra think that technological change is important?**

a) It's happening too fast.

b) It can solve major problems.

c) It's exciting.

**Q2. How often does Branden use social media?**

a) Always.

b) Never.

c) Not often

**Q3. What was Cassandra's last change?**

a) She changed her clothing style.

b) She trimmed her hair.

c) She dyed her hair black.

### Script

**Branden:** Hello, we're back for round 2. Guys, ready? Ok, so unfortunately, I have to report that Caoimhe won the first round, but we're going to change this. We're... it's not going to happen again. We still have round two and three. And, yeah, so we're going to be using the same rejoinders for asking questions, but the question is different. This time, we're asking each other, "Do you think that change is important?" So, it's kind of like a philosophical, general question. Change in, you know, people's appearance, society, you name it. Let's see where the conversation takes us. We're going to give ourselves three minutes to answer this question. Are you guys ready?

**Caoimhe:** Yes!

**Branden:** Ok, let's start now. Ok, so change. Is it important? What do you guys think?

**Caoimhe:** So what kind of change do you mean? Do you... are you... ahh! I can't use it in a question. Do you mean change in relation to appearance? Change in relation to lifestyle? What kind of change do you mean?

**Branden:** Well, let's talk about society, because, you know, it's changing so fast. I mean, just fifty years ago, we had like these old looking cars like... everything changes. So, uh, yeah. Where do you think we can see change in our lives?

**Caoimhe:** Well, in society I think change is coming too quickly in terms of things like technology, I don't think that technology, technological change is so important. What about you, Cass?

**Cassandra:** Oh, I'm somewhat of the opposite opinion. I think that this technological change is quite important to advance us as a species...

**Branden:** Why do you think so?

**Cassandra:** To solve some major problems that we have in the world, such as, you know, like the environmental issues.

**Caoimhe:** So how can technology change environmental issues?

**Cassandra:** I do not know precisely, but I have great faith in our scientists, people much smarter than me.

**Branden:** Ok, uh, what about social media? I think you referred to that before. Is it that important? The way it's changing our lives? Um, I think it is. Like, just twenty years ago, we didn't really have social media, we didn't have Instagram or did we have Facebook? I don't know.

Caoimhe: Well, who here has social media? Who uses social media?

Branden: I don't really use it that much.

Cassandra: Oh, why not?

Branden: Uh, so, yeah...maybe a different type of change? What other types of change have we seen in society or our lives?

Cassandra: Oh, it's hard to comment, especially when you say society because...

Branden: We don't have to talk about society. What about...

Cassandra: Yeah, it's such a big question.

Caoimhe: What about change in appearance? So did you change your appearance in any way recently, Branden?

Branden: Oh, yeah, well I used to wear a lot of suits and a lot of ties, but as I get older, I don't really dress up that much. It might be because I'm becoming lazy. Maybe I'm getting lazier as time goes on. I don't know. My hairstyle has pretty much stayed the same. So, I don't know. I don't dye my hair blue like Cassandra does.

Caoimhe: Cassandra when did you last make an appearance... a change to your appearance?

Cassandra: Uh, maybe just trimming my hair? I can't think of any major... major surgeries that I've done recently.

Branden: When did you trim your hair last?

Cassandra: When? Um, maybe three weeks ago? I try to get regular trims.

Caoimhe: Is that why you look so beautiful today?

Cassandra: Oh, goodness, goodness. Such a charmer, and I'm not able to use any of these.

Branden: Oh, no. I am so sad to say that we are out of time. Which is bad for me. Very bad for me. How much, how many cards do you guys have?

Caoimhe: Good for me.

Cassandra: I've used one card.

Branden: Oh, my goodness. What about you?

Caoimhe: I took over again! So, I only have three cards remaining.

Branden: Ok, so the result is Caoimhe, you're the winner. But I think the third round is going to be a tie-breaker, guys. So, let's stay tuned for round 3.

**[Answer]**

**Q1. Why does Cassandra think that technological change is important?**

a) It's happening too fast.

b) It can solve major problems.

c) It's exciting.

> **Cassandra:** I think that this technological change is quite important to advance us as a species... to solve some major problems that we have in the world.

**Q2. How often does Branden use social media?**

a) Always.

b) Never.

c) Not often.

> **Caoimhe:** Well, who here has social media? Who uses social media?
> **Branden:** I don't really use it that much.

**Q3. What was Cassandra's last change?**

a) She changed her clothing style.

b) She trimmed her hair.

c) She dyed her hair black.

> **Caoimhe:** When did you last make an appearance... a change to your appearance?
> **Cassandra:** Uh, maybe just trimming my hair?

## Conversation Question 3

▶ **Do you often rearrange the furniture in your house?**

**Q1. Why does Caoimhe rearrange her furniture often?**

a) She doesn't have enough furniture to fill the space.
b) She practices feng shui.
c) She likes it when her couch faces a wall.

**Q2. When does Cassandra rearrange her furniture?**

a) When she cleans.
b) Every week.
c) Never.

**Q3. Why doesn't Branden reorganize much?**

a) He practices feng shui.
b) He likes everything to be clean.
c) He's lazy.

### Script

**Branden:** Hello, everyone, and welcome back. So, it's round 3 and fortunately Caoimhe, you've won the last two rounds. I can't believe it. But, we're doing something different this time. Guys, we previously agreed that this round would be worth two points, right?

**Caoimhe:** We agreed, we agreed.

**Branden:** Even if you don't win this round, you can still tie, ok? So, it's going to be worth two points, and yeah, let's use these rejoinders, but we have a different question this time. Ok? A yes or no question. Do you often rearrange the furniture in your house? So, I'll say it again. Do you often rearrange the furniture in your house? Ok? Who would like to go? I'll start the timer now.

**Caoimhe:** Ok, yeah, I'll start. Um, I try to rearrange the furniture as much as possible, so I can feel like I'm in a different environment in my house.

Branden: When do you do that?

Caoimhe: Maybe once every couple of months? Um, I actually did it yesterday. But I have to be really careful because my house is pretty small, so I can only have certain arrangements, but I try to always have good feng shui in my house.

Branden: Ok, so what are the things that you usually change?

Caoimhe: Um, I usually change, especially in my living room, I change my sofa and chairs around a lot. And also my plants because I have a lot of plants and I try to reposition those.

Cassandra: Question. How does feng shui work?

Caoimhe: Oh, so feng shui is about the Chinese practice of putting things in certain positions in order to create harmony. So, for example, your sofa should face the door, for example, not face a wall, maybe?

Branden: But why harmony? Why is that so important?

Caoimhe: Well, this is something you should research, Branden. But it's very important for your well-being. So, don't ask me too many questions about it please.

Branden: Ok.

Caoimhe: That's your homework.

Branden: Point taken.

Cassandra: Do you find that it helps you when you rearrange your house in this manner?

Caoimhe: I do! And what about you, Cassandra?

Cassandra: Oh, about rearranging my house?

Caoimhe: Yeah.

Cassandra: I rearrange my furniture often enough but not excessively, I'm not changing my furniture around every weekend. But maybe like you said, once every few months. Just to, again like you said, just to have a different energy or different feeling in, in my house. And it's a good thing to do when you're cleaning.

Caoimhe: Oh! What about do you often buy new furniture? Or do you keep the same and rearrange it?

Cassandra: I think I keep the same and rearrange it. Because it's a little bit hard to dispose of furniture.

Caoimhe: Yeah, for sure.

Branden: Ok. Well, yeah, as for me I don't really change that often. Like I typically move my house every one or two years, and when I move, that's the time when I change a lot. Like, I organize everything. But after I move in and I get settled, I don't really reorganized that much, to be honest.

**Cassandra:** Ok. Is that because you're lazy?

**Branden:** Absolutely, Cassandra. Absolutely. You guys know this very well. I'm so lazy. What can I say?

**Caoimhe:** So, Cassandra, why did you assume that Branden was lazy?

**Cassandra:** Oh, no! I think - didn't he make that joke earlier? He may have. Or maybe off camera he made that joke. It's only a joke, guys.

**Branden:** What about you, Cassandra? Would you consider yourself a lazy person?

**Cassandra:** Sometimes. Yeah, why not.

**Branden:** How? In what way?

**Cassandra:** How? Are we getting off topic?

**Caoimhe:** This is getting personal.

**Branden:** Ok. So let's talk about, like, we're talking about rearranging our house. How important is it? Like, to rearrange our house, to clean our house, even? Like, what do you guys think?

**Caoimhe:** I think it's pretty important. Cleanliness is important. Who cleans their house the most here? Who do you think?

**Cassandra:** I think me, maybe.

**Branden:** Sorry, guys, I have to stop. I have to stop you.

**Caoimhe:** But we're just getting into it.

**Branden:** I know. So sad. Uh, how many cards do you have? I have five. So, you have five too. Cassandra?

**Cassandra:** Uh, seven.

**Branden:** Ok, so round number 3 is a tie. That means I get two points, Caoimhe gets two points, but in the end, the result, Caoimhe is the all-time winner! What can I say? You're the winner.

**Caoimhe:** Woo! I haven't won anything in so long. This feels good.

**Branden:** I'm… guys, I'm used to losing. I do it all the time. It's my specialty, so to speak. Alright, so that's it for today and hopefully you enjoyed that. It was great review, and we will see you next time.

**[Answer]**

**Q1. Why does Caoimhe rearrange her furniture often?**

a) She doesn't have enough furniture to fill the space.

b) She practices feng shui.

c) She likes it when her couch faces a wall.

> **Caoimhe:** so feng shui is about the Chinese practice of putting things in certain positions in order to create harmony.

**Q2. When does Cassandra rearrange her furniture?**

a) When she cleans.

b) Every week.

c) Never.

> **Cassandra:** I rearrange my furniture often enough but not excessively, I'm not changing my furniture around every weekend. And it's a good thing to do when you're cleaning.

**Q3. Why doesn't Branden reorganize much?**

a) He practices feng shui.

b) He likes everything to be clean.

c) He's lazy.

> **Branden:** But after I move in and I get settled, I don't really recognize that much, to be honest. I'm so lazy. What can I say?

## Lecture 2

### Follow-up Questions in Action

**1. What about...?**

- to ask about alternative options or opinions

**Game 1**

Caoimhe: It was at the beginning, it's getting easier. What about you, Cassandra? What was the last major change that you made in your life?

Cassandra: Hmm, major change. That's a hard question. Maybe the decision to stop dying my hair.

**Game 1**

Cassandra: Blonde, well a girl has her secrets. But this is my natural color.

Caoimhe: Did you get your money back when you went to the new experience, the hairdresser?

Cassandra: No, no. I think the stylist was embarrassed. I was embarrassed. So I went home and washed my hair many times.

Branden: What about a different color? Could you see yourself using a different color? Someday?

**2. Is that...?**

- to ask for clarification

**Game 1**

Cassandra: There's a little bit of a story behind it. Um, a year ago, my hair was dyed blue at a salon by mistake. I wanted to become blonde, but I ended up turning blue.

Branden: Oh, is that your natural color?

**Game 3**

Branden: I typically move my house every one or two years, and when I move, that's the time when I change a lot. Like, I organize everything. But after I move in and I get settled, I don't really

reorganize that much, to be honest.
Cassandra: Ok. Is that because you're lazy?

3. **Do you mean...?**
- to ask for clarification

**Game 2**
Branden: Ok, let's start now. Ok, so change. Is it important? What do you guys think?
Caoimhe: So, what kind of change do you mean? I can't use it in a question. Do you mean change in relation to appearance? Change in relation in lifestyle? What kind of change do you mean?

4. **Did you...?**
- to ask about facts and opinions

**Game 2**
Caoimhe: What about change in appearance? So did you change your appearance in any way recently, Branden?
Branden: Oh, yeah, well I used to wear a lot of suits and a lot of ties, but as I get older, I don't really dress up that much. It might be because I'm becoming lazy.

5. **Do you...?**
- to ask about facts and opinions

**Game 1**
Caoimhe: So, do you know about various types of alcohol, Cassandra?
Cassandra: I feel like this is a personal question. Um, I mostly know about wine.

6. **What...?**
- to ask about facts and opinions

**Game 1**
Caoimhe: So, you quit drinking... what is your favorite thing to drink or what do

you miss most about drinking?

**Branden:** Oh, I used to drink everything normally, wine, yeah, I used to be a wine drinker.

**Game 3**

**Branden:** Ok, so what are the things that you usually change?

**Caoimhe:** Um, I usually change, especially in my living room, I change my sofa and chairs around a lot and also my plants because I have a lot of plants and I try to reposition those.

### 7. When...?

- to ask about time

**Game 1**

**Branden:** Oh! When did you start that?

**Caoimhe:** Oh, I started it maybe about two months ago?

**Game 2**

**Branden:** When did you trim your hair last?

**Cassandra:** When? Uh, maybe three weeks ago? I try to get regular trims.

### 8. Where...?

- to ask about location

**Game 1**

**Cassandra:** Where? Where do you go hiking?

**Branden:** Uh, there are various mountains in Seoul, such as Suraksan, Bukhansan, Dobongsan, places like that.

**Game 1**

**Caoimhe:** And can I ask where was the hair salon? Because I do not want to go there.

**Cassandra:** Oh, just a little salon near my house. So, I think you wouldn't go there.

9. **Who...?**

- to ask about people

**Game 1**

**Caoimhe:** Oh, who do you go hiking with? I'm so competitive, sorry.

**Branden:** I usually go hiking alone, but sometimes friends will join me.

**Game 3**

**Branden:** I think it's pretty important. Cleanliness is important. Who cleans their house the most here? Who do you think?

**Cassandra:** I think me, maybe.

10. **How...?**

- to ask for explanations and methods

**Game 3**

**Cassandra:** Question. How does feng shui work?

**Caoimhe:** Oh, so feng shui is about the Chinese practice of putting things in certain positions in order to create harmony. So, for example, your sofa should face the door and not face a wall, maybe?

11. **Why...?**

- to ask about reasons

**Game 1**

**Caoimhe:** Oh, why did you make that decision?

**Cassandra:** There's a little bit of a story behind it. Um, a year ago, my hair was dyed blue at a salon by mistake. I wanted to become blonde, but I ended up turning blue.

## Word Power

1. **intermittent fasting**
   - to only eat for certain periods of time in the day

Caoimhe: So, I would say the last big change that I made in my life was intermittent fasting. So, I only eat during certain hours of the day.
Branden: Oh! When did you start that?
Caoimhe: Oh, I started it maybe about two months ago?

2. **There's a little bit of a story behind it.**
   - there are important details that you should know to understand what happened

Caoimhe: Oh, why did you make that decision?
Branden: Oh, oh.
Cassandra: There's a little bit of a story behind it. Um, a year ago, my hair was dyed blue at a salon by mistake. I wanted to become blonde, but I ended up turning blue.

3. **natural color**
   - the color that your hair grows naturally

Branden: Oh, is that your natural color?
Cassandra: Blue?
Branden: No, no.
Cassandra: Blonde.

4. **of the opposite opinion**
   - I disagree

Caoimhe: Well, in society I think change is coming too quickly. In terms of things like technology, I don't think that technological change is so important. What about you, Cass?
Cassandra: Oh, I'm somewhat of the opposite opinion. I think that this technological change is quite important to, you know, advance us as a species...

5. **such a charmer**

- a nice person; someone who compliments others a lot

Caoimhe: Is that why you look so beautiful today?
Cassandra: Oh, goodness, goodness.
Caoimhe: Such a charmer.
Cassandra: Such a charmer.

6. **point taken**

- I understand what you're trying to say

Caoimhe: Well, this is something you should research. But it's very important for your well-being. So, don't ask me too many questions about it please...
Branden: That's why, that's why, ok...
Caoimhe: That's your homework.
Branden: Point taken.

7. **getting off-topic**

- talking about something else

Branden: How? In what way?
Cassandra: How? Are we getting off-topic?
Branden: Ok, so...
Caoimhe: This is getting personal!

## Outro

### Dialogue

**Cassandra:** Hey, Branden!

**Branden:** Oh, hi Cassandra. I was wondering, did you have a chance to watch the movie I told you about last week?

**Cassandra:** Do you mean the horror film? Sorry, I try to avoid scary movies.

**Branden:** You don't like horror movies? Why is that?

**Cassandra:** I'm just really uncomfortable when I feel scared, and I also hate surprises! How can you enjoy a movie with ghosts popping up and people screaming every few minutes?

**Branden:** Not every horror movie is like that, you know. When was the last time you actually watched a horror movie from start to finish?

**Cassandra:** I am not sure... Anyway, that's enough about me! It's almost 12 o'clock. Where are you going for lunch today?

**Branden:** I'm thinking of trying out that new Thai restaurant up the street. I've heard good things about it.

**Cassandra:** Oh! Is that the restaurant that serves free iced coffees with your order?

**Branden:** That's the one! What are your plans for lunch? Why don't you join us?

**Cassandra:** Sure! Who are you going with?

**Branden:** Just Tim. You've met him before. We can leave now and pick him up on the way.

**Cassandra:** Actually, I still have a bit of work to do back at the office. What about meeting in front of the restaurant at noon?

**Branden:** That sounds fine. See you there.

## Wrap-up

1. **What about...?**
   - to ask about alternative options or opinions

2. **Is that...?**
   - to ask for clarification

3. **Do you mean...?**
   - to ask for clarification

4. **Did you...?**
   - to ask about facts and opinions

5. **Do you...?**
   - to ask about facts and opinions

6. **What...?**
   - to ask about facts and opinions

7. **When...?**
   - to ask about time

8. **Where...?**
   - to ask about location

9. **Who...?**
   - to ask about people

10. **How...?**
    - to ask for explanations and methods

11. **Why...?**
    - to ask about reasons

## Assignment

**1. Select the expression that best completes the passage.**

A: I have been thinking about travelling to Europe someday.
B: ____________ Italy? They have excellent food and many historical sites.

1) Why
2) Is that
3) What about
4) How

**2. Select the expression that best completes the passage.**

A: ____________ do you boil eggs?
B: Well, first, put the eggs in a pot of water and bring the water to a boil. Then let the eggs cook for 12 minutes.

1) How
2) Why
3) Do you mean
4) When

**3. Select the expression that best completes the passage.**

A: ____________ didn't you invite Jason to the party?
B: Have you seen how crazy Jason gets when he drinks? I thought it would be best to avoid that situation again.

1) What
2) Why
3) When
4) Who

**4. Select the expression that best completes the passage.**

A: ____________ know when World War 1 started?
B: I think it started in the year 1914.

1) How
2) Who
3) Did you
4) Do you

**5. Select the expression that best completes the passage.**

A: ____________ did you leave the toilet paper?
B: Check the cabinet above the fridge.

1) When
2) Where
3) How
4) By the way

**6. Select the expression that best completes the passage.**

A: I parked the car in the parking lot around the corner
B: ____________ the one by the gas station?

1) Are they
2) Who is
3) Toward
4) Do you mean

**7. Select the expression that best completes the passage.**

A: What are you doing?
B: I am playing a computer game.
A: ____________ the game you were playing yesterday?

1) How
2) Are those
3) Is that
4) Why

**8. Select the expression that best completes the passage.**

A: ____________ you know that Jason was caught cheating on his exam?
B: No but that doesn't surprise me at all.

1) Did you
2) What
3) Who
4) When

**9. Select the expression that best completes the passage.**

A: I think we have to clean this room.
B: It looks clean to me. ____________ do you think needs cleaning?
A: The floor needs to be mopped. There is so much dust on it.

1) Why
2) What
3) Who
4) When

**10.** **Select the expression that best completes the passage.**

A: It's getting late. ___________ do you want to sleep?
B: How about at midnight?

1) Who
2) When
3) Why
4) Where

**11.** **Select the expression that best completes the passage.**

A: Do you know ___________ left these flowers at my desk?
B: I don't know, but it looks like you have a secret admirer.

1) Why
2) Where
3) What
4) Who

Week 3

# Asking for Clarification

**Contents**
1. Clarification by using an example
2. Clarification by elaborating on the topic
3. Clarification through a yes-or-no question
4. Clarification with an open-ended question
5. Clarification by expressing disbelief
6. Clarification by expressing an alternative opinion
7. Clarification through an offer or request for more information

**Objectives**
1. To understand 7 types of clarification
2. To understand how 7 types of follow-up clarification are used in real conversations
   1) How do you like to celebrate your birthday?
   2) What is the next birthday gift you expect to receive?
   3) Did your parents give you birthday parties when you were a child?

## Intro

### Speaking Skills: Expressions for Clarification

**1. You're telling me...?**
- to ask for clarification by using an example

Example

A: I didn't get any birthday presents this year.

B: You're telling me even your mom didn't get you a present?

**2. It sounds like...**
- to ask for clarification by elaborating on the topic

Example

A: I got a ton of birthday presents when I was a teenager.

B: It sounds like you were a really popular kid in high school.

3. **... Is that it?**
   - to ask for clarification through a yes-or-no question

Example

A: I don't buy a lot of birthday presents, but I spend a lot on Christmas presents.

B: So you think Christmas is more important. Is that it?

4. **What do you mean...?**
   - to ask for clarification with an open-ended question

Example

A: I don't celebrate my birthday.

B: What do you mean you don't celebrate your birthday?

5. **What are you trying to say?**
   - to ask for clarification with an open-ended question

Example

A: If your girlfriend cared for you, she would have bought you a present.

B: What are you trying to say? My girlfriend doesn't love me?

6. **You think...?**
   - to ask for clarification with a yes-or-no question

Example

A: Birthday parties are dumb.

B: You think birthdays shouldn't be celebrated?

7. **Wait. What?**
   - to ask for clarification by expressing disbelief

Example

A: I've never bought my wife a gift.

B: Wait. What?

8. **I thought...**
   - to ask for clarification by expressing an alternative opinion

Example

A: I got a great birthday present last month.

B: Last month? I thought your birthday was in June.

**9. Okay, so...**

- to ask for clarification through request for more information

Example

A: I think birthday gifts are really important.

B: Okay, so I need to buy you a gift this year? When's your birthday?

**10. What kind of...?**

- to ask for clarification with an open-ended question

Example

A: I'd like some new books for my birthday.

B: What kind of books?

## Lecture 1

### Conversation Question 1

▶ **How do you like to celebrate your birthday?**

**Q1. How have Cassandra's birthday celebrations changed as she has gotten older?**

a) She used to have big parties, but now she keeps it low-key.

b) She used to keep it low-key, but now she has big parties.

c) She has always been low-key, so they're really the same.

**Q2. What does Caoimhe usually do to celebrate her birthday?**

a) Have a party.

b) Travel by herself.

c) Travel with friends.

**Q3. What did Branden usually eat on his birthday when he was a child?**

a) Cake

b) Cookies

c) Cupcakes

Script

**Branden:** Hello, everyone. Welcome back. I'm Branden Oland.

**Caoimhe:** I'm Caoimhe McCotter.

**Cassandra:** I'm Cassandra Nykyforak.

**Branden:** All right, so we're playing another game using the rejoinders that you learned in class. So this time these rejoinders deal with clarification questions. Okay, so you don't quite understand something and you need to clarify it to understand it more fully. Okay, you guys ready?

**Cassandra:** Sure.

**Branden:** All right. So just like last time, we're going to have a round for 3 minutes. But first, I will ask the question. How do you like to celebrate your birthday? Ok? How do you like to celebrate your birthday? Let's get started. Let's get started with Cassandra.

**Cassandra:** Ok, well, starting now, ok, so, well when I was young, I liked to celebrate, you know, with my friends, my family, have this big gathering. But now that I'm older, I prefer something a little more low-key. Something more quiet.

**Branden:** Ok, so you're saying that you don't like big crowds?

**Cassandra:** Perhaps I mean, I think it's more that as I'm getting older, I don't really want to acknowledge that time is passing. So I don't like to put a lot of focus on myself and my age on my birthday.

**Caoimhe:** What kind of things do you do that now? You said low-key?

**Cassandra:** Right.

**Caoimhe:** So what kind of things do you do to celebrate?

**Cassandra:** Um, maybe just a dinner, a really delicious dinner with some very close friends, or going to a spa, or spending the weekend doing something like that.

**Branden:** It sounds like you're a very laid-back person, you like more of a simple style celebration. Is that so?

**Cassandra:** Okay, simple. What are you trying to say? I'm not simple at all!

**Branden:** Oh, sorry, that didn't come out, right?

**Cassandra:** I was trying to use this.

**Caoimhe:** Getting personal. So you think Cassandra is simple?

**Branden:** Oh...

**Cassandra:** Wait, what? Where is this going?

**Branden:** Ah... so, yeah, we gotta be careful with these rejoinders. We could mean something saying something we really don't mean. All right, what about Caoimhe? Tell us about yourself. Your ideal birthday.

**Caoimhe:** Um... I would say also similar to Cassandra. Usually before COVID, I liked just going overseas on my own and just doing it that way because I don't really like the fuss of having a birthday party.

**Branden:** So, you're telling me you're like a traveller? You like to travel?

**Caoimhe:** I would say so, yeah, I really like travelling, yeah.

**Cassandra:** What kind of countries do you like to travel to?

**Caoimhe:** I'm... anywhere. Usually I just kind of pick somewhere and then I go. But I like going somewhere that has a very different culture and somewhere with good weather.

**Cassandra:** Sounds like you are adventurous.

**Caoimhe:** I would say so, but you're telling me that you're not adventurous?

**Cassandra:** I'm... not really.

**Branden:** You're not adventurous, is that it? Is that it, Cassandra?

**Cassandra:** I don't know what's going on here. Don't put words in my mouth. Okay, so, Branden. Did you answer this question?

**Branden:** I did not.

**Cassandra:** I can't remember. Why don't you go?

**Branden:** Yeah, so based on my experience, when we're younger, it's simple. We just get our friends together. You know, we had the cupcakes, did you guys have cupcakes? Western tradition. And then when we were younger we have large groups of friends. But I do have to agree with Cassandra. The older I get, the more low-key I want to keep it. So I tend to have smaller groups of people. I don't like to make a big fuss. Because, let's face it guys, birthdays, they celebrate a year older. A year older, closer to dying. Right?

**Caoimhe:** I thought you were still very young though, Branden?

**Cassandra:** You're telling me you're older that you look?

**Branden:** Oh, well, I may still be young, but I don't feel so. Anyway, that's it, guys. That's a really interesting talk surprisingly. But we're out of time. Let's count up the cards. Who's the winner? I have six. Oh, my goodness. I did not do well this time.

Caoimhe: I think Cassandra is the winner of this one. I still have five.
Cassandra: And I have four.
Branden: Ok, so Cassandra is the winner. We'll give it to her, but two more rounds remain. Let's see what happens next.

**[Answer]**

**Q1. How have Cassandra's birthday celebrations changed as she has gotten older?**

a) She used to have big parties, but now she keeps it low-key.

b) She used to keep it low-key, but now she has big parties.

c) She has always been low-key, so they're really the same.

Cassandra: well when I was young, I liked to celebrate, you know, with my friends, my family, have this big gathering. But now that I'm older, I prefer something a little more low-key. Something more quiet.

**Q2. What does Caoimhe usually do to celebrate her birthday?**

a) Have a party.

b) Travel by herself.

c) Travel with friends.

Caoimhe: Usually before COVID I liked just going overseas on my own and just doing it that way because I don't really like the fuss of having a birthday.

**Q3. What did Branden usually eat on his birthday when he was a child?**

a) Cake

b) Cookies

c) Cupcakes

Branden: Yeah, so based on my experience, when we're younger, it's simple. We just get our friends together. You know, we had the cupcakes, did you guys have cupcakes? Western tradition.

## Conversation Question 2

▶ **What is the next birthday gift you expect to receive?**

**Q1. Why does Cassandra accuse Branden of having expensive taste?**

a) He's offered to buy everyone a new PC game.

b) He saves more money than he spends on technology.

c) All of his expected gifts are expensive items.

**Q2. Why does Caoimhe usually receive money for her birthday?**

a) She is hard to buy gifts for.

b) She is really materialistic.

c) She hates her birthday.

**Q3. What does Cassandra prefer to receive for her birthday?**

a) An experience

b) A big, expensive gift

c) A puppy

### Script

**Branden:** All right. Welcome back to round 2. So, yeah. Last time, Cassandra was the winner, right? Yeah, congratulations. But it's not over yet. Okay, so we still have more chances to redeem ourselves. We're gonna practice using rejoinders for 3 minutes, but the question is different. I'll share that with you guys now. What is the next birthday gift you expect to receive? I'll say it again. What is the next birthday gift you expect to receive? Ok. Who would like to go first?

**Caoimhe, Cassandra:** How about you?

**Branden:** Oh, ok. Putting the pressure on Branden. Surprise, surprise. Ok, yeah, so birthday gift., What can I say? Games? Computer games? Technology? A new phone? A new computer, or whatever? A watch, maybe? All of those are good. Money? We usually don't receive money as a birthday gift, but...

**Caoimhe:** Okay, so I guess you have rich friends if you're expecting a computer for your birthday or a cell phone.

**Branden:** Oh, those are the best kinds of friends to have.

**Cassandra:** It sounds like you have expensive taste.

**Branden:** Well, what can I say... So, yeah, what are you trying to say, Cassandra? Am I too expensive?

**Cassandra:** No, I want to know more, so like what kind of technology are you into?

**Branden:** Sure. Well, these days you can buy games in an online marketplace and somebody from the convenience of their own computer can just use their credit card and send you a game.

**Caoimhe:** Wait, what? Someone can just send you a game?

**Branden:** Yeah, sure, things are becoming so convenient these days. Okay, I'm gonna take the pressure off to me. Caoimhe, please. What kind of birthday gift?

**Caoimhe:** Um, the next birthday gift I expect to receive... probably money. Like, I'm a pretty difficult person to buy for, so usually my friends and family just give me money.

**Branden:** Wait, what? Are you saying you're materialistic?

**Caoimhe:** No, I'm saying that it's difficult to buy a gift to suit me. So I like to just receive money. Not a large amount.

**Branden:** Okay, so you're saying that you don't want to think too much about it. You want it to be a little simpler.

**Caoimhe:** You think I don't like thinking about things?

**Branden:** It sounds like you're overthinking things, Caoimhe.

**Cassandra:** Wait, what? I think we're getting off topic again.

**Branden:** Okay. What about you, Cassandra?

**Cassandra:** Well, I agree with the both of you. I think money is the most practical gift to receive, but I'm also a fan of not getting an object or something physical for my birthday. I could get an experience. Like, like I said before, like a nice dinner, or, you know, time with friends. Like, that could give me an experience.

**Branden:** What kind of dinner are you referring to?

**Cassandra:** Oh, maybe lobster? Something nice.

**Branden:** That's good. Fine dining.

**Cassandra:** Fine dining, yeah.

**Caoimhe:** What kind of experiences have you received in the past for your birthday?

**Cassandra:** What kind of experience? Oh, I don't know offhand, but, like you said earlier, a trip. Travelling somewhere new for your birthday weekend is always fun, a different country.

Branden: Ok, so yeah. Uh, we have - we've talked about fancy dinners, travel. Is that it guys? Anything else?

Caoimhe: I'm… I would say it sounds like there are still more to talk about. Um, so, I would say also maybe, yeah, as Cassandra said, maybe a trip? Um, I would also quite like a puppy for my next birthday.

Branden: You're telling me you're going to get a puppy soon?

Caoimhe: I hope so, but I don't know.

Branden: I want a puppy too. This sounds cool. Oh, you guys hear that? It looks like time's up. So, I have three cards. What about you guys?

Caoimhe: I have used five and I have four leftover. No, I have five leftover.

Cassandra: Oh, it's exciting.

Branden: Yes, I'm so happy to say this, but Branden is the winner for round 2. So, I won round 2. What about in Cassandra? You did in round 1, right?

Caoimhe: I am losing hard, but I have one round to make up.

Branden: Yeah, perhaps you still have a chance. We'll have to see it. That's it for now.

**[Answer]**

**Q1. Why does Cassandra accuse Branden of having expensive taste?**

a) He's offered to buy everyone a new PC game.

b) He saves more money than he spends on technology.

c) All of his expected gifts are expensive items.

Branden: What can I say? Games? Computer games? Technology? A new phone? New computer, whatever? All of those are good.

Cassandra: It sounds like you have expensive taste.

**Q2. Why does Caoimhe usually receive money for her birthday?**

a) She is hard to buy gifts for.

b) She is really materialistic.

c) She hates her birthday.

> **Caoimhe:** the next birthday gift I expect to receive... probably money. Like, I'm a pretty difficult person to buy for, so usually my friends and family just give me money.

**Q3. What does Cassandra prefer to receive for her birthday?**

a) An experience

b) A big, expensive gift

c) A puppy

> **Cassandra:** I could get an experience. Like, like I said before, like a nice dinner, or, you know, time with friends. Like, give me an experience.

## Conversation Question 3

**▶ Did your parents give you birthday parties when you were a child?**

**Q1. Which of these did Cassandra not do for her birthday as a child?**

a) Wear green.

b) Go to an amusement park.

c) Go to a restaurant.

**Q2. On what day do Irish people typically wear green?**

a) Their birthday

b) Irish people never wear green.

c) St. Patrick's Day

**Q3. Why does Branden think birthday parties are important for kids?**

a) They can have expensive parties.

b) They can eat cupcakes.

c) They can learn social skills.

Script

**Branden:** Hello, everyone, and welcome back. So this is round three of your game with the rejoinders that you learned in class. So, so far, Cassandra, you won one round. Is that correct?

**Cassandra:** Correct.

**Branden:** Good. I did that, I was the victor in round 2. So, don't worry, Caoimhe. You have a chance. If you win round 3, you can tie.

**Caoimhe:** Okay, keep confident!

**Branden:** Ok, good good. So we have a different question. I'm going to share that with you now. Did your parents give you birthday parties when you were a child? I'll say that one more time. Did your parents give you birthday parties when you were a child? Ok, so, yeah, I'll start the timer now and I'll start. Yeah. So, in my experience, birthday parties were pretty typical when I was a child, the parents would invite the children over to the house or whoever, whichever kid was having the birthday, they would have pizza, cupcakes, I don't know. Just like in the movies, really.

**Caoimhe:** Ok, so were those your classmates or your friends that came to your house?

**Branden:** Both. Yeah, there was some mixing going on there.

**Cassandra:** It sounds like my experience in Canada, you know, just all your friends are  coming over, some classmates, maybe even some relatives like your family members, cousins. Everyone's mixing together

**Branden:** Sure. So maybe you can tell us more about the Canadian birthday.

**Cassandrea:** The Canadian birthday? I don't think there's a typical Canadian birthday, but, yeah, my experience, like Branden said, you know, parties with your friends. Maybe doing something outdoors, such as an amusement park or going camping. Going to a restaurant. Sitting on a patio.

Branden: It sounds like there's really no real traditional birthdays in either Canada or America. They're all different.

Cassandra: I guess so. It depends on the family.

Branden: True. Family.

Cassandra: Yeah, how about in Ireland?

Caoimhe: Um, it sounds, yeah, pretty much the same. So I guess I would just have a birthday party usually at my house each year with my classmates or friends and just invite them to my house. Just have cake, play games.

Branden: I thought that Ireland, the Irish people used a lot of green in there.

Caoimhe: Ah··· I think that might be a stereotype. Wait, what? What are you trying to say about Ireland?

Braden: I must have thought, I must be talking about St. Patrick's Day, right?

Caoimhe: Yeah, on St. Patrick's Day. So, you're telling me you know St. Patrick's Day?

Branden: Oh, I do. Yeah, it's, you guys go to a pub and you know wear green and hang out together.

Caoimhe: It sounds like you have seen a lot of people in green from Ireland, but have you ever seen me wear in green?

Branden: Ok. I have to admit. I'm ignorant of many things, guys. Yeah, perhaps we can change the subject a little bit. We're not children anymore. Let's imagine. If we had children, what kind of birthday parties would we throw for our kids? What do you think is the best type of birthday party?

Caoimhe: So, I think from what I've heard in Korea, a lot of kids these days have like sleepovers at hotels. So, it's···

Branden: Wait, what? Hotels? That's expensive.

Caoimhe: Yeah, you think so too? I think that they must cost so much money. So I don't know if I would be spending so much money on a kid's party.

Branden: I do think it's really important for them, for especially when the kids are younger, for them to have those social opportunities because that's where they learn social skills and learn how to be little humans.

Caoimhe: What do you mean little humans?

Branden: Well, they are little humans. They gotta learn how to interact in society. So, yeah, I think that birthday parties are important. We should make our kids socialize.

**Caoimhe:** So, what kind of parties do you think kid should have these days, Cassandra?

**Cassandra:** Oh, goodness. I don't know what children should have, but I mean, I can only talk about what I think my future children would want to have. And I think something similar to have I celebrated on my birthday. I think I would keep that tradition going, kind of give them something similar to what I experienced.

**Branden:** Oh, what are you trying to say? You want children someday?

**Cassandra:** Um, perhaps.

**Branden:** Perhaps. Ok, yeah. You think it's a good idea?

**Cassandra:** You're just trying to use all your cards, is that it?

**Caoimhe:** You're just using all your cards, is that it?

**Branden:** Yeah, you guys caught me. Just because I want to win. I'm a winner. Ok, well.

**Caoimhe:** I thought I was going to win this one and it looks like I'm right. So, all of my cards are gone.

**Branden:** You just had to ruin it, didn't you, Caoimhe.

**Caoimhe:** I'm sorry.

**Branden:** No, it's ok.

**Cassandra:** We have a winner.

**Branden:** So, yeah, it's fine. Sometimes we don't win all the games, you know, I'm actually very, I lose quite frequently. So this is no surprise, but I didn't lose this time because it is a draw. You won one, one point, one point, and one point, right? So, yeah, we can all feel good about ourselves.

**Caoimhe:** That's true.

**Branden:** So guys, this is the end. We learned all about rejoinders for asking clarification questions. And hopefully you enjoyed that and stay tuned for the next part.

**[Answer]**

**Q1. Which of these did Cassandra not do for her birthday as a child?**

a) Wear green.

b) Go to an amusement park.

c) Go to a restaurant.

> **Cassandra:** Maybe doing something outdoors, such as an amusement park or going camping. Going to a restaurant. Sitting on a patio.

**Q2. On what day do Irish people typically wear green?**

a) Their birthday

b) Irish people never wear green.

c) St. Patrick's Day

> **Branden:** I must have thought, I must be talking about St. Patrick's Day, right? ... you guys go to a pub, and you know wear green, and hang out together.

**Q3. Why does Branden think birthday parties are important for kids?**

a) They can have expensive parties.

b) They can eat cupcakes.

c) They can learn social skills.

> **Branden:** I do think it's really important for them to have those social opportunities because that's where they learn social skills and learn how to be little humans.

## Lecture 2

### Words in Action

**1. You're telling me...?**

- to ask for clarification by using an example

**Game 2**

Caoimhe: Um, so, I would say also maybe, yeah, as Cassandra said, maybe a trip? Um, I would also quite like a puppy for my next birthday.

Branden: You're telling me you're going to get a puppy soon?

**Game 1**

Caoimhe: Um, I would say also similar to Cassandra. Usually before COVID I liked just going overseas on my own and just doing it that way because I don't really like the fuss of having a birthday.

Branden: So, you're telling me you're a traveller? You like to travel?

Caoimhe: I would say so, yeah, I really like travelling, yeah.

**2. It sounds like...**

- to ask for clarification by elaborating on the topic

**Game 1**

Cassandra: Maybe just a dinner, a really delicious dinner with some very close friends, or going to a spa, or spending the weekend doing something like that.

Branden: It sounds like you're a very laid-back person. You like more of a simple style celebration. Is that so?

**Game 3**

Cassandra: The Canadian birthday? I don't think there's a typical Canadian birthday, but, yeah, my experience, like Branden said, you know, parties with your friends. Maybe doing something outdoors, such as an amusement park or going camping. Going to a restaurant. Sitting on a patio.

Branden: It sounds like there's really no real traditional birthdays in either Canada or America. They're all different.

3. ... Is that it?

- to ask for clarification through a yes-or-no question

**Game 2**

Cassandra: What experiences? Oh, I don't know offhand, but, like you said earlier, a trip. Travelling somewhere new for your birthday weekend is always fun, a different country.

Branden: Ok, so yeah. Uh, we have – we've talked about fancy dinners, travel. Is that it, guys? Anything else?

**Game 3**

Caoimhe: You're just trying to use all your cards, is that it?

Branden: Yeah, you guys caught me. Just because I want to win. I'm a winner. Ok, well.

4. What do you mean...?

- to ask for clarification with an open-ended question

**Game 3**

Branden: I do think it's really important for them, for especially when the kids are younger, for them to have those social opportunities because that's where they learn social skills and learn how to be little humans.

Caoimhe: What do you mean little humans?

5. What are you trying to say?

- to ask for clarification with an open-ended question

**Game 2**

Cassandra: It sounds like you have expensive taste.

Branden: Well, what can I say. So, yeah, what are you trying to say, Cassandra? Am I too expensive?

Cassandra: No, I want to know more, so like what kind of technology are you into?

**Game 1**

Cassandra: Maybe just a dinner, a really delicious dinner with some very close friends, or going to a spa, or spending the weekend doing something like that.

**Branden:** It sounds like you're a very laid-back person. You like more of a simple style celebration. Is that so?

**Cassandra:** Ok, simple. What are you trying to say? I'm not simple at all!

**6. You think...?**

- to ask for clarification with a yes-or-no question

**Game 1**

**Branden:** It sounds like you're a very laid-back person. You like more of a simple style celebration. Is that so?

**Cassandra:** Ok, simple. What are you trying to say? I'm not simple at all!

**Branden:** Oh, sorry, that didn't come out right.

**Caoimhe:** Getting personal. So you think Cassandra is simple?

**7. Wait. What?**

- to ask for clarification by expressing disbelief

**Game 1**

**Branden:** Oh, sorry, that didn't come out right.

**Caoimhe:** Getting personal. So you think Cassandra is simple?

**Cassandra:** Wait, what? Where is this going?

**Game 3**

**Caoimhe:** Um, it sounds, yeah, pretty much the same. So I guess I would just have a birthday party, usually at my house each year with my classmates or friends and just invite them to my house. Just have cake, play games.

**Branden:** I thought that Ireland, the Irish people used a lot of green in their...

**Caoimhe:** Uh, I think that might be a stereotype. Wait, what? What are you trying to say about Ireland?

**8. I thought...**

- to ask for clarification by expressing an alternative opinion

**Game 1**

**Branden:** The older I get, the more low-key I want to keep it. So, I tend to have smaller groups of people, I don't like to make a big fuss. Because, let's face it guys, birthdays, they celebrate a year older. A year older, closer to dying. Right?

**Caoimhe:** I thought you were still very young, though, Branden?

**Game 3**

**Caoimhe:** You're just trying to use all your cards, is that it?

Branden: Yeah, you guys caught me. Just because I want to win. I'm a winner. Ok, well.

**Caoimhe:** I thought I was going to win this one and it looks like I'm right. So, all of my cards are gone.

**9. Okay, so...**

- to ask for clarification through an offer or request for more information

**Game 3**

**Branden:** So, in my experience, birthday parties were pretty typical when I was child, the parents would invite the children over to the house or whoever, whichever kid was having the birthday, they would have pizza, cupcakes, I don't know. Just like in the movies, really.

**Caoimhe:** Ok, so were those your classmates or your friends that came to your house?

**Game 1**

**Cassandra:** Ok, well, starting now, ok, so, well when I was young, I liked to celebrate, you know, with my friends, my family, have this big gathering. But now that I'm older, I prefer something a little more low-key. Something more quiet.

Branden: Ok, so you're saying that you don't like big crowds?

**10. What kind of...?**

- to ask for clarification with an open-ended question

**Game 1**

**Caoimhe:** I would say so, yeah, I really like travelling.

**Cassandra:** What kind of countries do you like to travel to?

**Game 2**

**Cassandra:** Well, I agree with the both of you. I think money is the most practical gift to receive, but I'm also a fan of not getting an object or something physical for my birthday. I could get an experience. Like, like I said before, like a nice dinner, or, you know, time with friends. Like, give me an experience.

**Branden:** What kind of dinner would you be referring to?

**Cassandra:** Oh, maybe lobster? Something nice.

## Word Power

**1. low-key**

- relaxed; quiet; not a big deal

**Cassandra:** when I was young, I liked to celebrate, you know, with my friends, my family, have this big gathering. But now that I'm older, I prefer something a little more low-key. Something more quiet.

**Branden:** Ok, so you're saying that you don't like big crowds?

**2. fuss**

- a lot of effort; a big deal

**Caoimhe:** Um, I would say also similar to Cassandra. Usually before COVID I liked just going overseas on my own and just doing it that way because I don't really like the fuss of having a birthday.

**Branden:** So, you're telling me you're a traveler? You like to travel?

### 3. expensive taste
- to like expensive things

| | |
|---|---|
| Caoimhe: | Ok, so I guess you have rich friends if you're expecting a computer for your birthday. |
| Branden: | Oh, those are the best kind of friends to have. |
| Cassandra: | It sounds like you have expensive taste. |
| Branden: | Well, what can I say. |

### 4. materialistic
- to value objects over experiences

| | |
|---|---|
| Caoimhe: | Uh, the next birthday gift I expect to receive...probably money. Like, I'm a pretty difficult person to buy for, so usually my friends and family just give me money. |
| Branden: | Wait, what? Are you saying you're materialistic? |
| Caoimhe: | No, I'm saying that it's difficult to buy a gift to suit me. So I like to just receive money. |

### 5. ignorant
- uninformed; don't know about

| | |
|---|---|
| Caoimhe: | It sounds like you have seen a lot of people in green from Ireland, but have you ever seen me wearing green? |
| Branden: | Ok, I have to admit I am ignorant of many things, guys. So, perhaps we can change the subject a little sure. |
| Cassandra: | Sure. |

### 6. be into
- to be interested in

| | |
|---|---|
| Caoimhe: | You think so, too? Yeah. I think that they must cost so much money. But that's just... |
| Cassandra: | Yeah, right. |
| Caoimhe: | So, I don't know if I would be into spending so much money on a kid's party. |

## Outro

### Dialogue

**Cassandra:** I'm ready for the weekend!

**Branden:** What do you mean?

**Cassandra:** This weekend is my birthday weekend. So, I plan on doing something relaxing.

**Branden:** Oh? I thought your birthday wasn't until the summer. Anyway, it sounds like you have a nice weekend ahead of you. What kind of relaxation do you have in mind?

**Cassandra:** I love booking an expensive hotel and having a spa weekend every time I turn a year older.

**Branden:** That sounds good. And, I think you could use the rest!

**Cassandra:** Huh? What are you trying to say? Do you think I look tired and horrible all of the time?

**Branden:** Wait. What? That's not what I said. I just think that you should take good care of yourself.

**Cassandra:** You think that I don't get enough rest? Is that it?

**Branden:** No. Don't get upset. I'm just talking generally, here. Everyone could benefit from sleeping more.

**Cassandra:** I guess I misunderstood you. Okay, so how about you? How many hours of sleep do you get a night?

**Branden:** I normally geta good 8 or 9 hours.

**Cassandra:** What? You're telling me that you sleep that much, even though you're so busy all of the time?

**Branden:** Definitely. I really prioritize my health, above all else.

**Cassandra:** I only sleep 5 hours a night. Hmm. Maybe I should get more rest.

### Wrap-up

1. **You're telling me...?**
   - to ask for clarification by using an example

2. **It sounds like...**
   - to ask for clarification by elaborating on the topic

3. **... Is that it?**
   - to ask for clarification through a yes-or-no question

4. **What do you mean...?**
   - to ask for clarification with an open-ended question

5. **What are you trying to say?**
   - to ask for clarification with an open-ended question

6. **You think...?**
   - to ask for clarification with a yes-or-no question

7. **Wait. What?**
   - to ask for clarification by expressing disbelief

8. **I thought...**
   - to ask for clarification by expressing an alternative opinion

9. **Okay, so...**
   - to ask for clarification through request for more information

10. **What kind of...?**
   - to ask for clarification with an open-ended question

## Assignment

**1. Select the option that best completes the passage.**

A: I saw on the news that an asteroid is going to hit earth next week.
B: ________ it's going to hit earth?

1) What do you mean
2) I thought
3) What kind of
4) Where

**2. Select the option that best completes the passage.**

A: I was wondering if I could give you my phone number.
B: ________? Do you like me?

1) You think
2) I thought
3) It sounds like
4) What are you trying to say

**3. Select the option that best completes the passage.**

A: I studied English in Canada for several years.
B: ________ your English must be pretty good.

1) You think
2) I didn't think
3) It sounds like
4) How can

**4. Select the option that best completes the passage.**

> **A:** I think reading good books is important for our intellectual development.
> **B:** ________ I need to read a book to get smarter? Which book do you suggest?

1) I thought
2) Okay, so
3) It's sounding that
4) How can

**5. Select the option that best completes the passage.**

> **A:** Social media is so superficial.
> **B:** ________ I should delete my social media accounts?

1) Is that
2) How about
3) I thought
4) You think

**6. Select the option that best completes the passage.**

> **A:** I'd like to get some jewelry for my birthday.
> **B:** ________ jewelry?

1) What kind of
2) I thought
3) You think
4) How about

**7. Select the option that best completes the passage.**

A: I got a raise yesterday.
B: How could you get a raise already? ____________ you just started working a month ago.

1) What kind of
2) I thought
3) You think
4) How about

**8. Select the option that best completes the passage.**

A: I didn't get sick last year.
B: ____________ you didn't even get a cold? For an entire year?

1) I thought
2) You thought
3) What are you trying to say
4) You're telling me

**9. Select the option that best completes the passage.**

A: I've never cooked anything before
B: ____________ Not even Ramyeon?
A: Well... Ramyeon isn't really cooking. That doesn't count.

1) Wait. What?
2) It sounds like it.
3) Exactly what I thought.
4) Is that it?

**10. Select the option that best completes the passage.**

> **A:** I never hang out with my coworkers. I spend most of my time with my family.
>
> **B:** So you think family is more important. ______________

1) Is that what I'm saying.
2) It sounds like it.
3) So you're trying to say.
4) Is that it?

Week 4

# Interrupting

**Contents**
1. To interrupt by using an imperative sentence
2. To interrupt by using a suggestive sentence
3. To interrupt by using a declarative sentence
4. To interrupt by using a conjunction
5. To interrupt by using a yes-no question Objectives

**Objectives**
1. To understand 5 types of interruption
2. To understand how 5 types of interruption are used in real conversations
   1) Do you usually remember your dreams?
   2) Do you usually have pleasant dreams or nightmares?
   3) Do you think your dreams have special meaning?

## Intro

### Speaking Skills: Interrupting

**1. Hold up.**

- to interrupt by using an imperative sentence

Example

A: Yesterday my husband and I had dinner at Disco Pizza.
B: Hold up. Are you married?

**2. Wait a second.**

- to interrupt by using an imperative sentence

Example

A: I'm going to be home from work late tonight.
B: Wait a second. You promised you'd make dinner!

**3. Let me interrupt you.**

- to interrupt by using a suggestive sentence

Example

A: With ten mouths to feed, my single mother never spent money on new clothes for herself.

B: Let me interrupt you. Do you mean that there were 9 kids in your family?

**4. Excuse me.**

- to interrupt by using an imperative sentence

Example

A: I wish I had a fancy car.

B: Excuse me. Do you even have a driver's license?

**5. Wait. I'm sorry...**

- to interrupt by using a declarative sentence

Example

A: I'm thinking of getting the new Gucci bag.

B: Wait. I'm sorry. How can you afford that?

**6. Sorry to interrupt, but...**

- to interrupt by using a conjunction

Example

A: I saw Psy in Gangnam last night.

B: Sorry to interrupt, but isn't he currently touring in China?

**7. But....**

- to interrupt by using a conjunction

Example

A: I just got a raise.

B: But didn't you get a raise last month?

**8. May I say something?**

- to interrupt by using a yes-no question

Example

A: I'm going to Jeju-do in a few weeks.

B: May I say something? I think it's better to visit in spring.

**9. Could I say something?**

- to interrupt by using a yes-no question

Example

A: I think I'll go camping this weekend.

B: Could I say something? The forecast shows it's supposed to rain.

**10. Can I ask something?**

- to interrupt by using a yes-no question

Example

A: I'm so sad. I lost my cat.

B: Can I ask something? Have you put up signs around the neighborhood?

## Lecture 1

### Conversation Question 1

▶ **Do you usually remember your dreams?**
**What was your most recent dream?**

**Q1. Which of these does Cassandra NOT dream about?**

a) Her daily life.

b) Going to the gym.

c) Tsunamis.

**Q2. Who has nightmares the most often?**

a) Caoimhe

b) Branden

c) Cassandra

**Q3. What did Caoimhe and Song Joong-ki do in her last dream?**

a) They had a baby together.

b) They appeared in a commercial together.

c) They got married.

### Script

**Branden:** Hello, everyone, welcome back. I'm Branden Noland.

**Caoimhe:** I'm Caoimhe McCotter.

**Cassandra:** I'm Cassandra Nykyforak.

**Branden:** Alright, so we're playing another game with rejoinders that you learned in class. These rejoinders talk about - help us interrupt people so that we can share our opinion. We can politely disagree using rejoinders. Ok? With that said, let's get started. We're going to have a round that lasts for three minutes and our question for today⋯actually, there are two questions for this first round. Do you usually remember your dreams? Ok? When we sleep, we have dreams, right? What was your recent dream? Your most recent dream, I guess. Ok? So, do you usually remember your dreams and what was your most recent dream?

**Caoimhe:** Ok. Mhm.

**Branden:** Let's talk about that. Alright, so I will start, uh, the timer. Professor, would anyone like to start?

**Caoimhe:** How about Cassandra?

**Cassandra:** Ok, sure, well, um, I actually usually remember my dreams. And, um, I don't have any particularly interesting dreams to tell you about because I normally dream about my daily life. So, the people in my life, going to work, going to the gym, cooking food, just very normal situations.

**Branden:** Excuse me, are you saying that you dream every night?

**Cassandra:** I definitely dream every night, and I think I remember my dreams almost every night.

**Branden:** Wow, that's amazing.

**Cassandra:** Yeah, how - sorry, you go ahead?

**Caoimhe:** But do you never have exciting dreams? You only dream about your daily routine? That's a bit depressing.

**Cassandra:** Ok, ok, occasionally I'll have an exciting dream, like I'm flying in the air or I'm in a video game, or, I don't know, I'm doing something amazing like playing with a bunch of puppies in a field.

**Branden:** Oh, can I ask you something? Can I ask you something?

**Cassandra:** Yes.

**Branden:** Do you ever have a nightmare? Do you ever have bad dreams?

**Cassandra:** Um, I rarely have nightmares.

**Branden:** Oh, ok.

**Cassandra:** Yeah. How about you?

**Branden:** All the time. Yeah, most of my dreams are kind of like nightmares. I don't usually dream. I don't dream every day. Or, at least, I can't remember when I do dream. But, yeah, it's usually like depressing nightmares like growing old and not remembering who I am and··· yeah. Anyway, what about you, Professor Caoimhe?

**Caoimhe:** Whoa, ok, um, very contrasting.

**Branden:** Sorry.

**Cassandra:** Very contrasting.

**Caoimhe:** Um, I would say I remember at least one dream from every night, and my most recent dream is a little bit embarrassing, but my most recent dream was that I got married to a famous Korean celebrity.

**Branden:** Oh!

**Cassandra:** Can I ask something? Which celebrity?

**Caoimhe:** Um, it's a little bit embarrassing because this celebrity has already been married, but it was Song Joong-ki.

**Branden:** Ok, ok. So···.

**Cassandra:** That's cute.

**Branden:** So, yeah, so may I ask you something?

**Caoimhe:** Mhm.

**Branden:** Are you attracted to celebrities, like, are they attractive to you?

**Caoimhe:** Wait a second, are you saying I'm superficial? But, yes, I'm attracted to celebrities.

**Branden:** Oh, ok, well a lot of people are. They're beautiful, aren't they?

**Cassandra:** Wait, wait a minute, Branden. Have you seen Song Joong-ki? You know what he looks like, correct?

**Branden:** I'm sorry I actually don't know who he is.

**Caoimhe:** Hold up! You don't know who Song Joong-ki is?

**Branden:** Yeah, yeah, I'm sorry but I don't. Is he really handsome? I guess, tall?

**Caoimhe:** Wait, I'm sorry, but he is like the most famous celebrity and he is very, very handsome.

**Branden:** Ok.

**Cassandra:** I, I do agree. Yes, yes. I'm shocked, I'm shocked.

**Branden:** Can I say something, guys? Could I say something? I don't really follow, like, mainstream pop culture. So, yeah, I'm sorry I wish I could understand his handsomeness to the greatest extent possible.

Caoimhe: Let me interrupt you, yeah, I totally understand. I don't really follow it either, but it's hard to ignore or escape him because he's in a lot of advertisements in Korea.

Branden: Oh.

Cassandra: May I say something? Um, Caoimhe, do you often dream about other people?

Caoimhe: All the time, yes. The other dream I often have is that a tsunami is coming, and I feel like that has some kind of meaning? I have recurring dreams about tsunamis. And Song Joong-ki.

Branden: Wait, I'm sorry. Wait, I'm sorry, that is very terrible. Tsunamis. Bad dreams, but we had some good dreams, too. But we're out of time, guys. We've got to stop.

Cassandra: Oh, ok.

Branden: So, the time, I have five cards here. What about you guys?

Caoimhe: Oh, I only have four remaining.

Cassandra: Seven.

Branden: Oh, no, so that means that Caoimhe is unfortunately the winner of round number one, but there are more chances remaining. Ok? So, let's stay tuned for the next round.

**[Answer]**

**Q1. Which of these does Cassandra NOT dream about?**

a) Her daily life.

b) Going to the gym.

c) Tsunamis.

Cassandra: I normally dream about my daily life. So, the people in my life, going to work, going to the gym, cooking food, just very normal situations.

**Q2. Who has nightmares the most often?**

a) Caoimhe

b) Branden

c) Cassandra

> **Branden:** All the time. Most of my dreams are kind of like nightmares. I don't usually dream. But, yeah, it's usually like depressing nightmares like growing old and not remembering who I am and... yeah.

**Q3. What did Caoimhe and Song Joong-ki do in her last dream?**

a) They had a baby together.

b) They appeared in a commercial together.

c) They got married.

> **Caoimhe:** But my most recent dream was that I got married to a famous Korean celebrity. Um, it's a little bit embarrassing because this celebrity has already been married, but it was Song Joong-ki.

## Conversation Question 2

**▶ Do you usually have pleasant dreams or nightmares?**

**Q1. What should you do if you dream of a pig, according to Caoimhe?**

a) Buy a lottery ticket.

b) Retire early.

c) Have children.

**Q2. Who recently dreamed about puppies?**

a) Caoimhe

b) Branden

c) Cassandra

**Q3. What superstition does Caoimhe's mom have about dreams?**

a) That eating bacon gives her good dreams.

b) That eating cheese gives her strange dreams.

c) That eating dairy gives her nightmares.

Script

**Branden:** Hello, everyone, and welcome back. So now we have round two. The last round, unfortunately Caoimhe was the winner. You should feel happy about that.

**Caoimhe:** I do.

**Branden:** But not for long because Cassandra and I have another chance. We'll see what happens. Anyway, we're going to use the rejoinders for a round that last three minutes, but the question will be different, guys. Let me share that with you. The question is "Do you think that your dreams have special meaning?" Ok? So throughout history, you know, pe- there have been superstitions, superstitions that dreams have special meaning. They can predict our future, something like that. What do you think? Let's start the timer at three minutes.

**Caoimhe:** Excuse me, what does superstition mean?

**Branden:** That is, that's like a belief that you have that's not based on scientific evidence. Yeah.

**Caoimhe:** Oh, ok. Ok.

**Branden:** Can I ask you something? What kind of superstitions regarding dreams are you familiar with?

**Caoimhe:** Um, in the west, I haven't heard many, but I have heard that in Korean culture if you dream of a pig, it means that money may be coming your way. So you should buy a lottery ticket if you have a dream about a pig.

**Branden:** Oh. Excuse me, so you're saying that I should watch a lot of images of pigs so that I can dream of a pig so that I can be rich?

**Caoimhe:** Let me interrupt you. That would be very strange, to just start watching pigs. I think there are easier ways to get money. I think we just have to leave it up to fate.

**Branden:** Ok. You're right.

Caoimhe: Wait a minute. Do you like watching images of pigs?

Branden: Let me, let me interrupt you right there. I like eating pigs. I like bacon. I like bacon. Alright, so, yeah, dreams. Special meanings. I don't think they have special meanings. I think it's just our brain recharging from like a long day. So, it's just a natural process, but does it have any special spiritual meaning, anything like that? Do you guys agree?

Cassandra: You want to go first?

Caoimhe: I would say - so I'm curious about Cassandra's dreams, because in the last class, you talked about your dreams of puppies? You had a dream about being around puppies?

Cassandra: Yeah, yeah. There's nothing special there.

Caoimhe: Do you think it has a special meaning?

Cassandra: No, no, I think that I just dream about what's on my mind, what I like, or sometimes what's bothering me. So, I think that dreams do have a special meaning in the sense that they kind of tune you in to what's going on in your brain and maybe what's happening in your subconscious. So, it helps you to know more about yourself by maybe studying your dreams. That's my -

Caoimhe: Oh.

Branden: Oh, I see.

Caoimhe: Can I say something?

Branden: Yeah, sure.

Caoimhe: So, in Ireland we believe that if you eat cheese during the day you have very strange dreams. So, have you guys heard that as well?

Cassandra: No, never.

Branden: No, I've never heard of that.

Cassandra: That's interesting.

Branden: So, wait, I'm sorry, I'm sorry to interrupt you, but what kind of strangeness are we talking about here?

Caoimhe: I'm not sure, but every time my mom has a strange dream and she thinks back, she remembers that she ate cheese previously that day. So, I was just wondering if it's like an international thing or if it's an Irish kind of superstition. But, you've never heard that before?

Branden: Uh, I never have. I never have.

Caoimhe: I feel weird.

Cassandra: No, no, no.

**Branden:** I'm sorry to interrupt, but Cassandra, are there any ideas about dreams in Canadian culture?

**Cassandra:** In Canadian culture? I think that Canadian culture is kind of western culture, right?

**Branden:** Oh, right.

**Cassandra:** Um, well, I don't have a good answer for you. I think that…

**Caoimhe:** Hold up, I think our time is up.

**Branden:** Wait a second, it's not over until it's over. No, just kidding. Yeah, our time is up. Yeah, so…

**Cassandra:** What happened?

**Branden:** Let's see how many points we have. I have four, what about…what do you have?

**Caoimhe:** I also have four.

**Cassandra:** Zero. I couldn't use any. I was just thinking about dreams. Those dreams in the question.

**Branden:** Oh, this is what happens when you daydream during a competition. Ok, so this is great. Caoimhe, you have two points and I have one point because we tied this time, right? So, we'll end it there and move on to round three.

**[Answer]**

**Q1. What should you do if you dream of a pig, according to Caoimhe?**

a) Buy a lottery ticket.

b) Retire early.

c) Have children.

> **Caoimhe:** So you should buy a lottery ticket if you have a dream about a pig.

**Q2. Who recently dreamed about puppies?**

a) Caoimhe

b) Branden

c) Cassandra

Caoimhe: I'm curious about Cassandra's dreams, because in the last class, you talked about your dreams of puppies?
Cassandra: Yeah, yeah. There's nothing special there.

**Q3. What superstition does Caoimhe's mom have about dreams?**

a) That eating bacon gives her good dreams.
b) That eating cheese gives her strange dreams.
c) That eating dairy gives her nightmares.

Caoimhe: Every time my mom has strange dream, she remembers that she ate cheese previously that day. So, I was just wondering if it's like an international thing or if it's an Irish kind of superstition.

## Conversation Question 3

**▶ Do you think your dreams have special meaning?**

**Q1. What does Cassandra have recurring dreams about?**

a) Being old.
b) Being in high school.
c) Her first job.

**Q2. Who has recurring dreams about being old?**

a) Caoimhe
b) Branden
c) Cassandra

**Q3. Where did Caoimhe work part-time?**

a) A coffee shop.
b) A restaurant.
c) A gas station.

### Script

**Branden:** Hello, and welcome back to round three. So, uh, yeah, we're pretty close. Well, Cassandra isn't, but Caoimhe and I···Caoimhe has two, Caoimhe has two points, right? And I have one point. Um, but to sort of mix things up, because I feel really bad for Cassandra, we're going to change the point system. Ok?

**Caoimhe:** Fine.

**Cassandra:** Sure.

**Branden:** Yeah, so, this round will be worth two points. So at least, Cassandra, you have a chance to tie.

**Cassandra:** Much appreciated.

**Branden:** Better than nothing, right?

**Cassandra:** Right.

**Branden:** Ok. So, yeah, we're going to be using these rejoinders. Interrupting each other. But the question is different. I'll read that right now. Could you tell us your experience of having bad dreams? Ok? So, we've been talking about dreams, but now we're talking about nightmares. Could you tell us your experience of having bad dreams? Ok? I might have already talked about this, but anyway, let's start the timer.

**Caoimhe:** Wait, I'm sorry, so we're specifically just talking about bad dreams and nightmares?

**Branden:** Uh, yeah, I think so.

**Cassandra:** Looks like it.

**Branden:** Yeah, but if you want to talk about something else, some other kind of dreams, feel free to do so as well.

**Caoimhe:** Ok, so, excuse me. Um, Cassandra maybe you can go first this time.

**Cassandra:** Ok.

**Branden:** Ok.

**Cassandra:** Sure, sure. Um, as I said before, I usually do not have bad dreams. Um, and when I do have a bad dream, honestly, it's usually something not that scary. For example, I have recurring dreams about being in high school again and failing a test or being unable to open my locker, the lock on my locker to get my books. So, it's just stuff like that. Nothing too scary.

**Branden:** So, hold up, are you saying that when you were in high school you had trouble academically? Was that like a reoccurring thing for you?

**Cassandra:** That's - no, I was a student who cared very much about her grades, so…

**Branden:** Oh, ok, I see.

**Cassandra:** I was afraid of not meeting a certain standard, so maybe that's why…

**Branden:** Oh, excuse me, I'm sorry. Sorry for making assumptions.

**Cassandra:** It's ok.

**Caoimhe:** Can I say something?

**Cassandra:** Sure, sure.

**Branden:** Of course.

**Caoimhe:** It's really interesting, I think a lot of people have dreams about high school and I'm really curious about what it means. Branden, do you ever have dreams about, like, high school, or academic dreams?

**Branden:** Oh, yeah, so, I really, like very often I have dreams about my past, and I think I may have mentioned this before, like a reoccurring bad dream in my case is just like…I know this is depressing, guys, bear with me, but I imagine myself as being like an old senile man, and then I don't really realize…I think I'm still young, and I don't realize that I'm old and about to die, and I'm, like, looking back at the past. Isn't that depressing?

**Caoimhe:** But, Branden, you're still in your prime! You're still so young. Is this something you really worry about?

**Branden:** I know, but think about it. What if we're actually older right now, but we don't know it? We may all be in a coma, right?

**Caoimhe:** That is so depressing!

**Branden:** This whole thing may just be a memory.

**Cassandra:** It sounds like The Matrix.

**Branden:** I know, right?

**Cassandra:** I do not like this.

**Caoimhe:** Oh, my gosh.

**Branden:** Ok.

**Cassandra:** Let's change the, the conversation.

**Branden:** Yeah, ok.

**Cassandra:** Caoimhe? Your bad dreams?

**Caoimhe:** Um, I often have a dream that I am forced to work in my part-time job when I was in high school. So, I worked in like a gas station. And I have a dream that somehow my career fails and I have to work in that gas station for the rest of my life. And it's almost every week, it's crazy.

**Branden:** Wait a, wait a second. Are you saying that there's something wrong with working at a gas station?

**Caoimhe:** Let me interrupt you. There's absolutely nothing wrong, but it was the people that worked in the gas station. That was it.

**Branden:** Oh, I see.

**Cassandra:** You didn't like your coworkers.

**Caoimhe:** Yeah, they still work there, and so I know that I would be going back to that.

**Branden:** Oh, I see. Yeah.

**Caoimhe:** So, yeah. So, can I ask something? Are you judging me? Because of my dreams?

**Branden:** Oh, no! Oh, please, please understand that I just want to win. I just want to win one time. But, it looks like it's not going to happen because we are out of time and I have too many cards. What do you guys have?

**Cassandra:** Too many cards as well.

**Caoimhe:** I have three cards left. I'm sorry guys. It looks like I'm cleaning up.

**Branden:** Yeah, really, really unfortunate. Anyway, without a doubt, Caoimhe is the winner. You should pat yourself on the shoulder. You deserve it.

**Cassandra:** On the back, yeah.

**Branden:** And, uh, yeah. That's it for today. Hopefully you enjoyed that and it helped you out.

**[Answer]**

**Q1. What does Cassandra have recurring dreams about?**

a) Being old.

b) Being in high school.

c) Her first job.

**Cassandra:** I have recurring dreams about being in high school again and failing a test or being unable to open my locker, the lock on my locker to get my books. So, it's just stuff like that. Nothing too scary.

**Q2. Who has recurring dreams about being old?**

a) Caoimhe

b) Branden

c) Cassandra

Branden: I think I may have mentioned this before, like a reoccurring bad dream in my case is just like...I know this is depressing, guys, bear with me, but I imagine myself as being like an old senile man.

**Q3. Where did Caoimhe work part-time?**

a) A coffee shop.

b) A restaurant.

c) A gas station.

Caoimhe: I often have a dream that I am forced to work in my part-time job when I was in high school. So, I worked in like a gas station.

## Lecture 2

### Words in Action

**1. Hold up.**

- to interrupt by using an imperative sentence

**Game1**

Cassandra: wait a minute, Branden. Have you seen Song Joong-ki? You know what he looks like, correct?

Branden: I'm sorry I actually don't know who he is.

Caoimhe: Hold up! You don't know who Song Joong-ki is?

**Game3**

**Cassandra:** For example, I have recurring dreams about being in high school again and failing a test or being unable to open my locker.

**Branden:** So, hold up, are you saying that when you were in high school you had trouble academically?

**Cassandra:** That's – no, I was a student who cared very much about her grades, so...

2. **Wait a second.**
   - to interrupt by using an imperative sentence

**Game1**

**Branden:** Are you attracted to celebrities, like, are they attractive to you?

**Caoimhe:** Wait a second, are you saying I'm superficial? But, yes, I'm attracted to celebrities.

3. **Let me interrupt you.**
   - to interrupt by using a suggestive sentence

**Game1**

**Branden:** Oh. Excuse me, so you're saying that I should watch a lot of images of pigs so that I can dream of a pig so that I can be rich?

**Caoimhe:** Let me interrupt you. That would be very strange, to just start watching pigs. I think there are easier ways to get money. I think we just have to leave it up to fate.

4. **Excuse me.**
   - to interrupt by using an imperative sentence

**Game2**

**Caoimhe:** So you should buy a lottery ticket if you have a dream about a pig.

**Branden:** Oh. Excuse me, so you're saying that I should watch a lot of images of pigs so that I can dream of a pig so that I can be rich?

**5. Wait. I'm sorry...**

- to interrupt by using a declarative sentence

**Game1**

Branden: yeah, I'm sorry but I don't. Is he really handsome? I guess, tall?

Caoimhe: Wait, I'm sorry, but he is like the most famous celebrity and he is very, very handsome.

**6. Sorry to interrupt, but...**

- to interrupt by using a conjunction

**Game2**

Branden: I'm sorry to interrupt, but Cassandra, are there any ideas about dreams in Canadian culture?

Cassandra: In Canadian culture? I think that Canadian culture is kind of western culture, right?

**7. But...**

- to interrupt by using a conjunction

**Game3**

Branden: I imagine myself as being like an old senile man, looking back at the past. Isn't that depressing?

Caoimhe: But, Branden, you're still in your prime! You're still so young. Is this something you really worry about?

**8. May I say something?**

- to interrupt by using a yes-no question

**Game1**

Cassandra: May I say something? Um, Caoimhe, do you often dream about other people?

Caoimhe: All the time, yes. The other dream I often have is that a tsunami is coming, and I feel like that has some kind of meaning? I have recurring dreams about tsunamis. And Song Joong-ki.

**9. Could I say something?**

- to interrupt by using a yes-no question

**Game1**

Caoimhe: He is like the most famous celebrity and he is very, very handsome.

Branden: Can I say something, guys? Could I say something? I don't really follow, like, mainstream pop culture. So, I'm sorry I wish I could understand his handsomeness to the greatest extent possible.

**10. Can I ask something?**

- to interrupt by using a yes-no question

**Game1**

Branden: Can I ask you something? What kind of superstitions regarding dreams are you familiar with?

Caoimhe: I have heard that in Korean culture if you dream of a pig, it means that money may be coming your way. So you should buy a lottery ticket if you have a dream about a pig.

## Word Power

**1. nightmares**

- bad or scary dreams

Branden: Do you ever have a nightmare? Do you ever have bad dreams?

Cassandra: Um, I rarely have nightmares.

**2. (to be) superficial**

- to be attracted to people for only their appearances

Branden: Are you attracted to celebrities, like, are they attractive to you?

Caoimhe: Wait a second, are you saying I'm superficial? But, yes, I'm attracted to celebrities.

3. **superstition**

- a cultural belief based on stories

| | |
|---|---|
| Caoimhe: | Excuse me, what does superstition mean? |
| Branden: | That is, that's like a belief that you have that's not based on scientific evidence. Yeah. |

4. **subconscious**

- the part of one's brain that they are not fully aware of, but which influences their actions

| | |
|---|---|
| Cassandra: | So, I think that dreams do have a special meaning in the sense that they kind of tune you in to what's going on in your brain and maybe what's happening in your subconscious. |

5. **bear with me**

- be patient with me

| | |
|---|---|
| Branden: | I know this is depressing, guys, bear with me, but I imagine myself as being like an old senile man, and then I don't really realize...I think I'm still young, and I don't realize that I'm old and about to die, and I'm, like, looking back at the past. Isn't that depressing? |

6. **still in your prime**

- in the best years of your life; young and full of potential

| | |
|---|---|
| Caoimhe: | But, Branden, you're still in your prime! You're still so young. Is this something you really worry about? |
| Branden: | I know, but think about it. What if we're actually older right now, but we don't know it? We may all be in a coma, right? |

## Outro

### Dialogue

**Cassandra:** I was just reading this article about electric cars. I think I might consider buying one in the future.

**Branden:** Hold up. You are actually considering buying an electric car? You should be careful when investing in new technology. I prefer gasoline cars. As far as I know, they are cheaper and more reliable.

**Cassandra:** Wait a second. You can't just say that gasoline cars are more reliable without any evidence to back your opinion. I see people driving electric cars all the time. They seem to work just fine. They are also better for the environment...

**Branden:** Let me interrupt you. What about the batteries? How long do they last? How much money does it take to replace them? We don't know because electric cars haven't been around long enough to determine whether the technology is more economical in the long run. And what happens when we have to dispose of used batteries? I bet that is not good for the environment either!

**Cassandra:** Excuse me, but I'm not sure you are considering all the possibilities. We can recycle used batteries. And anyway, electric power must be better than burning more fossil fuels...

**Branden:** Wait, I'm sorry. But even if we recycle batteries, they won't last forever. Then we will be forced to throw them away. And what about cost? With how much it takes to replace a battery on an electric car, you could just buy a new car! If I am going to spend 40 thousand dollars on a car, I want it to last...

**Cassandra:** Sorry to interrupt, but I don't agree with you. These days electric cars are becoming more cost-effective.

**Branden:** But they are still not at the point where they can compete with traditional gas-powered vehicles.

**Cassandra:** May I say something?

**Branden:** Sure....

**Cassandra:** Just because something cost a little more, isn't it still worth it if it reduces global warming and air pollution?

Branden: Can I ask something?

Cassandra: Ok. Go ahead.

Branden: Where does the electricity to recharge the electric cars come from? Most power plants still use fossil fuels to produce electricity.

Cassandra: That may be true, but could I say something? I think there is one thing you haven't considered yet.

Branden: Sure. What is it?

Cassandra: Well, we are developing new ways to produce electricity from renewable power sources. I hope that one day fossil fuels will become obsolete.

Branden: I hope so, too. But my next car is still going to be gasoline!

## Wrap-up

1. **Hold up.**
   - to interrupt by using an imperative sentence

2. **Wait a second.**
   - to interrupt by using an imperative sentence

3. **Let me interrupt you.**
   - to interrupt by using a suggestive sentence

4. **Excuse me.**
   - to interrupt by using an imperative sentence

5. **Wait. I'm sorry.**
   - to interrupt by using a declarative sentence

6. **Sorry to interrupt, but...**
   - to interrupt by using a conjunction

7. **But...**
   - to interrupt by using a conjunction

**8. May I say something?**

- to interrupt by using a yes-no question

**9. Could I say something?**

- to interrupt by using a yes-no question

**10. Can I ask something?**

- to interrupt by using a yes-no question

## Assignment

**1. Select the option that best completes the passage.**

A: I'm thinking of getting a Rolex watch.
B: ______________ How can you afford that?

1) Hold down.
2) Wait. Sounds good.
3) Wait. I'm sorry.
4) Wait an hour.

**2. Select the option that best completes the passage.**

A: My company is managing the construction of a new hospital.
B: ______________ Do you mean you work for a construction company?

1) Hold it.
2) Let me interrupt you.
3) May I speak something?
4) Could I tell something?

**3. Select the option that best completes the passage.**

A: I'm going to major in Art History.
B: ______________ I think it's better to study something more practical.

1) May I say something?
2) Can you hold.
3) If I would interrupt.
4) Excuse it.

**4. Select the option that best completes the passage.**

A: Yesterday I went straight home after class.
B: ______________ Are you a student?

1) May I speak something?
2) Hold this.
3) Hold up.
4) Can I tell something?

**5. Select the option that best completes the passage.**

A: I'm going to play a computer game with my friend.
B: ______________ We agreed that you would finish your homework before playing games.

1) Excuse you.
2) Sorry to admit, but.
3) Hold something.
4) Wait a second.

## 6. Select the option that best completes the passage.

A: It is so hard to get practice speaking English.
B: ______________ Have you tried making some foreign friends?

1) Can I ask something?
2) Can you hold for a second?
3) Could I be excused?
4) I wasn't thinking about this.

## 7. Select the option that best completes the passage.

A: I got a new Samsung phone last week.
B: ______________ aren't Apple phones better?

1) Can I ask though
2) Sorry to interrupt, but
3) Excuse this, but
4) I always thought, but

## 8. Select the option that best completes the passage.

A: I have been thinking about getting a dog.
B: ______________ Don't you live in a one room and work every weekday? Dogs need lots of space an attention.

1) Can I ask though.
2) Sorry to interrupting.
3) Hold me.
4) Excuse me.

**9. Select the option that best completes the passage.**

> A: I just got a new motorcycle.
> B: ________ don't you already have a car?

1) But
2) Therefore
3) Since
4) Excuse this

**10. Select the option that best completes the passage.**

> A: I want to go hiking now.
> B: ________ It's too hot right now. How about waiting a few hours for the weather to cool down.

1) Can I tell something?
2) Let me interrupt someone.
3) Could I say something?
4) Sorry to wait.

Week 5

# Accepting a Question or Interruption

**Contents**
1. To accept a question or interruption with exclamations
2. To accept a question or interruption with imperative sentences
3. To accept a question or interruption with wh-questions
4. To elicit agreement with yes-no questions

**Objectives**
1. To understand 4 types of accepting skills
2. To understand how 4 types of accepting skills are used in real conversations
   1) How do you use body language in your daily life?
   2) Do different cultures have different body language?
   3) How important do you think eye contact is?

## Intro

### Speaking Skills: Accepting a Question or Interruption

**1. Sure.**

- to accept a question or interruption with exclamations

Example

A: Can I ask you a question?

B: Sure.

**2. Yes.**

- to accept a question or interruption with exclamations

Example

A: Could I say something?

B: Yes.

**3. Yes?**

- to accept a question or interruption with exclamations

Example

A: Would you do me a favor?

B: Yes?

**4. Go ahead.**

- to accept a question or interruption with imperative sentences

Example

A: Can I interrupt you?

B: Go ahead.

**5. Ask away.**

- to accept a question or interruption with imperative sentences

Example

A: Would you mind if I asked you something?

B: Ask away.

**6. Fire away!**

- to accept a question or interruption with imperative sentences

Example

A: Could I ask you a personal question?

B: Fire away!

**7. Yes, what is it?**

- to accept a question or interruption with wh-questions

Example

A: I need to ask you something.

B: Yes, what is it?

**8. You don't agree?**

- to elicit agreement with yes-no questions

Example

A: You really believe that he will pass the examination?

B: You don't agree?

**9. No problem.**

- to accept a question or interruption with exclamations

Example

A: Sorry, can I interrupt for a second?

B: No problem.

**10. Be my guest.**

- to accept a question or interruption with imperative sentences

Example

A: Can I say something?

B: Be my guest.

## Lecture 1

### Conversation Question 1

▶ **How do you use your body language in your daily life?**

**Q1. Which of these is NOT one of the ways that the professors use body language?**

a) public speaking

b) trying to communicate in a foreign language

c) watching a movie

**Q2. Who does not usually use body language when taking a selfie?**

a) Caoimhe

b) Branden

c) Cassandra

**Q3. How has Caoimhe's body language changed since moving to Korea?**

a) She uses more cute gestures.

b) She uses bigger gestures.

c) She uses less gestures than before.

### Script

**Branden:** Hello, everyone. Welcome back. So, time for another quiz game. My name is Branden.

**Caoimhe:** I'm Caoimhe.

**Cassandra:** Cassandra.

**Branden:** Alright. So, we're going to have a little competition today using some of those rejoinders that you learned in class. Ok? So, like last time, we have three minutes to complete the round. Whoever uses the most rejoinders in that time will be the winner of round 1. And we'll have three rounds. Right, guys?

**Caoimhe:** Ok. Sounds good.

**Branden:** Ok. So, let's get started with our first question, which is: How do you use body language in your daily life? Ok? I'll say it one more time. How do you use your body language in your daily life? Let's get started. Ok, three minutes. Ok, who would like to get it started? I, I can.

**Cassandra:** Go for it.

**Branden:** Well, I don't know, I don't have like a really systematic way of how I use body language, but I do notice when I talk, I'm always gesturing a little bit. Absolutely when I use public speaking, when I do public speaking, I think, gesturing is important to sort of, express yourself, express your ideas.

**Caoimhe:** Sure.

**Branden:** Oh, there you go. That's our word, guys. Caoimhe pulled a fast one. She has one point.

**Caoimhe:** Ok, yeah, so public speaking, I think also when I'm trying to, I guess, communicate because my Korean isn't so good, sometimes I use body language to try to express what I'm saying. For example, 'no.' Well, I can say 'no' in Korean, but sometimes I find myself doing this kind of gesture.

**Branden:** Ok.

**Caoimhe:** And I use a lot of Korean body language now like the heart symbol like this kind of cute things.

**Branden:** Alright. So, can I ask a question?

**Caoimhe:** Go ahead.

**Branden:** Oh, I gave that to her. I gave it.

**Cassandra:** Ask away, ask away.

**Branden:** So have you found that your body language has actually changed since you moved to Korea?

**Caoimhe:** Oh, definitely, sure.

**Cassandra:** Oh, Good question. I think so, too.

**Caoimhe:** What do you think, Cass?

**Cassandra:** Well, I agree with what Caoimhe said that we're using our bodies in a way to, you know, help us when language isn't enough. So, we're, you know, for English speakers in a Korean environment, yeah, we're truly, you know, always trying to make our point known, so we have, kind of naturally fallen to using gestures.

**Caoimhe:** So, what kind of body language do you think that you use a lot in your daily life?

**Cassandra:** Oh, I, I don't really know. I think I'm not really conscious of that, I'm not really paying attention to how I move my body when I'm communicating with people. I, I, I do do this sometimes, actually, to say 'no.'

**Caoimhe:** Yeah, haha…

**Branden:** And guys, I do you want to remind you that our rejoinders today have to do with questions. So I think we're going to have to ask some questions here. Like, just to give our - give me a chance.

**Caoimhe:** Yes?

**Cassandra:** Do you have a question? Something you want to talk about with someone?

**Branden:** Ah, so, oh, oh, yes, but I don't really know. Can you ask away? Ask away. Let me know, let me, if you give a specific question, may it'll help me out.

**Caoimhe:** I'm curious about something. So, Branden, when I take selfies or photos…

**Branden:** Go ahead.

**Caoimhe:** Oh! I often do like this, like cute…so I want to know what kind of body language you use when you're taking a selfie or when you're taking a photo.

**Branden:** Oh, sure, uh, yeah I, you know, you know guys, I'm really terrible with the whole cutesy thing. I don't really know, I just, I don't, I don't do that to be honest.

**Caoimhe:** Really?

**Cassandra:** You never? You never do some cute gesture in picture? And if you're with a friend.

**Caoimhe:** Ah, time is up. We'll never know.

Branden: The time is up. I'll tell you guys later. Anyway, so the time is up, guys. This was hard. This was hard.
Caoimhe: This was very tricky.
Branden: This was very close. So, I have two points. Oh, Cassandra one. Good try.
Caoimhe: And I have three! I was sneaky.
Branden: Oh, no! I can't believe it! Alright, guys. That's it. Caoimhe won the first round, but it is not over. Let's move on to the next question.

**[Answer]**

**Q1. Which of these is NOT one of the ways that the professors use body language?**

a) public speaking

b) trying to communicate in a foreign language

c) watching a movie

Branden: When I do public speaking, gesturing is important to sort of, express yourself.
Caoimhe: For example, 'no.' Well, I can say 'no' in Korean, but sometimes I find myself doing this kind of gesture.

**Q2. Who does not usually use body language when taking a selfie?**

a) Caoimhe

b) Branden

c) Cassandra

Caoimhe: Oh! I often do like this, like cute...so I want to know what kind of body language you use when you're taking a selfie or taking a photo.
Branden: I'm really terrible with the whole cutesy thing. I don't do that to be honest.

**Q3. How has Caoimhe's body language changed since moving to Korea?**

a) She uses more cute gestures.

b) She uses bigger gestures.

c) She uses less gestures than before.

| | |
|---|---|
| Caoimhe: | when I take selfies... |
| Caoimhe: | Oh! I often do like this, like cute... |

## Conversation Question 2

▶ **Do different cultures have different body language?**

**Q1. What is another meaning for the 'OK' sign in a different culture?**

a) Money

b) You're having a bad day.

c) You're angry at the person.

**Q2. What is a new greeting that has started since COVID?**

a) shaking hands

b) bowing

c) bumping elbows

**Q3. Which of these is not a universal trait, according to Cassandra?**

a) making eye contact

b) crouching when you're scared

c) bowing

### Script

**Branden:** Hello, everyone and welcome back. So, it's time for round 2 of our game today. Now, Caoimhe, you were the winner of the last round, weren't you?

**Caoimhe:** I was, indeed.

**Branden:** That makes me really sad. I'm sure Cassandra too. Ah, so, we're going to move on to the next question and practice using some of the rejoinders that you learned in class. You guys, ready?

**Caoimhe:** Yes.

**Branden:** Ok, I'm ready to win! Alright, so the next question is: Do different cultures have different body language? So, do different cultures have different body language? And, just like last time, we have three minutes to answer. Are you guys ready?

**Cassandra, Caoimhe:** Yes!

**Branden:** Ok, let's get started! Ok!

**Caoimhe:** So, who's going first?

**Branden:** Oh, can I, I guess I can go first. Is that ok?

**Caoimhe:** Fire away!

**Branden:** Ok, so I'm asking for permission, and they're granting it. Ah, yeah, so, different cultures, I think, in some cultures, this means 'ok,' right? From our countries. This means 'yeah, ok,' but in some cultures it means something else, like 'money.' Does it mean 'money'?

**Cassandra:** Possibly?

**Branden:** Possibly? I think we're talking about this earlier.

**Cassandra:** But I'm not sure which culture.

**Branden:** Alright, that's why I'm looking at you because you told me about this.

**Caoimhe:** Can I mention something about Korea?

**Cassandra:** Sure.

**Branden:** Go ahead.

**Caoimhe:** Oh, you're good. I think greetings, like different cultures have different body languages in terms of greeting. So, for example, in the west, we often shake hands. Whereas in Korea, bowing is more common greeting. So, I think in terms of greetings, the body language differs between cultures. You don't agree?

**Branden:** Uh, no, I completely agree. It seems like every culture sort of has its own customs, you know? Um, bowing, sha-uh, and even there's like company culture, right? Shaking hands, that's part of the culture in that context. Um, can I add something?

**Caoimhe:** Sure.

**Cassandra:** Be my guest.

**Branden:** Oh, I'm just, I'm just helping them out now. Uh, so, would you say that there's a new kind of gesture, like, we've seen some alternatives to shaking hands. Like, I've seen some people doing this.

**Caoimhe:** Oh, yes, since COVID?

**Cassandra:** Ah-ha, yeah, because it's not really safe actually. Right, right.

**Braden:** Sure, I guess so. I guess it depends on the situation too.

**Caoimhe:** So I read the different countries have, like, different things of that. So, some countries have their like an elbow bump, and in some countries say bump feet instead.

**Cassandra:** Ok.

**Branden:** Ok, can I ask, can I ask something?

**Cassandra:** Ask away.

**Caoimhe:** No problem.

**Branden:** I'm just helping them out. Which countries are you referring to? Can you list any examples?

**Caoimhe:** Have you?

**Cassandra:** No, I'm···

**Caoimhe:** Um, I think from what I understand in my country in Ireland, I think they do the elbow bump, but I'm not sure. But, yeah, so, we have to be careful, I guess, in countries, in terms of like the body language, because sometimes something in one country can be rude, and it can be too refined in other country.

**Cassandra:** Yeah. Could I say something, though?

**Branden:** Oh, fire away.

**Caoimhe:** Be my guest.

**Cassandra:** Because we keep talking about, like, gestures and kind of equating that with body language, and but body language encompasses a whole lot of other things, you know, like eye contact, like, crouching if you're scared, like I think some things are just universal to humans. They're not only in certain cultures, I think, every human, you know, naturally, maybe expands when they're happy and proud of something for example. So, what do you think of that? There are some universal traits that are obviously shared

| | |
|---|---|
| | between humans? |
| **Branden:** | I, Caoimhe, what do you think about that? Be my guest. |
| **Caoimhe:** | Oh, hahaha, nice. |
| **Branden:** | Unfortunately, we have to stop the round now. So, who's the winner? I have three points right here. And Caoimhe? |
| **Caoimhe:** | Sorry, guys. |
| **Cassandra:** | Once again? |
| **Caoimhe:** | I have five. |
| **Branden:** | No! And then, Cassandra has three. |
| **Cassandra:** | Also three. |
| **Branden:** | So, Caoimhe, good job. |
| **Caoimhe:** | I'll let you win the next time. |
| **Cassandra:** | Really? |
| **Branden:** | Alright, guys. Time for the next round. |

**[Answer]**

**Q1. What is another meaning for the 'OK' sign in a different culture?**

a) Money

b) You're having a bad day

c) You're angry at the person

**Branden:** Our countries. This means 'ok,' but in some cultures this means something else, like money. Does it mean money?

**Q2. What is a new greeting that has started since COVID?**

a) shaking hands

b) bowing

c) bumping elbows

**Branden:** Oh, I'm just helping them out now. Uh, so, would you say that there's a new kind of gesture, like, we've seen some alternatives to shaking hands. Like, I've seen some people doing this.

**Caoimhe:** Oh, yes, since COVID?

**Q3. Which of these is not a universal trait, according to Cassandra?**

a) making eye contact

b) crouching when you're scared

c) bowing

> **Cassandra:** Body language encompasses a whole lot of other things, you know, like eye contact, like, crouching if you're scared, like I think some things are just universal to humans.

## Conversation Question 3

▶ **How important do you think eye contact is?**

**Q1. According to Branden, what is the only animal that will make eye contact with humans?**

a) cats

b) dogs

c) birds

**Q2. In the west, what is eye contact a sign of, according to Caoimhe?**

a) dishonesty

b) honesty

c) aggression

**Q3. When is eye contact weird, according to Caoimhe?**

a) when it's a stranger who makes too much eye contact

b) when it's a family member

c) when it's a stranger who makes too little eye contact

### Script

**Branden:** Alright, everyone. Time for round 3. So, Caoimhe, you won two times.

**Caoimhe:** I'm sorry. Yes, that is correct.

**Branden:** Don't worry. You're forgiven. So, we're going to do something special for round 3. Round 3 is going to be worth two points to give Cassandra and I a chance. Is that ok?

**Caoimhe:** Ok, fine fine.

**Branden:** At least we can tie you. Alright. Just like the last time, we'll have three minutes to answer the question using these rejoinders. Let's get started. The question is: How important do you think eye contact is? Let's get started.

**Caoimhe:** Ok, who would like to go first?

**Cassandra:** Can I go first?

**Caoimhe:** Be my guest.

**Cassandra:** I think eye contact is fundamental, I mean, don't infants die without lack of eye contact from daycare? I think I read this statistics somewhere. It's just natural for humans. We require eye contact, right? Like, it's need.

**Caoimhe:** I've never heard that before. But, yes, I guess, it's basic human need.

**Cassandra:** Yeah, basic human need.

**Branden:** Yeah, I heard, I heard that that's something that, that's very… hopefully if you don't mind if I butt in here with something totally unrelated…but I heard that that's why dogs evolved to stare humans in the eyes because eye contact is so important, right?

**Cassandra:** Interesting!

**Branden:** Yeah, so the dogs are like the only animals that will make eye contact with us. Anyway!

**Caoimhe:** You guys are going deep. Can I interrupt with something a little more trivial?

**Cassandra:** What is it?

**Branden:** Fire away.

**Caoimhe:** I'll just go something a little less scientific. So, I think, I don't know if this is across all cultures, but I know that in the west we believe that eye contact is a sign of like honesty? So, if you're not making eye contact with someone, the other person might think that you're lying or being like shifty or dishonest.

Branden: Ok, can I just add something to that?

Caoimhe: Go ahead.

Branden: So, do you think that there's such a thing, too much eye contact?

Caoimhe: Oh, for sure!

Cassandra: Definitely!

Branden: Oh, really?

Caoimhe: I think 90% if you know someone really well, 90% is kind of like a good ratio. You don't agree?

Cassandra: Sure, sure.

Branden: I agree, but I just want to ask you one more question about that. Have you known many people who give too many eye contact, too much eye contact? This is a very common thing. What about you, Cassandra?

Cassandra: I don't know. I haven't met any with that problem, for me, like, I never really think about eye contact. I just do it naturally and hope it's not too much and hope it's not enough.

Branden: Right. Definitely I don't want bull's eyes like this.

Caoimhe: Yeah, I would say that sometimes on the subway, for example, you might catch eyes with someone and then they, they don't follow the 90% ratio, they are just staring like very directly for a long time. And, when it's a stranger, then, that becomes weird. Never happened to you?

Branden: Oh, I've never had that problem. I wish people would stare me more often. Ok. Alright. Um, yeah, so eye contact. Very important, I think, we can all agree. But we just have to do the right amount. Um, do you guys mind if I talk about public speaking?

Caoimhe: No problem.

Cassandra: Be my guest.

Branden: Yeah, no problem, good. So, one thing that I tried to do when I'm speaking is to make eye contact with not just one person but just, sort of, just move around the audience to individual members. So, not enough to creep them out. Just to make them think that we're interacting properly.

Cassandra: Good tip.

Braden: Good. So, I, this is not good. I have one point.

Cassandra: Once again.

Braden: I was talking too much.

Caoimhe: Oh, my gosh. Maybe I was talking too little. Sorry.

Braden: Caoimhe, good for you. Sometimes I lose. It's ok. Alright, guys. That's the end of round 3. Hope for you enjoyed that. And now let's move on to the next part.

**[Answer]**

**Q1. According to Branden, what is the only animal that will make eye contact with humans?**

a) cats

b) dogs

c) birds

**Branden:** Yeah, so the dogs are like the only animals that will make eye contact with us.

**Q2. In the west, what is eye contact a sign of, according to Caoimhe?**

a) dishonesty

b) honesty

c) aggression

**Caoimhe:** I know that in the west we believe that eye contact is a sign of like honesty? So, if you're not making eye contact with someone, the other person might think that you're lying.

**Q3. When is eye contact weird, according to Caoimhe?**

a) when it's a stranger who makes too much eye contact

b) when it's a family member

c) when it's a stranger who makes too little eye contact

**Caoimhe:** you might catch eyes with someone and they, they don't follow the 90% ratio, they are just staring like very directly for a long time. And, when it's a stranger, then, that becomes weird.

## Lecture 2

### Words in Action

1. **Sure.**
   - to accept a question or interruption with exclamations

**Game2**
Caoimhe: Can I mention something about Korea?
Cassandra: Sure.

2. **Yes.**
   - to accept a question or interruption with exclamations

**Game2**
Branden: Ok, I'm ready to win! Alright, so the next question is: Do different cultures have different body language? So, do different cultures have different body language. And, just like last time, we have three minutes to answer. Are you guys ready?
Caoimhe: Yes.

3. **Yes?**
   - to accept a question or interruption with exclamations

**Game1**
Branden: I do want to remind you that our rejoinders today have to do with questions. So, I think we're going to have to ask some questions here. Like, just to give our – give me a chance.
Caoimhe: Yes?

4. **Go ahead.**
   - to accept a question or interruption with imperative sentences

**Game1**
Branden: Oh, right. So, can I ask a question?
Caoimhe: Go ahead.

**Game3**
Branden: Ok, can I just add something to that?
Caoimhe: Go ahead.

5. **Ask away.**
- to accept a question or interruption with imperative sentences

**Game2**
Branden: Oh! Can I ask something?
Cassandra: Ask away.

6. **Fire away!**
- to accept a question or interruption with imperative sentences

**Game2**
Cassandra: Yeah. Could I say something, though?
Branden: Oh, fire away.

7. **Yes, what is it?**
- to accept a question or interruption with wh-questions

**Game3**
Caoimhe: You guys are going deep. Can I interrupt with something a little more trivial?
Cassandra: What is it?

8. **You don't agree?**
- to elicit agreement with yes-no questions

**Game2**
Caoimhe: So, I think in terms of greetings, the body language differs between cultures. You don't agree?
Branden: Uh, no, I completely agree. It seems like every culture sort of has its own customs, you know?

**Game3**

Caoimhe: I think 90% if you know someone really well, 90% is kind of like a good ratio. You don't agree?

Cassandra: Sure, sure.

**9. No problem.**

- to accept a question or interruption with exclamations

**Game3**

Branden: so eye contact. Very important, but we just have to have the right amount. Um, do you guys mind if I talk about public speaking?

Caoimhe: No problem.

**10. Be my guest.**

- to accept a question or interruption with imperative sentences

**Game3**

Caoimhe: Oh. Ok, so who would like to go first?

Cassandra: Can I go first?

Caoimhe: Be my guest.

## Word Power

**1. customs**

- cultural behaviors and practices; traditions

Branden: Uh, no, I completely agree. It seems like every culture sort of has its own customs, you know? Um, bowing, uh, sha – uh, even there's like company culture, right?

**2. crouching**

- to squat down and make yourself appear as small as possible; to hide behind something by squatting down

**Cassandra:** Because we keep talking about, like, gestures and like equating that with body language, but body language encompasses a whole lot of other things, you know, like eye contact, like, crouching if you're scared, like I think some things are just universal to humans.

### 3. systematic
- planned and careful; like a system

**Branden:** Well, I don't know, I don't have like a really systematic way of how I use body language, but I do notice when I talk, I'm always gesturing a little bit.

### 4. curious
- interested in; would like to ask a question

**Caoimhe:** I'm curious about something.
**Branden:** Ok.
**Caoimhe:** So, Branden, when I take selfies...

### 5. butt in
- to interrupt (casual)

**Branden:** I heard that that's something that's very...hopefully you don't mind if I butt in here on a totally unrelated...but I heard that's why dogs evolved to stare humans in the eyes because eye contact is so important, right?

### 6. shifty
- acting uncertain or untrustworthy

**Caoimhe:** So, if you're not making eye contact with someone, the other person might think that you're lying or being like shifty or dishonest.

## Outro

### Dialogue

**Branden:** Hey, Cassandra. I need to ask you something.
**Cassandra:** Sure! Be my guest.
**Branden:** It's about work. Do you have a few minutes to talk right now?
**Cassandra:** Yes, what is it?
**Branden:** Well, to be honest, this monthly report is killing me. I have so much data to analyze and not enough time to do anything – I'm barely sleeping. Do you think you could help me out?
**Cassandra:** No problem at all. I'd be glad to help! I've got some question, thought.
**Branden:** Fire away!
**Cassandra:** Well, most importantly: when is the report due?
**Branden:** Actually... it's due tomorrow. Sorry I realize this is sort of last minute. Are you still able to help me?
**Cassandra:** Well... actually... can I...?
**Branden:** Go ahead. It's okay to refuse. Don't worry.
**Cassandra:** Can I say something.
**Branden:** Please do.
**Cassandra:** I can help write the report, but next time please don't wait so long before you reach out for help. Okay?
**Branden:** Yes. Of course. Thank you. I really appreciate it.
**Cassandra:** So, since the two of us will have to work late tonight, is dinner on you?
**Branden:** Naturally. I'll order us some steaks.
**Cassandra:** Steaks? I can't agree to that. Can we get something else?
**Branden:** You don't agree? Oh! That's right. You don't eat meat. Sorry about that. I'll order whatever you'd like. What do you want? Ask away!

## Wrap-up

1. **Sure.**
   - to accept a question or interruption with exclamations

2. **Yes.**
   - to accept a question or interruption with exclamations

3. **Yes?**
   - to accept a question or interruption with exclamations

4. **Go ahead.**
   - to accept a question or interruption with imperative sentences

5. **Ask away.**
   - to accept a question or interruption with imperative sentences

6. **Fire away!**
   - To accept a question or interruption with imperative sentences

7. **Yes, what is it?**
   - to accept a question or interruption with wh-questions

8. **You don't agree?**
   - to elicit agreement with yes-no questions

9. **No problem.**
   - to accept a question or interruption with exclamations

10. **Be my guest.**
   - to accept a question or interruption with imperative sentences

## Assignment

**1. Select the option that best completes the passage.**

A: Would you mind if I asked you a few questions?
B: ______________

1) Ask to be.
2) Ask therefore.
3) Ask away.
4) Ask afar.

**2. Select the option that best completes the passage.**

A: Can I suggest something?
B: ______________

1) Be my guest.
2. Be my friend.
3) Ask me.
4) Ask my guest.

**3. Select the option that best completes the passage.**

A: Can I say something?
B: ______________

1) To be honest.
2) Sure.
3) Nevermore.
4) For certain.

**4. Select the option that best completes the passage.**

> A: You really believe that he is a good candidate?
> B: ____________

1) Agreed.
2) You agree?
3) Are you thinking?
4) You don't agree?

**5. Select the option that best completes the passage.**

> A: Could I ask you a personal question?
> B: ____________

1) Fire away!
2) You're fired.
3) Go away!
4) Get over it.

**6. Select the option that best completes the passage.**

> A: Can I interrupt you for a second?
> B: ____________

1) Go far.
2) Go long.
3) Go to it.
4) Go ahead.

**7. Select the option that best completes the passage.**

A: Would you do something for me?
B: ____________

1) Of course, I have something.
2) What is there?
3) Affirmation.
4) Yes?

**8. Select the option that best completes the passage.**

A: Sorry, can I interrupt for a second?
B: ____________

1) Yes, there is.
2) Yes, you are.
3) No, problem.
4) Probably.

**9. Select the option that best completes the passage.**

A: Could I say something?
B: ____________

1) Yes.
2) Nowhere.
3) Yes, it is.
4) Just a moment ago.

**10. Select the option that best completes the passage.**

A: I need to ask you something.
B: ____________

1) Whatever you do.
2) Yes, where is it?
3) Yes, what is it?
4) Ask for me.

Week 6

# Expressing Opinions

**Contents**

1. To simply express an opinion
2. To emphatically express an opinion
3. To express an opinion out of personal compulsion
4. To express an opinion based on the information available
5. To express unexpected news or opinion
6. To express an opinion from a simple perspective
7. To express an opinion from a personal perspective
8. To express a considerate opinion
9. To politely express an impression
10. To express an individual preference over other preferences

**Objectives**

1. To understand 10 types of expressing skills
2. To understand how 10 types of expressing skills are used in real conversations
   1) If any, what different kinds of art do you like?
   2) Have you ever been to a museum before? If so, describe your experience.
   3) Do you think it's important to have art in our home, restaurants, or public places?

## Intro

### Speaking Skills: Expressing Opinions

**1. I think...**

- to simply express an opinion

Example

A: What should I do?

B: I think you should ask your parents for help.

**2. I do think...**

- to emphatically express an opinion

Example

A: You don't care about politics, right?

B: Not really, but I do think it's important to read the news.

**3. I have to say...**

- to express an opinion out of personal compulsion

Example

A: I'm going to ask Marcy to marry me.

B: I have to say I think it's too soon.

**4. As far as I can tell...**

- to express an opinion based on the information available

Example

A: Is this a good time to buy stocks?

B: As far as I can tell, it is.

**5. You know what?**

- to express unexpected news or opinion

Example

A: Do you think BTS will win a Grammy award?

B: You know what? They've got a good chance.

**6. In my opinion...**

- to express an opinion from a simple perspective

Example

A: Is she good enough to pass her driving test?

B: In my opinion, she definitely is.

**7. If you ask me...**

- to express an opinion from a personal perspective

Example

A: Should we take a taxi?

B: If you ask me, it's better to walk.

8. **It seems to me...**

- to express a considerate opinion

Example

A: My kids are so lazy!

B: It seems to me they just need to get outside more.

9. **I feel...**

- to politely express an impression

Example

A: I feel you should take the subway instead of driving.

B: Okay, I'll think about it.

10. **As for me...**

- to express an individual preference over other preferences

Example

A: I think running is the best exercise.

B: Maybe for you, but as for me, running hurts my knees.

## Lecture 1

### Conversation Question 1

**▶ If any, what different kinds of art do you like?**

**Q1. What kind of art has always intrigued Branden?**

a) Renaissance art

b) Canadian art

c) Performance art

**Q2. Who is interested in modern art?**

a) Caoimhe

b) Branden

c) Cassandra

**Q3. Which of these does Cassandra not mention as a type of Canadian art?**

a) Nature-themed art

b) Aboriginal art

c) Animated art

Script

**Branden:** Hello, everyone. Welcome back. We're going to have another review game based on the rejoinders you learned in class. I'm Branden.

**Caoimhe:** I'm Caoimhe.

**Cassandra:** I'm Cassandra.

**Branden:** Alright. So, just like last time, we'll have three minutes to answer the question. Whoever uses the most rejoinders will be the winner. Probably me, but we'll see. Ok, so, these rejoinders have to do with expressing our opinion. Let's get started. Alright. So, the question is: If any, what different kinds of art do you like? Ok, so there are so many different kinds of art. What kind of art do you like? Let's get started. Ok.

**Caoimhe:** Ok. So, what about you, Cass?

**Cassandra:** I have to say. This is kind of a difficult question to answer, because I think I like all forms of art, you know, from performance art to comics, if you count that is art, to visual, to music, so, I don't really know how to answer this question, I don't know where to start.

**Branden:** So, is there such a thing as bad art though, some are just really bad, right?

**Cassandra:** Oh, that's a hard question to answer.

**Branden:** Yeah. What is - what is bad art? Because it's subjective, right?

**Cassandra:** Right, right.

**Caoimhe:** I mean, for me, as for me, I'm, yeah, sometimes I go to a museum, for example, and I see like this very expensive painting, but it looks like I could've done that when I was in, like, elementary school. So, for me, maybe that's not bad art, but I just don't really understand, like, that kind of art.

**Branden:** Sure. It seems to me that just like beauty is in the eye of the beholder. Art, too, is in the eye of the beholder. Wouldn't you say so?

**Cassandra:** Yeah. I think that's well said.

**Branden:** Oh, thank you. I appreciate that.

**Caoimhe:** What about you, Branden? Do you have like a favorite kind of art or artist?

**Branden:** Well, as for me, I, I feel that the Renaissance art has always been quite interesting to look at. Just the way it takes like all these figures from literature and then puts them in a, sort of a European situation. I've always found that intriguing for some reason, you know, just like all these classical gods and stuff. So, yeah, that's personal, my personal preference.

**Caoimhe:** It seems to me you're like a very highbrow, like, intellectual kind of guy.

**Branden:** Ah, probably not, probably not. I have to say, however, I've been watching some animations on Netflix, and I think that some animations have really good standards of production, so, yeah, I do, I do like some of that.

**Caoimhe:** Uhm, ok, great. What about you, Cass? Do you like animation?

**Cassandra:** Oh, sure. I'm a big fan of animation. I don't want to bore you about kind of naming awful ones I like, I'll tell you, I'll tell you later all about that. Um, as for me, I just want to be a little bit of a patriot for a second and mention Canadian art. Canadian visual art. So, I'm a pretty big fan of, yeah, like the Canadian painters like the group of seven.

**Branden:** You know what? I'm not familiar with that kind of art. So, what kind of themes does it involve?

**Cassandra:** Honestly, lots of nature. You know, it's Canada, so, yeah, lots of nature, and also the artwork of aboriginal peoples in Canada. The mythology, that sort of thing. Yeah, what are you into, Caoimhe?

**Caoimhe:** Um, I would say, if you ask me, I'm really into modern…time is up! Modern art.

**Branden:** Modern art, ok, we'll have to continue the discussion later.

**Cassandra:** Definitely, definitely.

**Branden:** That's great. So, I have, guys, I have five points. What about you?

**Caoimhe:** Oh, I have three.

**Branden:** Three, three. Yes! I'm the winner of round 1, but you guys still have a chance. We have two more questions to go over. Let's get started on that.

**[Answer]**

**Q1. What kind of art has always intrigued Branden?**

a) Renaissance art
b) Canadian art
c) Performance art

> **Branden:** Well, as for me, I feel that the Renaissance art has always been quite interesting to look at. Just the way it takes like all these figures from literature and puts them in a, sort of a European situation.

**Q2. Who is interested in modern art?**

a) Caoimhe
b) Branden
c) Cassandra

> **Cassandra:** the artwork of aboriginal peoples in Canada. The mythology, that sort of thing. Yeah, what are you into, Caoimhe?
> **Caoimhe:** Um, I would say, if you ask me, I'm really into modern...time is up! Modern art.

**Q3. Which of these does Cassandra not mention as a type of Canadian art?**

a) Nature-themed art
b) Aboriginal art
c) Animated art

> **Branden:** You know what? I'm not familiar with that kind of art. What kind of themes does it involve?
> **Cassandra:** Honestly, lots of nature. The artwork of aboriginal peoples in Canada. The mythology, that sort of thing.

## Conversation Question 2

▶ **Have you ever been to a museum before? If so, describe your experience?**

**Q1. Who took Branden to the Egyptian museum when he was a child?**

a) Caoimhe

b) His grandparents

c) It was a school trip.

**Q2. Who lives near the war museum in Yongsan?**

a) Caoimhe

b) Branden

c) Cassandra

**Q3. Why did Cassandra go to the war museum for Valentine's Day?**

a) She needed to do an assignment.

b) She and her boyfriend are history buffs.

c) Her boyfriend works at the museum.

### Script

**Branden:** Alright, it's time for question number two using the rejoinders that we learned in class. Yeah, so, we have a new question, and we have three minutes to answer. Guys: Have you ever been to a museum before? If so, describe your experience. Have you ever been to a museum before? If so, describe your experience. Let's get started. Ah-ha, good. Alright!

**Caoimhe:** Ok, who's going first?

**Branden:** Ok, I'll start. Um, yeah, as for me, as for me, I always, yeah, when I was a kid, I went to museum that had to do with Egyptian, ancient Egyptian relics and mummies, you know, mummy is a, sort of like a dead body that has been preserved for a long time. So, yeah, it was very intriguing, although, as a child, I was scared because, you know, just the realization that these used be real-life humans and now they're dead, right, that was kind of morbid when you think about it.

**Cassandra:** I have to say, Branden, I think you're a big f an of history, aren't you?

**Branden:** Oh, yeah. I do enjoy various parts of history, yeah.

**Caoimhe:** I feel like we often go to those kinds of museums for like a school trip. So, was it a school trip or did you actually go there of your own free will?

**Branden:** Oh, no, my grandparents took me. So, I didn't go as a school trip. What about you guys? Do you have any experience with museums?

**Caoimhe:** Um, you know what? I actually live really close to the war museum. Like I don't know if you guys have been in Yongsan in Seoul?

**Branden:** Oh, ok, so that's the one that commemorates the Korean War?

**Caoimhe:** Yeah. So, I've been there for a few times. So, I went there with previous students, and I've been with friends as well. It was a really impressive museum. And I think they actually like re-did it a few years ago. So, it's a really really great museum.

**Branden:** Yeah, you know what? You know what? Now that you mentioned it, it's so interesting how much this country has changed in such a short amount of time. It could be interesting to see that.

**Caoimhe:** Yeah, for sure.

**Cassandra:** Oh, and you know what, as well? The war museum was where I spent my last Valentine's Day. I went on a date to the war museum.

**Caoimhe:** Oh, in my opinion, that's a very educational romantic Valentine's Day.

**Branden:** I thought about doing that one, but I was afraid that it wouldn't be romantic enough. But you enjoyed it?

**Cassandra:** Uh, yeah, we're both history buffs, so...it was enjoyable.

**Branden:** Ok, I feel that could be interesting, yeah.

**Cassandra:** Yeah, as far as I can tell, there are a lot of various museums in Korea. In my neighborhood, we have like a furniture museum, a museum of these stone guardians, a museum of art, so many various museums.

**Caoimhe:** I do think, yeah, Korea has like a really good variety. There's also like the kimchi museum...

**Branden:** I haven't heard about that. Kimchi.

**Caoimhe:** And there are also really random, like, trick-eye museums with like optical illusions. So, I have to say, like I love the museum culture in Korea.

**Cassandra:** I do think so too, I love museums too.

**Branden:** I think I have to get out more because all these museums we're talking about, except for the war museum, I don't really know, I've never heard of it. Yeah, thanks for the suggestion.

**Caoimhe:** Ok, what about, have you guys been to like any famous art museums? Oh, time's up!

**Branden:** Oh, I thought, Caoimhe, we'll talk about that later. Ok, so, I have four points. What about you guys?

**Cassandra:** Four also.

**Caoimhe:** Five.

**Branden:** Ok, so, you guys may remember that I won last round, which is good. Caoimhe won this round, bad. Anyway, we have a next round to look forward to. Alright! Let's move on to the next part.

**[Answer]**

**Q1. Who took Branden to the Egyptian museum when he was a child?**

a) Caoimhe

b) His grandparents

c) It was a school trip.

**Caoimhe:** So, was it a school trip or did you actually go there of your own free will?

**Branden:** Oh, no, my grandparents took me. So, I didn't go as a school trip.

**Q2. Who lives near the war museum in Yongsan?**

a) Caoimhe

b) Branden

c) Cassandra

**Branden:** What about you guys? Do you have any experience with museums?

**Caoimhe:** I actually live really close to the war museum. Like I don't know if you guys have been. In Yongsan?

**Q3. Why did Cassandra go to the war museum for Valentine's Day?**

a) She needed to do an assignment.

b) She and her boyfriend are history buffs.

c) Her boyfriend works at the museum.

> **Branden:** But you enjoyed it?
> **Cassandra:** Uh, yeah, we're both history buffs, so...it was enjoyable.

## Conversation Question 3

▶ **Do you think it's important to have art in our home, restaurants or public places?**

**Q1. Which of these is above art on Branden's importance scale?**

a) A cell phone

b) Candles

c) Food

**Q2. Who thinks art is important because it can 'cheer you up'?**

a) Caoimhe

b) Branden

c) Cassandra

**Q3. What is Cassandra's desktop background?**

a) A painting of an old building

b) A picture of her boyfriend

c) A Canadian landscape

**Script**

**Branden:** Alright, guys. Welcome back. This is round 3. So, last time I won and then Caoimhe won. Ok? We used the most rejoinders. Cassandra, zero, but she still has a chance because this round is worth two points. So, there's a chance you can outdo, Cassandra. Don't give up hope.

**Cassandra:** Thank you.

**Branden:** Alright, so we have three minutes to answer the question. You guys, ready?

**Caoimhe, Cassandra:** Yes.

**Branden:** Ok. Do you think it's important to have art in your home or restaurants or public places? Do you think it's important? Let's get started. Good! So, yeah, I'll start. If you ask me, come on, it's not that important. Like, what's essential for us to live? Food, air, you know, water? But art isn't essential for our survival, so I would rank it a little lower in the – on the important scale. Personally.

**Caoimhe:** Um, you know what? I kind of, I disagree. I think it can really... especially in public places, I think that art can really cheer you up. So, for example, like recently because people were feeling a bit gloomy because of COVID, like Seoul, they did some like light projections and things in the city to boost people's moods. So, I guess for me, it can really cheer people e up.

**Cassandra:** Yeah, in my opinion, I agree with Caoimhe. I think like while it's not essential, as in it's not like sunlight or shelter, but I think it played a really important role in human history. I mean like, think of cave people. They were communicating with each other and teaching each other through stories and art by drawing on, you know, the cave walls. So I think humans have natural need to storytell through art.

**Caoimhe:** Oh, interesting!

**Branden:** I do think that art can affect our emotions and plant ideas into our heads. So, it can really, um, convey complex concepts possibly.

**Caoimhe:** What about in your home? Do you guys have any artwork in your house? Or do you think that is important?

**Cassandra:** Um, yes, I have artwork but it's not, like, they're not real prints. I didn't spend a lot of money. I'm not a collector. But I have just you know the regular prints that you can buy from stores or order online. Canadian art, mostly.

**Caoimhe:** You're really selling that Canadian art. I do think you're very patriotic.

**Branden:** You know what? You know what? Now that you mentioned it, I do have art, but not in my house, on my desktop computer, sometimes I put arts as my wallpaper. So, yeah, sort of, yeah, it's nice to look at. You know.

**Caoimhe:** So, like a painting? What do you have?

**Branden:** I usually like, just old buildings, like paintings, paintings of old buildings. I like, like, old stuffs, so, yeah, I enjoy that.

**Caoimhe:** So, in my opinion, a desktop, like the background, says a lot about a person. So, Cass, what is your background on your computer?

**Cassandra:** A Canadian landscape.

**Caoimhe:** Is it? Really?

**Cassandra:** Yeah, it's nature.

**Branden:** Oh, as far, as far as I can tell that you're really proud to be Canadian, right? Because I heard about Cana-, you know, you know a lot about it.

**Cassandra:** Sure, I'm pro Canadian, but I'm also happy to live in Korea. Um... ok, can we, can we talk a bit about like, uh, in restaurants or in cafes when you see some art displayed. How does it make you feel?

**Branden:** I feel it's important. When people go to cafes, they want to have a good feeling, so art definitely contributes to that. Alright, guy. We're going to have to stop there. That's three minutes is up. So, I have five points, three, and two.

**Cassandra:** Oh, two, you're generous! I have, I thought I have just one.

**Branden:** Oh, I miscounted. One point. Yes! So, I am the winner. I have two points, one, and zero. Alright, but that's not over. We'll probably have a game in the future. Ok, let's move on to the next part.

**[Answer]**

**Q1. Which of these is above art on Branden's importance scale?**

a) A cell phone

b) Candles

c) Food

**Branden:** If you ask me, it's not that important. Like, what's essential for us to live? Food, air, you know, water? But art isn't essential for our survival, so I would rank it a little lower in the – on the importance scale. Personally.

**Q2. Who thinks art is important because it can 'cheer you up'?**

a) Caoimhe

b) Branden

c) Cassandra

**Caoimhe:** I think that art can really cheer you up. So, for example, like recently because people were feeling a bit gloomy because of COVID, like Seoul, they did some like light projections and things in the city.

**Q3. What is Cassandra's desktop background?**

a) A painting of an old building

b) A picture of her boyfriend

c) A Canadian landscape

**Caoimhe:** in my opinion, a desktop, like the background, says a lot about a person. So, Cass, what is your background on your computer?

**Cassandra:** A Canadian landscape.

## Lecture 2

### Words in Action

**1. I think...**

- to simply express an opinion

**Game1**

Branden: I feel that the Renaissance art has always been quite interesting to look at. I've been watching some animations on Netflix, and I think that some animations have really good standards of production.

**2. I do think...**

- to emphatically express an opinion

**Game2**

Caoimhe: I do think, yeah, Korea has like a really good variety. There's also like the kimchi museum...

**3. I have to say...**

- to express an opinion out of personal compulsion

**Game2**

Caoimhe: And there are also really random, like, trick-eye museums with like optical illusions. So, I have to say, like I love the museum culture in Korea.

**4. As far as I can tell...**

- to express an opinion based on the information available

**Game2**

Cassandra: Yeah, as far as I can tell, there are a lot of various museums in Korea. In my neighborhood, we have like a furniture museum, a museum of these stone guardians, a museum of art, so many various museums.

**5. You know what?**

- to express unexpected news or opinion

**Game1**

Cassandra: As for me, I just want to be a little bit of a patriot for a second and mention Canadian art. Canadian visual art. So, I'm a pretty big fan of, yeah, like the Canadian painters like the group of seven.

Branden: You know what? I'm not familiar with that kind of art. What kind of themes does it involve?

**6. In my opinion...**

- to express an opinion from a simple perspective

**Game3**

Caoimhe: So, I guess for me, it can really cheer people up.

Cassandra: Yeah, in my opinion, I agree with Caoimhe. I think like while it's not essential, as in it's not like sunlight or shelter, but I think it played a really important role in human history.

**7. If you ask me...**

- to express an opinion from a personal perspective

**Game1**

Cassandra: So, I'm a pretty big fan of, yeah, like the Canadian painters like the group of seven. Yeah, what are you into, Caoimhe?

Caoimhe: Um, I would say, if you ask me, I'm really into modern art.

**8. It seems to me...**

- to express a considerate opinion

**Game1**

Branden: I feel that the Renaissance art has always been quite interesting to look at. I've always found that intriguing for some reason.

Caoimhe: It seems to me you're like a very highbrow, like, intellectual kind of guy.

**9. I feel...**

- to politely express an impression

**Game3**

Cassandra: Um, ok, can we, can we talk a bit about like, uh, in restaurants or in cafes when you see some art displayed.

Branden: I feel it's important. When people go to cafes, they want to have a good feeling, so art definitely contributes to that.

**10. As for me...**

- to express an opinion individual preference over other preferences

**Game3**

Caoimhe: Ok. Who's going first?

Branden: Um, yeah, as for me I always...yeah, when I was a kid I went to a museum that had to do with ancient Egyptian relics and mummies.

## Word Power

**1. subjective**

- dependent on personal opinions

Cassandra: Oh, that's a hard question to answer.

Branden: Yeah. What is – what is bad art? Because it's subjective, right?

Cassandra: Right, right.

**2. highbrow**

- fancy; of a high social status

Branden: I feel that the Renaissance art has always been quite interesting to look at. Just the way it takes like all these figures from literature and puts them in a, sort of a European situation. I've always found that intriguing for some reason.

Caoimhe: It seems to me you're like a very highbrow, like, intellectual kind of guy.

3. **commemorate**

- to recall and show respect for

> **Caoimhe:** I actually live really close to the war museum. Like I don't know if you guys have been. In Yongsan?
>
> **Branden:** Oh, ok, so that's the one that commemorates the Korean war?

4. **history buffs**

- people who are really interested in history

> **Branden:** But you enjoyed it?
>
> **Cassandra:** Uh, yeah, we're both history buffs, so...it was enjoyable.
>
> **Branden:** ok. I feel that could be interesting, yeah.

5. **cheer [someone] up**

- to improve someone's mood; to make someone happy

> **Caoimhe:** I think it can really...especially in public places, I think that art can really cheer you up. So, for example, like recently because people were feeling a bit gloomy because of COVID, like Seoul, they did some like light projections and things in the city.

6. **prints**

- copied versions of original pieces of art

> **Cassandra:** Um, yes, I have artwork but it's not, like, they're not real prints. I didn't spend a lot of money. I'm not a collector. But I have just you know the regular prints that you can buy from stores or order online. Canadian art, mostly.

## Outro

### Dialogue

Branden: It's so hot outside! I think that global warming is making our weather more extreme.

Cassandra: Oh? It seems to me that today is just a normal summer day.

Branden: I feel you aren't as sensitive to weather as I am, and that's fine. But you cannot deny the reality of climate change.

Cassandra: If you ask me, climate change is just a big hoax!

Branden: Are you serious? I have to say I'm disappointed in you, Cassandra. I thought you believed in science.

Cassandra: I do think that the climate is changing, but in my opinion rising sea levels and increasing temperatures are just natural changes that the earth goes through, regardless of us humans.

Branden: You know what? You're totally wrong! Based on the evidence, about 97 percent of climate scientists agree that human-caused climate change is happening right now. It's a serious problem.

Cassandra: As far as I can tell, everything is fine. The earth is over 4 billion years old! I am sure the Earth can continue to protect itself without any involvement from us humans.

Branden: Suit yourself, but as for me, I'll continue to believe in what our scientist have to say on this matter.

### Wrap-up

1. **I think...**
   - to simply express an opinion

2. **I do think...**
   - to emphatically express an opinion

3. **I have to say...**
   - to express an opinion out of personal compulsion

**4. As far as I can tell...**

- to express an opinion based on the information available

**5. You know what?**

- to express unexpected news or opinion

**6. In my opinion...**

- To express an opinion from a simple perspective

**7. If you ask me...**

- to express an opinion from a personal perspective

**8. It seems to me...**

- to express a considerate opinion

**9. I feel...**

- to politely express an impression

**10. As for me...**

- to express an opinion individual preference over other preferences

## Assignment

**1. Select the option that best completes the passage.**

A: I hate my coworkers. I think I'm going to quit my job soon.
B: ______________ I think you should keep your job. The pay is good and you don't have any other options right now.

1) I tell you
2) I am saying
3) As far as I can tell
4) I have to say

**2. Select the option that best completes the passage.**

A: Do you think my son will get married someday?
B: ______________ He has a decent personality. I think there's a chance.

1) You know what?
2) You know?
3) You know about it?
4) I know about it.

**3. Select the option that best completes the passage.**

A: ____________________ you should take a taxi instead of walking. This neighborhood can be dangerous at night.
B: Ok, you have a good point.

1) I know
2) I feel
3) I am thinking so
4) As for me

**4. Select the option that best completes the passage.**

A: Should we go see a movie or take a walk in the park?
B: ________________, it's better to see a movie. I heard it's going to rain later today.

1) As my opinion
2) When you ask me
3) If you ask me
4) It seems for me

**5. Select the option that best completes the passage.**

A: My dog is puking all over the floor. What should I do?
B: ______________ you should take it to a veterinarian.

1) I ask
2) That seems
3) As far as I can think
4) I think

**6. Select the option that best completes the passage.**

A: Do you think this computer is a worthy investment?
B: ______________, it isn't. It's way too expensive.

1) In my opinion
2) As I think
3) In my thought
4) I have to tell

**7. Select the option that best completes the passage.**

A: You never take public transportation, do you?
B: No, I always drive my own car. But ______________ it's important to improve the public transportation system. A lot of people rely on it every day.

1) If you ask
2) As far as I think
3) Seems
4) I do think

**8.** **Select the option that best completes the passage.**

A: I think gym membership is totally worth it.
B: Maybe for you, but ________________, working out in a gym is too boring. I would rather hike outside for my daily exercise.

1) as I think
2) as for me
3) as you see
4) as it seems

**9.** **Select the option that best completes the passage.**

A: I wonder if it's a good time to travel.
B: ________________, it is

1) As far as I tell
2) As far as I can tell
3) You know when
4) It's like

**10.** **Select the option that best completes the passage.**

A: I am getting so fat.
B: ________________ that you gained some weight over the vacation. But it's not that bad.

1) It seems as far
2) I say
3) It seems to me
4) If feel as

Week 7

# Agreeing

**Contents**

1. To informally agree
2. To emphatically agree
3. To agree and express frustration
4. To completely agree
5. To show that you share exactly the same opinion
6. To show partial agreement
7. To agree and acknowledge a good point
8. To agree and confirm a fact
9. To agree in an official way
10. To agree in a defensive way

**Objectives**

1. To understand 10 types of agreeing skills
2. To understand how 10 types of agreeing skills are used in real conversations
    1) What are the pros and cons of having pets?
    2) Do you have any animal phobias? Please discuss your fears.
    3) What do you think about keeping animals in zoos or aquariums?

## Intro

### Speaking Skills: Agreeing

**1. Yeah.**

- to informally agree

Example

A: This cafeteria has the best bagels.

B: Yeah.

**2. Of course.**

- to emphatically agree

Example

A: Pine nuts are so much more expensive than almonds.

B: Of course.

**3. That is what I've been saying.**

- to agree and express frustration

Example

A: It is raining. We should probably take a taxi.

B: That is what I've been saying.

**4. I totally agree.**

- to completely agree

Example

A: It looks like it's going to rain.

B: I totally agree.

**5. I'm totally with you.**

- to show that you share exactly the same opinion

Example

A: The best way to lose weight is by eating healthier.

B: I'm totally with you.

**6. I guess so.**

- to show partial agreement

Example

A: You need more dairy in your diet.

B: I guess so.

**7. That's a good point.**

- to agree and acknowledge a good point

Example

A: Technology can be harmful.

B: That's a good point.

**8.** **That's true.**

- to agree and confirm a fact

Example

A: She didn't even graduate from high school.

B: That's true.

**9.** **I concur.**

- to agree in an official way

Example

A: It's an expensive restaurant but well worth it.

B: I concur.

**10.** **Yes, (Yeah) I know.**

- to agree in a defensive way

Example

A: You should drink less coffee.

B: Yeah, I know.

## Lecture 1

### Conversation Question 1

▶ **What are the pros and cons of having pets?**

**Q1.** **What pet would Branden like to have?**

a) A bird

b) A dog

c) A cat

**Q2.** **Why doesn't Cassandra want a pet right now?**

a) Her apartment is too noisy.

b) Her apartment is too big.

c) Her apartment is too small.

**Q3. Why doesn't Caoimhe want to get a cat?**

a) She's allergic to their hair.

b) She wants a big dog instead.

c) She thinks that her apartment is too small for a cat.

**Script**

**Branden:** Hello! I'm Branden.

**Caoimhe:** I'm Caoimhe.

**Cassandra:** I'm Cassandra.

**Branden:** Good. So, we're going to have a game using the rejoinders that you learned in class for showing agreement. Ok? So, whoever uses the most rejoinders in three minutes will be the winner. You guys ready?

**Caoimhe:** Yes. Let's do it.

**Cassandra:** Mmhmm.

**Branden:** Good. Glad to hear. Ok, so let's start with the first question. What are the pros and cons of having pets? So, pros and cons, that means what are the good points and bad points of having pets. Ok? I'm going to set the timer now. Ok, let's get started. Uh, yeah, who would like to start us off in our discussion?

**Caoimhe:** Um, I will say I would love to have a pet, but I think for me because I love travelling, it's very difficult to know who would take care of that animal while I'm overseas.

**Branden:** Oh, that's a good point. A lot of responsibility.

**Caoimhe:** Responsibility, yeah. Mmhmm. So, how about you guys? What do you think?

**Cassandra:** Well, sure, a con, I guess, of pets is that you have to care for them...

**Caoimhe:** Yeah.

**Cassandra:** Um, physically be there to, you know, watch over them. Pay for their medical expenses. So, yeah, they're a big responsibility but the pros are so great.

**Branden:** Yeah.

**Cassandra:** Right?

**Caoimhe:** Mmhmm. Yeah, I'm totally with you.

**Branden:** That's true. I would love to have a pet. A dog. I don't know if you remember, I had a bird? Do you remember that?

**Caoimhe:** Yes, I remember. I remember. That's a good point.

**Branden:** Yeah, I had a bird. Unfortunately, it passed away several years ago, but I like animals, you know. I even thought about getting a dog one of these days.

**Caoimhe:** Oh, wow.

**Branden:** Uh, Cassandra, you said you would love – you like pets. Would you ever consider getting a pet in the future?

**Cassandra:** Um, It's hard to answer because it depends on the amount of space that I have. So, at the moment my apartment is too small, I think, to ethically keep an animal.

**Caoimhe:** Yeah.

**Branden:** Yeah.

**Cassandra:** In the future, if I have space, I would love to have some pets.

**Caoimhe:** I totally agree. I think...

**Branden:** I'm also totally with you. It's kind of hard to have a big enough place, especially when we're living in the city. Right?

**Caoimhe:** Yeah, like the people who live above me have the same size of apartment, but they have two big dogs, and I feel like as soon as they open the door, the dogs are like really dying to get outside. So, yeah, I think space is a big factor as well.

**Branden:** Sure.

**Caoimhe:** Yeah, so any other pros? Why do you guys want to have a pet? What other pros do you think they have?

**Branden:** Uh...

**Cassandra:** Companionship.

**Branden:** Companionship, that's a good one. Just, yeah, what can I say? If you're not ready for a child, you have a pet. No, I'm just...

**Caoimhe:** Oh, my god.

**Cassandra:** That's true, actually.

**Caoimhe:** I guess so. Yeah. I have one friend who wanted to have a baby and I said maybe get a dog first. The dog isn't going so well, so I think she's learned. So, it can also be a kind of like a life lesson.

**Branden:** Sure, sure.

**Cassandra:** Yeah, yeah.

**Caoimhe:** I think also like they, pets motivate you, especially dogs, to stay healthier because obviously you need to take that dog for a walk and things.

**Cassandra:** Oh, that's a good point.

**Branden:** I concur.

**Caoimhe:** But I guess particularly with dogs. Yeah.

**Branden:** So, we've been talking about dogs, you know, they're big, usually. What about other pets, like cats? Do they have different pros and cons? They're small! They're small, right?

**Cassandra:** They require less space, for sure...

**Branden:** Less space.

**Caoimhe:** Yeah, for sure, yeah.

**Cassandra:** But, I have issues with their litter box.

**Caoimhe:** Oh, yeah!

**Branden:** Yeah. It can be a little smelly.

**Cassandra:** Yeah, a little smelly.

**Caoimhe:** That's true, yeah.

**Cassandra:** Again, that's why I need a big apartment. A giant apartment where they can, you know, go off and do their business somewhere far from me.

**Caoimhe:** For me, I'm allergic to cat hair and then also dislike the smell of the litter box, so I totally concur.

**Branden:** I totally agree. I've – I've visited people who have that problem. They don't clean it, it smells. Not good, let me tell you. Alright, so, we're out of time. Uh, let's see here. I have three points, no, I have six points.

**Caoimhe:** Five, six, seven...I have eight! I don't know how I did it, but...

**Branden:** And Cassandra how...

**Cassandra:** Just two.

**Branden:** Two? Ok, we're going to have to give this one to Caoimhe. She's the winner. However, there will be two more questions. So, let's see how we do.

**[Answer]**

**Q1. What pet would Branden like to have?**

a) A bird

b) A dog

c) A cat

Branden: Yeah, I had a bird. Unfortunately, it passed away several years ago, but I like animals, you know. I even thought about getting a dog one of these days.

**Q2. Why doesn't Cassandra want a pet right now?**

a) Her apartment is too noisy.

b) Her apartment is too big.

c) Her apartment is too small.

Cassandra: It's hard to answer because it depends on the amount of space that I have. So, at the moment my apartment is too small, I think, to ethically keep an animal.

**Q3. Why doesn't Caoimhe want to get a cat?**

a) She's allergic to their hair.

b) She wants a big dog instead.

c) She thinks that her apartment is too small for a cat.

Caoimhe: For me, I'm allergic to cat hair and then also dislike the smell of the litter box, so I totally concur.

## Conversation Question 2

▶ **Do you have any animal phobias?**

**Q1. What is Caoimhe's biggest animal phobia?**

a) Cockroaches

b) Cats

c) Rats

**Q2. Who doesn't really have any animal phobias, except maybe cockroaches?**

a) Cassandra

b) Caoimhe

c) Branden

**Q3. Who claims that they are an 'insect killer'?**

a) Cassandra

b) Caoimhe

c) Branden

### Script

**Branden:** Hello, everyone. Welcome back. It's time for question number two. Are you guys ready?

**Caoimhe:** Yes.

**Branden:** Good. So, we're going to have three minutes to use as many rejoinders as we possibly can with the next question. Do you have animal phobias? Please discuss your fears. Animal phobias. So, that is, like, an animal that you're afraid of, right? Ok? So, something that you're afraid of is a phobia. Alright, let's get started. We have three minutes, starting now. Ok, animal phobias. Who would like to start?

**Caoimhe:** Ok, well I have a huge phobia of rats. So, if I see a rat on the street, like, I will cry. Like, it totally ruins my day. Like, I get a kind of trauma from it. So, I'm absolutely terrified of rats.

**Branden:** I guess so. I understand why you would say that, but they're kind of cute, right?

**Caoimhe:** There's nothing cute. Even like...

**Branden:** Just their little chubby face?

**Caoimhe:** Even like the movie Ratatouille, like the animated rat, I can't watch that. So, I'm totally terrified.

**Cassandra:** Ok, that sounds like a true phobia and not just a dislike of them.

**Branden:** Yeah. I suppose they could be considered dirty, you know. Who knows where they've been, you know?

**Cassandra:** Yeah, I guess so.

**Caoimhe:** It's everything. Ok, so I have others, but what about Cass?

**Cassandra:** I don't think I have any phobias, actually, of animals. I grew up, kind of like in the countryside of Canada where we have so many animals, insects, fish...

**Branden:** But, you know Cassandra, insects are animals. You're not scared of any insects?

**Cassandra:** There are insects that I don't like.

**Branden:** Oh, ok.

**Cassandra:** But I'm not terrified – I think maybe cockroaches.

**Branden:** Yeah, I was going to mention...

**Cassandra:** Are...they're not my favorite thing.

**Branden:** eah, sure.

**Cassandra:** So, you agree with me?

**Branden:** I concur. I concur. Cockroaches are quite...distasteful. I actually – now that we mention cockroaches – I have a fear, a terrible fear of cockroaches. Um, I just think...I don't really know. They're small. Why am I afraid of these little insects?

**Cassandra:** That's true.

**Branden:** Spiders are ok. Spiders, even flies. I also don't like houseflies. So... yeah.

**Caoimhe:** Ok.

**Branden:** What – what about cockroaches? You like them?

**Caoimhe:** For me, like, yeah, I'm not really bothered by, kind of, insects. And when I was in Australia, like, the cockroaches fly.

**Cassandra:** Oh, my.

**Caoimhe:** Which is, so, but it didn't really bother me, so, like I'm usually the one, like if one of my friends is scared, I'm the one that like lifts it and places it outside. Because I don't really like killing any animals except for mosquitos. Mosquitos are the only animal I would ever kill.

**Branden:** Ok, so, even insects, you won't do it.

Caoimhe: Yeah, no, I won't kill any insects.
Branden: Wow, ok, quite a pacifist. Ok.
Cassandra: No, I'm totally with you. I try not to kill any beings. Like if it's kind of a mosquito flying around, I'll...I'll do it but I, if I can like actually capture the insect and bring it outside, like a spider, I can like catch it and bring it outside and release it. It's better.
Branden: Sure, well, sorry, I have to disagree. I kill them. I kill them. I'm an insect killer.
Caoimhe: I was going to say, I think the one insect I do have a phobia of is, like, wasps. Because I was badly stung when I was a kid. So, I think, I don't know. I think everybody is kind of scared of being stung by a wasp.
Cassandra: Sure, for sure.
Branden: I'm totally with you. I was also stung when I was a kid.
Caoimhe: Oh, really?
Branden: Yeah.
Caoimhe: Was it painful?
Branden: Oh yeah, yeah.
Caoimhe: It's not comfortable.
Branden: It wasn't a fun time, let me...
Caoimhe: Yeah. I totally – I need to get some points here – I totally agree.
Branden: Oh, ok, yeah.
Caoimhe: Um, so for me probably just like wasps and then just like natural phobias. Like, I think most people are scared of sharks.
Branden: Oh, sure.
Cassandra: For sure, yeah. Yeah, that's a good point.
Branden: Yeah.
Caoimhe: So, what about, Cass, in....ok, guess I'll never get to ask that question.
Branden: Well we'll have to....ask that question after class. Uh, yeah, so that's it for question two. I have three points.
Caoimhe: I have two points.
Cassandra: Oh, I have three. Wow.
Branden: Wow, you know what this means? We are tied! Yeah, one, one, one. Great.
Caoimhe: Uh, ok. Yup.
Branden: So, that brings us to the end of question two. Let's move on to the next question.

[Answer]

**Q1. What is Caoimhe's biggest animal phobia?**

a) Cockroaches

b) Cats

c) Rats

Caoimhe: I have a huge phobia of rats. So, if I see a rat on the street, like, I will cry. Like, it totally ruins my day. Like, I get a kind of trauma from it. So, I'm absolutely terrified of rats.

**Q2. Who doesn't really have any animal phobias, except maybe cockroaches?**

a) Cassandra

b) Caoimhe

c) Branden

Cassandra: I don't think I have any phobias, actually, of animals. There are insects that I don't like. I think maybe cockroaches.

**Q3. Who claims that they are an 'insect killer'?**

a) Cassandra

b) Caoimhe

c) Branden

Cassandra: I can like catch it and bring it outside and release it. It's better.
Branden: Sure, well, sorry, I have to disagree. I kill them. I'm an insect killer.

## Conversation Question 3

**▶ What do you think about keeping animals in zoos or aquariums?**

**Q1. What does Branden say is good about zoos and aquariums?**

a) They can be educational.

b) They can be dangerous.

c) They can be expensive.

**Q2. Who saw the giant pandas at Everland?**

a) Cassandra

b) Caoimhe

c) Branden

**Q3. Which of these were not mentioned as an intelligent ocean animal?**

a) Dolphins

b) Blowfish

c) Octopuses

### Script

Branden: Alright, everyone. Welcome back. This time, we're going to consider question number three, and you may remember that we are tied. We all have one point, so whoever wins this round will win the game for this week. Ok? You guys ready?

Caoimhe: Yes. Ok.

Branden: Alright, so the next question. What do you think about keeping animals in zoos or aquariums? Ok? So, keeping animals in an unnatural habitat for our enjoyment. Ok? So, let's get started. Uh, we have the timer here. Good. We're good to go. So, zoos, aquariums, good or bad?

Cassandra: Tough question.

Branden: Yeah.

Caoimhe: Who wants to start?

Branden: Ok, I'll start. I like – I like going to aquariums. I like zoos. I think they're interesting. Like, where else can we see animals, exotic animals, from...in a safe environment? Yeah, I think it's great. Great learning experience.

**Caoimhe:** That's a good point, but you say safe environment for us.

**Branden:** For us.

**Caoimhe:** But it's not always necessarily safe. Especially watching documentaries about these places – I'll not mention any names – where they, like, aquariums where they have performance animals and often those like, dolphins, for example, have been captured, and, um, so, yeah. I, for me, I'm not a big fan.

**Cassandra:** Yeah.

**Branden:** Yes, I know. I see what you're saying, but yeah, I think nowadays they're getting a little better, right? Like, we're more aware of the... I don't know I haven't been...to be honest, guys, I haven't been to an aquarium in a long time, so....

**Caoimhe:** Yeah.

**Cassandra:** Yeah.

**Branden:** The problems still continue today, probably.

**Caoimhe:** Yeah, there are a few, yes, obviously, very secretive, but...

**Branden:** Good.

**Caoimhe:** What about Cass?

**Cassandra:** Yeah, case by case, I guess. Um, so for me, it's hard to answer this question, but I think that zoos, yeah they overall could be a good thing, if they're providing, like Branden said, education...

**Branden:** I concur.

**Cassandra:** Some entertainment in a way that's safe for both the human and the animal, but I think ideally, I mean, it's not in the, usually not in the best interest of the animal. So, I'm sure the animals would like to be free, but sometimes there are these places that keep like endangered species and help them.

**Caoimhe:** I totally agree.

**Cassandra:** So, I think that these are all, yeah, kind of on a case by case basis, but I agree with you. I don't like seeing the performances, you know. They train the dolphin to jump through the hoop. That makes me a little sad.

**Branden:** That's a good point.

**Caoimhe:** Yeah, I think you're definitely right about the endangered thing, so, for example, the last time I went to Everland, they're keeping like giant pandas, which are an endangered species. So, and I believe that they had a baby, like last year, so it's great that they're using it to like repopulate, and...

**Cassandra:** Yeah, I totally agree. Yeah.

**Branden:** That's great, yeah, because otherwise they, that species would disappear. So, preserving...

**Caoimhe:** Yeah, of course.

**Branden:** Yeah, very nice.

**Caoimhe:** I think as long as the animals have enough space as well. Sometimes, you go to a zoo, and, like, the cage is so small. Or, the, like, you know, the area for like the lion or whatever, so, it's, it's sad to see animals in such a small space.

**Branden:** Yeah, yeah I understand what you're saying. But I don't know, what about, aquariums are not so bad though, because usually fish don't have high intelligence, right? So, it's...

**Caoimhe:** Well...

**Branden:** Except dolphins! Dolphins are extremely intelligent, but...normally, like sharks and stuff...

**Cassandra:** Octopuses are extremely intelligent.

**Branden:** Oh, octopus...

**Caoimhe:** Yeah, I was just going to say, have you seen My Octopus Teacher?

**Branden:** Oh, really?

**Cassandra:** We watched the same documentary.

**Branden:** That's true, that's true.

**Caoimhe:** I guess so, yeah.

**Cassandra:** They have feelings.

**Branden:** Octopi are quite intelligent. Ok, guys.

**Caoimhe:** I'm very passionate about that documentary.

**Branden:** That's it for this round. Three minutes is up. So, I have four points.

**Caoimhe:** I have five.

**Cassandra:** Two.

**Branden:** Ok, so, yeah, Caoimhe, you're the winner. Good job, yeah.

**Caoimhe:** Thank you.

**Branden:** Ok, so that's it for these rejoinders and these questions. Uh, let's move on to the next part.

**[Answer]**

**Q1. What does Branden say is good about zoos and aquariums?**

a) They can be educational.

b) They can be dangerous.

c) They can be expensive.

Branden: Ok, I'll start. I like going to aquariums. I like zoos. I think they're interesting. Like, where else can we see animals, exotic animals, from...in a safe environment? Yeah, I think it's great. Great learning experience.

**Q2. Who saw the giant pandas at Everland?**

a) Cassandra

b) Caoimhe

c) Branden

Caoimhe: Yeah, I think you're definitely right about the endangered thing, so, for example, the last time I went to Everland, they're keeping like giant pandas, which are an endangered species.

**Q3. Which of these were not mentioned as an intelligent ocean animal?**

a) Dolphins

b) Blowfish

c) Octopuses

Branden: Except dolphins! Dolphins are extremely intelligent, but...normally, like sharks and stuff...

Cassandra: Octopuses are extremely intelligent.

## Lecture 2

### Words in Action

1. **Yeah.**
   - to informally agree

**Game1**
Cassandra: Octopuses are extremely intelligent.
Branden: Oh, octopus...
Caoimhe: Yeah, I was just going to say, have you seen *My Octopus Teacher*?

2. **Of course.**
   - to emphatically agree

**Game3**
Caoimhe: I went to Everland, they're keeping like giant pandas, which are an endangered species. So, and I believe that they had a baby, like last year, so it's great that they're using it to like repopulate, and...
Branden: That's great, yeah, because otherwise they, that species would disappear.
Caoimhe: Yeah, of course.

3. **I totally agree.**
   - to completely agree

**Game1**
Cassandra: Again, that's why I need a big apartment. A giant apartment where they can, you know, go off and do their business somewhere far from me.
Branden: I totally agree. I've visited people who have that problem. They don't clean it, it smells.

**4. I'm totally with you.**

- to show that you share exactly the same opinion

**Game2**

**Caoimhe:** Yeah, no, I won't kill any insects.

**Cassandra:** No, I'm totally with you. I try not to kill any beings. Like if it's kind of a mosquito flying around, I'll do it but I, if I can like actually capture the insect and bring it outside, like a spider, I can like catch it and bring it outside and release it.

**5. I guess so.**

- to show partial agreement

**Game1**

**Caoimhe:** Yeah, so any other pros? Why do you guys want to have a pet? What other pros do you think they have?

**Cassandra:** Companionship.

**Caoimhe:** I guess so. Yeah. I have one friend who wanted to have a baby and I said maybe get a dog first. The dog isn't going so well, so I think she's learned. So, it can also be a kind of like a life lesson.

**6. That's a good point.**

- to agree and acknowledge a good point

**Game1**

**Caoimhe:** I think also like they, pets motivate you, especially dogs, to stay healthier because obviously you need to take that dog for a walk and things.

**Cassandra:** Oh, that's a good point.

**7. That's true.**

- to agree and confirm a fact

**Game2**

**Branden:** I concur. Cockroaches are quite distasteful. I actually – now that we mention cockroaches – I have a fear, a terrible fear of cockroaches. I just think...I don't really know. They're small. Why am I afraid of these little insects?

**Cassandra:** That's true.

**8. I concur.**

- to agree in an official way

**Game3**

**Cassandra:** Yeah, case by case, I guess. so for me, it's hard to answer this question, but I think that zoos, yeah they overall could be a good thing, if they're providing, like Branden said, education...

**Branden:** I concur.

**9. Yes, (Yeah) I know.**

- to agree in a defensive way

**Game3**

**Caoimhe:** But it's not always necessarily safe. Especially watching documentaries about these places where they have performance animals and often those dolphins have been captured. I'm not a big fan.

**Branden:** Yes, I know. I see what you're saying, but yeah, I think nowadays they're getting a little better, right?

## Word Power

**1. pros and cons**

- the good and bad points; benefits and drawbacks; positives and negatives

> **Branden:** Glad to hear. Ok, so let's start with the first question. What are the pros and cons of having pets? So, pros and cons, that means what are the good points and bad points of having pets. Ok? I'm going to set the timer now. Ok, let's get started. Uh, yeah, who would like to start us off in our discussion?

**2. a life lesson**

- something that is important to learn to have a good life

> **Caoimhe:** I guess so. Yeah. I have one friend who wanted to have a baby and I said maybe get a dog first. The dog isn't going so well, so I think she's learned. So, it can also be a kind of like a life lesson.

**3. trauma**

- long-lasting negative emotions around a specific topic or event

> **Caoimhe:** Ok, well I have a huge phobia of rats. So, if I see a rat on the street, like, I will cry. Like, it totally ruins my day. Like, I get a kind of trauma from it. So, I'm absolutely terrified of rats.

**4. pacifist**

- people who avoid doing physical harm at all times

> **Branden:** Ok, so, even insects, you won't do it.
> **Caoimhe:** Yeah, no, I won't kill any insects.
> **Branden:** Wow, ok, quite a pacifist. Ok.

**5. nowadays**

- these days; recently

> **Branden:** Yes, I know. I see what you're saying, but yeah, I think nowadays they're getting a little better, right? Like, we're more aware of the... I don't know I haven't been...to be honest, guys, I haven't been to an aquarium in a long time, so....

**6. case by case**

- each example should be treated differently according to the facts of their situation

> **Cassandra:** Yeah, case by case, I guess. Um, so for me, it's hard to answer this question, but I think that zoos, yeah they overall could be a good thing, if they're providing, like Branden said, education...

## Outro

### Dialogue

**Branden:** Do you know what's wrong with Jason? His work performance has been declining these days.

**Cassandra:** That's what I've been saying. He hasn't been meeting deadlines or contributing to our team project. He always seems so... distracted...

**Branden:** Yeah... I know what you mean. We were in a meeting the other day and it looked like he wasn't paying attention. I think there may be something going on in his personal life.

**Cassandra:** That's true. I heard he's going through a divorce. And he lost a lot of money in the stock market. But that's no excuse, really. When he's at work he should carry his own weight.

**Branden:** Of course. Everyone has problems. I have problems. You have problems. But that doesn't stop us from doing our job.

**Cassandra:** I totally agree. Life is hard. Sometimes we just got to deal with it.

Branden: That's a good point. I've had plenty of financial troubles. And I've been divorced too, twice. That never stopped me from taking pride in my work.

Cassandra: I'm totally with you, but do you think there's a possibility we're being too hard on him?

Branden: Yeah, I know. I don't usually talk behind someone's back. But I'm just a little annoyed. I couldn't help it. Maybe we should tell our supervisor what's been going on.

Cassandra: I concur. I will mention this to the boss tomorrow.

Branden: Before his life fell apart, Jason was an excellent worker. We should give him a chance.

Cassandra: That's a good point. Maybe one of us should talk to him.

Branden: I guess so... Sometimes it helps just to have someone to talk to. I am sure he will be back to his old self in no time.

## Wrap-up

1. **Yeah.**
   - to informally agree

2. **Of course**
   - to emphatically agree

3. **That is what I've been saying**
   - to agree and express frustration

4. **I totally agree.**
   - to completely agree.

5. **I'm totally with you.**
   - to show that you share exactly the same opinion

6. **I guess so.**
   - To show partial agreement

**7.** **That's a good point**

- to agree and acknowledge a good point

**8.** **That's true.**

- to agree and confirm a fact

**9.** **in concur**

- to agree in an of official way

**10.** **Yes, (Yeah) I know.**

- to agree in a defensive way

## Assignment

**1.** **Select the option that best completes the passage.**

A: This party is boring. I think we should leave.
B: ______________

1) That's what I saying.
2) I totally agree.
3) So I guessed.
4) Of course so.

**2.** **Select the option that best completes the passage.**

A: I have a terrible headache.
B: Maybe you shouldn't drink so much.
A: ______________

1) So I seem.
2) That's a point.
3) Yes, concur.
4) I guess so.

**3. Select the option that best completes the passage.**

A: I like this brand. It's expensive but very classy.
B: ____________

1) I concur.
2) It's the way.
3) Yeah, I have.
4) That's sufficient.

**4. Select the option that best completes the passage.**

A: Jason is starting to get on my nerves. He never knows when to close his mouth.
B: ____________

1) That's what he said.
2) I'm totally agreeable.
3) That's what I've been saying.
4) That's what I say.

**5. Select the option that best completes the passage.**

A: He never cleans up after himself.
B: ____________

1) I guessed it.
2) I'm totally with him.
3) Yes, I'm totally at a point.
4) That's true.

**6.** **Select the option that best completes the passage.**

A: The best way to live well is to focus on friends and family.
B: ______________

1) I'm totally with you.
2) That's a sharp point.
3) Yes, you concur.
4) Of course I do.

**7.** **Select the option that best completes the passage.**

A: Don't you think you spend too much time playing computer games?
B: ______________

1) Yeah, I see it.
2) Yeah, I know.
3) Of course it is.
4) That's a good agreement.

**8.** **Select the option that best completes the passage.**

A: Getting lots of regular exercise is good for your health.
B: ______________

1) That's a good thinking.
2) I'm knowing it.
3) I see it.
4) That's a good point.

**9. Select the option that best completes the passage.**

A: This restaurant has the best pizza in town.
B: ____________

1) Yeah.
2) That's it.
3) I'm totally by you.
4) That's what I've been doing.

**10. Select the option that best completes the passage.**

A: It's always better to finish our work as soon as possible.
B: ____________

1) Yeah, I see it.
2) That's what it is.
3) Of course.
4) In course.

Week 8

# Midterm Exam

## 1-2. Listen to the conversation and choose the best answers. (Week 1)

| | |
|---|---|
| Woman: | So, what are your hopes for the future? Anything specific? |
| Man: | Well, I really want to learn how to play the piano. I also hope that I'll become fluent in Korean. And I hope that I'll be able to retire early... |
| Woman: | Seriously? You've got some high hopes for your future. |
| Man: | I thought they were reasonable. Why? What are your aspirations for the future? |
| Woman: | Well, let's see. This weekend I am hoping to meet some friends in Apgujeong to go shopping. Then after that I am hoping to try a new restaurant I heard about. Oh, and Sunday I am really hoping to relax and watch Netflix. |

**1. Which sentence is true according to the dialogue?**

1) The man is fluent in Korean.
2) The man thinks he can achieve his goals.
3) The woman has high hopes for the future.
4) The woman wants to learn a new skill.

**2. What will the woman do on the weekend?**

1) go to a movie theatre
2) spend time with her family
3) work at a part-time job
4) go shopping

## 3-4. Listen to the conversation and choose the best answers. (Week 3)

| | |
|---|---|
| **Woman:** | I love booking an expensive hotel and having a spa weekend every time I turn a year older. |
| **Man:** | That sounds good. And, I think you could use the rest! |
| **Woman:** | Huh? What are you trying to say? Do you think I look tired and horrible all of the time? |
| **Man:** | Wait. What? That's not what I said. I just think that you should take good care of yourself. |
| **Woman:** | You think that I don't get enough rest? Is that it? |
| **Man:** | No. Don't get upset. I'm just talking generally, here. Everyone could benefit from sleeping more. |
| **Woman:** | I guess I misunderstood you. |

**3. Why will the woman book an expensive hotel?**

1) to celebrate her wedding anniversary
2) because she likes to travel
3) to celebrate her birthday
4) because she doesn't get enough rest at home

**4. Why does the woman get upset?**

1) The man comments on her appearance.
2) She thinks the man doesn't like her.
3) She feels tired.
4) She doesn't want to go to the spa.

## 5-6. Listen to the conversation and choose the best answers. (Week 5)

| | |
|---|---|
| Man: | This monthly report is killing me. I have so much data to analyze and not enough time to do anything. Do you think you could help me out? |
| Woman: | Well, when is the report due? |
| Man: | Actually... it's due tomorrow. Sorry I realize this is sort of last minute. Are you still able to help me? |
| Woman: | I can help write the report, but next time please don't wait so long before you reach out for help. Okay? |
| Man: | Yes. Of course. Thank you. I really appreciate it. |
| Woman: | So, since the two of us will have to work late tonight, is dinner on you? |
| Man: | Naturally. I'll order us some steaks. |

**5. Which sentence is not true according to the dialogue?**

1) The woman will help write the monthly report.
2) They will work late into the night.
3) The man does not have enough time to do all of his work.
4) The monthly report is due next week.

**6. Which sentence is true according to the dialogue?**

1) The man will pay for dinner.
2) They will have pizza for dinner.
3) The man doesn't want to help with the monthly report.
4) The man doesn't want help.

## 7-8. Listen to the conversation and choose the best answers. (Week 6)

| | |
|---|---|
| Woman: | **It seems to me** that today is just a normal summer day. |
| Man: | But you cannot deny the reality of climate change. |
| Woman: | **If you ask me**, climate change is just a big hoax! |
| Man: | Are you serious? **I have to say** I'm disappointed in you. I thought you believed in science. |
| Woman: | **I do think** that the climate is changing, but in my opinion rising sea levels and increasing temperatures are just natural changes that the earth goes through, regardless of us humans. |
| Man: | **You know what?** You're totally wrong! Scientists agree that human-caused climate change is happening right now. It's a serious problem. |

**7. What does the woman think about climate change?**

1) Climate change is mostly caused by humans.
2) Climate change is a natural phenomenon.
3) There is no such thing as climate change.
4) The day is too hot because of climate change.

**8. Which statement is <u>true</u> according to the dialogue?**

1) The man thinks climate change is a hoax.
2) The woman thinks climate change is a serious problem.
3) Scientists agree that humans cause climate change.
4) The man agrees with the woman.

## 9-10. Listen to the conversation and choose the best answers. (Week 7)

| | |
|---|---|
| Woman: | **Jason** always seems so... distracted... |
| Man: | **Yeah...** We were in a meeting the other day and it looked like he wasn't paying attention. I think there may be something going on in his personal life. |
| Woman: | **That's true.** I heard he's going through a divorce. And he lost a lot of money in the stock market. But that's no excuse, really. When he's at work he should carry his own weight. |
| Man: | **Of course.** Everyone has problems. |
| Woman: | **I totally agree.** Life is hard. Sometimes we just got to deal with it. |
| Man: | **That's a good point.** I've had plenty of financial troubles. And I've been divorced too, twice. That never stopped me from taking pride in my work. |

**9. Which sentence is true according to the dialogue?**

1) Jason has been underperforming at work.
2) Jason is getting married soon.
3) Jason made some money on the stock market.
4) Jason's coworkers are happy with his performance.

**10. What is not true about the male speaker?**

1) He has been divorced twice.
2) He has had financial troubles in the past.
3) He takes pride in his work.
4) He has no problems in his personal life.

## 11-12. Listen to the conversation and choose the best answers. (Week 2)

| | |
|---|---|
| Man: | Oh, hi. <u>Did you</u> have a chance to watch the movie I told you about last week? |
| Woman: | <u>Do you</u> mean the horror film? Sorry, I try to avoid scary movies. |
| Man: | You don't like horror movies? |
| Woman: | I'm just really uncomfortable when I feel scared, and I also hate surprises! |
| Man: | Not every horror movie is like that, you know. **<u>When</u>** was the last time you actually watched a horror movie from start to finish? |
| Woman: | I am not sure... Anyway, that's enough about me! It's almost 12 o'clock. **<u>Where</u>** are you going for lunch today? |
| Man: | I'm thinking of trying out that new Thai restaurant up the street. I've heard good things about it. |

**11. Why is <u>true</u> about the woman?**

1) She loves surprises.
2) She can't remember the last time she watched a horror movie.
3) She likes horror movies.
4) She enjoys being scared.

**12. What will the speakers do in the afternoon?**

1) drink coffee
2) watch a movie
3) try out a new restaurant
4) get back to work

**13. Select the expression that best completes the passage. (Week 1)**

> A: The musical was not interesting at all.
> B: ____________________ It was hard to stay awake while watching it.

1) I'm glad to hear that.
2) Yeah.
3) No!
4) Why?

**14. Select the expression that best completes the passage. (Week 1)**

> A: I finally bought a new car.
> B: ____________________ It's about time you got a new car. Your old one was terrible.

1) That's great.
2) Oh, no!
3) I'm sorry to hear that.
4) Suddenly.

**15. Select the expression that best completes the passage. (Week 2)**

> A: What are you doing?
> B: I'm listening to music on my phone.
> A: ____________ the song you showed me on YouTube yesterday?

1) How
2) Are those
3) Why
4) Is that

**16.** **Select the expression that best completes the passage. (Week 2)**

> **A:** ___________ did you put the file?
> **B:** It's in the filing cabinet over there.

1) By the way
2) How
3) Where
4) When

**17.** **Select the expression that best completes the passage. (Week 3)**

> **A:** I love animals so I never eat meat.
> **B:** So you think eating meat is cruel. __________________

1) Is that it?
2) Is that what I'm saying.
3) So you're trying to say.
4) It sounds alike.

**18.** **Select the expression that best completes the passage. (Week 3)**

> **A:** Did you know cigarettes can cause lung cancer?
> **B:** __________________ I should stop smoking?

1) Is that
2) I thought
3) You think
4) How about

**19.** **Select the expression that best completes the passage. (Week 3)**

> A: I am getting married next week.
> B: How can you be getting married already? ______________ you just started dating a few weeks ago.

1) How about
2) What kind of
3) You think
4) I thought

**20.** **Select the option that best completes the passage. (Week 3)**

> A: I'd like to get my mom something special for her birthday.
> B: _____________________ gift are you thinking about?

1) How about
2) What kind of
3) I thought
4) You think

**21.** **Select the option that best completes the passage. (Week 4)**

> A: It's not easy to work and study at the same time. My grades are falling!
> B: _____________ Have you tried reducing your working hours? Maybe you just need more time to study.

1) Could I be excused?
2) I wasn't thinking about this.
3) Can I ask something?
4) Can you hold this for a second?

**22.** **Select the option that best completes the passage. (Week 4)**

> A: I decided to major in history.
> B: ____________ I thought you wanted to be an engineer?

1) Sorry to interrupt, but
2) I always thought, but
3) Excuse this, but
4) Can I ask so

**23.** **Select the option that best completes the passage. (Week 4)**

> A: I am thinking about buying a tablet PC.
> B: ____________ don't you already have a laptop?

1) Excuse it
2) But
3) Since
4) Therefore

**24.** **Select the option that best completes the passage. (Week 5)**

> A: Do you really think this is a good idea?
> B: ____________________________
> A: I am not sure.

1) You don't agree?
2) That's what I'm saying.
3) Are you thinking?
4) So you're saying that?

**25.** **Select the option that best completes the passage. (Week 5)**

A: Is it ok if I ask just one question?
B: ____________________

1) Get over it.
2) You're fired.
3) I'm sorry to hear that.
4) Fire away !

**26.** **Choose the most appropriate expression to complete the following blank. (Week 7)**

A: I love Black Pink's new song! It's so catchy!
B: ____________________

1) I'm totally beside you.
2) I so guess.
3) That is what I've been telling.
4) I totally agree.

**27.** **Select the option that best completes the passage. (Week 5)**

A: Sorry, can I just say on thing?
B: ____________________

1) No problem.
2) Where is it?
3) Yes, there is.
4) Ask for me.

**28.** **Select the option that best completes the passage. (Week 6)**

> A: Do you think it's better to get as dog or a cat?
> B: ____________, it's better to not have a pet at all. They are too much work and responsibility!

1) When you ask me
2) As my opinion
3) It seems for me
4) If you ask me

**29.** **Select the option that best completes the passage. (Week 6)**

> A: Do you think I should accept this job offer?
> B: ____________, it isn't worth it. The salary is too low.

1) In my opinion
2) I have to tell
3) In my thought
4) As I think

**30.** **Select the option that best completes the passage. (Week 6)**

> A: What do you think about our new co-worker?
> B: ________________, he seems like a nice guy.

1) As far as I tell
2) As far as I can tell
3) As I know
4) As far as I say

**31-40. Fill in the blanks by using one of the words on the list. There is only ONE correct answer for each question. Choose the BEST answer. (Week 1~7)**

| pacifist | materialistic |
|---|---|
| intermittent | bear |
| subjective | prime |
| into | butt |
| buff | obsessed |

**31.** My brother knows all about the events leading up to the first world war. He is somewhat of a history ____________.

**32.** My dog is past his _____________. He is too old to run.

**33.** I think my girlfriend is too ______________. She always wants the best and most expensive things so that she can show off to her friends.

**34.** I didn't know that you're __________ K-pop. What is your favorite girl group?

**35.** I'm sorry to ______________ in, but I have some information that might help.

**36.** I didn't know you were so ________ with watches. You have so many!

**37.** I think ___________ fasting is a great way to lose weight.

**38.** I think success is ________. It means different things to different people.

**39.** If you could just ________________ with me for a moment I will get you that information as soon as I finish this phone call.

**40.** As a ____________ I strongly believe that war is never the answer.

## Answer: Midterm Exam

| | | | | | | | |
|---|---|---|---|---|---|---|---|
| 1 | ② | 2 | ④ | 3 | ③ | 4 | ① |
| 5 | ④ | 6 | ① | 7 | ② | 8 | ③ |
| 9 | ① | 10 | ④ | 11 | ② | 12 | ③ |
| 13 | ② | 14 | ① | 15 | ④ | 16 | ③ |
| 17 | ① | 18 | ③ | 19 | ④ | 20 | ② |
| 21 | ③ | 22 | ① | 23 | ② | 24 | ① |
| 25 | ④ | 26 | ④ | 27 | ① | 28 | ④ |
| 29 | ① | 30 | ② | | | | |

| | | | |
|---|---|---|---|
| 31 | buff | 32 | prime |
| 33 | materialistic | 34 | into |
| 35 | butt | 36 | obsessed |
| 37 | intermittent | 38 | subjective |
| 39 | bear | 40 | pacifist |

Week 9

# Disagreeing

| | |
|---|---|
| **Contents** | 1. To directly disagree<br>2. To indirectly disagree<br>3. To politely disagree |
| **Objectives** | 1. To understand 3 types of disagreeing skills.<br>2. To understand how 3 types of disagreeing skills are used in real conversations<br>1) What are some characteristics of your personality?<br>2) What would you like to change about your personality?<br>3) What personality traits do you consider important in a friend? |

## Intro

### Speaking Skills: Disagreeing

**1. I don't agree.**

- to directly disagree

Example

A: Men make the best politicians.

B: I don't agree.

**2. I'm afraid I disagree.**

- to directly disagree

Example

A: On Sundays, there are no good TV shows.

B: I'm afraid I disagree.

**3. I'm not sure I agree.**

- to indirectly disagree

Example

A: This mask will protect you from pollution.

B: I'm not sure I agree.

**4. I hear you, but...**

- to indirectly disagree

Example

A: You should keep a diary to reduce your stress.

B: I hear you, but I don't have the time.

**5. On the other hand...**

- to indirectly disagree

Example

A: These apples look really good.

B: On the other hand, the grapes look even better and are cheaper.

**6. I know what you're saying, but...**

- to indirectly disagree

Example

A: It's too hot to go outside.

B: I know what you're saying but we could cool off in a pool.

**7. I get that, but...**

- to indirectly disagree

Example

A: You complain too much.

B: I get that, but you never help out around the house.

**8. Perhaps, but...**

- to indirectly disagree

Example

A: This humidity is great for my skin.

B: Perhaps, but it's also likely to give you foot fungus.

**9. I don't know about that.**

- to politely disagree

Example

A: My mom makes the best kimchi.

B: I don't know about that.

**10. I'm not sure that's true.**

- to indirectly disagree

Example

A: Driving a car is safer than taking a plane.

B: I'm not sure that's true.

## Lecture 1

### Conversation Question 1

▶ **What are some characteristics of your personality?**

**Q1. What characteristic of Cassandra's personality changes at work?**

a) She's shy at work, but outgoing in social spaces.

b) She's shy in social spaces, but tries to be outgoing at work.

c) She's shy in both social spaces and at work.

**Q2. Which of the speakers says they always try to be positive?**

a) Cassandra

b) Branden

c) JiYoung

**Q3. Which of these does not describe Branden?**

a) Optimistic

b) Low energy

c) Quiet

### Script

**Branden:** Hello, everyone, and welcome back. So, today we're going to practice using the key expressions that you learned in class. So, these have to do with disagreements, and I'm here today with my colleagues, ok? So, my name is Branden. You may remember...

**Cassandra:** Cassandra.

**JiYoung:** And I'm Jiyoung Kang.

**Branden:** Alright, welcome. Ok, guys, so, just like last time, round one will be three minutes long, and whoever uses the most expressions will be the winner. So, I wonder who that's going to be. We'll just have to wait and see. Alright, so, the first question. Ok. What are some characteristics of your personality? I'll say it one more time. What are some characteristics of your personality? Ok, so I will start the timer right now. There we go. Um, who would like start? What about – what about Cassandra?

**Cassandra:** Oh, I was hoping I wouldn't have to go first.

**Branden:** Tell us about yourself.

**Cassandra:** Ok, well...

**Branden:** Sorry we're putting you on the spot there.

**Cassandra:** Uh, actually, I think that I'm a pretty shy person. That is a major characteristic of my personality. But, when I warm up to somebody, then I show more of my friendly side and my sense of humor.

**Branden:** Ok. You know, Cassandra, I get that. But, when you need to be heard, you can be quite talkative.

**Cassandra:** Oh, really?

**Branden:** And, I've seen you in social situations. You seem to do ok.

**Cassandra:** Ok, but I don't agree. In my head, I feel so shy.

**Branden:** Oh.

**Cassandra:** And I feel like I'm saying all the wrong things.

**Branden:** I see.

**JiYoung:** Oh, I get that. But, when I saw you the first time, you said hello to me first, so yeah. So, I think you aren't shy a like. So, you're a brave person, I think.

**Branden:** Right.

**Cassandra:** Uh, perhaps, but, in the workplace, I try to be outgoing, but in my personal life, I'm quite quiet, I think.

**Branden:** Oh, I see, I see. Well, on the other hand, in the office, you may be a different, you may be a different way, right? We don't know.

**Cassandra:** Fair enough, fair enough. How about...

**Branden:** So, I guess, I guess I can go next. Uh, so, some characteristics of my personality, I have to think about myself. Um, yeah I think like Cassandra, at first I may be a little quiet. I don't know if I'm shy, though. I'm usually not afraid to talk in front of people, unless it's a huge group of people, then I can be a little nervous. But, yeah, I'm a little bit of a quiet person. Um, not that much energy. Low energy. You disagree, JiYoung?

**JiYoung:** I hear you, but, you're a very good talkative person I think.

**Branden:** Oh, you think so? I'm not sure that's true, but in professional contexts, like in, during work or in class, I try to be talkative, you know?

**JiYoung:** Yeah.

**Branden:** It's what I have to do, you know. We've gotta do what we've gotta do.

**JiYoung:** Ok.

**Branden:** Alright, so, JiYoung, what about your personality?

**JiYoung:** Oh, ok. My personality is, when I do something, when I meet someone, I'm thinking too much. What happens next, what's going on. So, I'm really worried about that. But, I'm trying to think positively a lot, too. So I think my personality is pretty positive.

**Branden:** Ok, you're very optimistic.

**JiYoung:** Yes, I think so, yeah.

**Branden:** Good, good. Well, I can't agree with you there, right? Uh, perhaps, but, perhaps but there's always those times in our lives when, you know, the negativity sort of creeps up on us. So...

**Cassandra:** Oh! Time.

**Branden:** Just like the time. So, anyway, we're going to stop there. That's round one. Let's see how many rejoinders...that last one was a little iffy but I'll keep that one for myself. So, I have four.

**JiYoung:** I have two.

**Branden:** Yes.

**Cassandra:** Two, also.

**Branden:** Yes. I'm the winner. I love being the winner. Alright, guys, so, let's wait a moment and move on to the next part. We're going to round two.

**[Answer]**

**Q1. What characteristic of Cassandra's personality changes at work?**

a) She's shy at work, but outgoing in social spaces.

b) She's shy in social spaces, but tries to be outgoing at work.

c) She's shy in both social spaces and at work.

**Cassandra:** Uh, perhaps, but, in the workplace, I try to be outgoing, but in my personal life, I'm quite quiet, I think.

**Q2. Which of the speakers says they always try to be positive?**

a) Cassandra

b) Branden

c) JiYoung

**JiYoung:** My personality is, when I do something, when I meet someone, I'm thinking too much. But, I'm trying to think positively a lot, too. So I think my personality is pretty positive.

**Q3. Which of these does not describe Branden?**

a) Optimistic

b) Low energy

c) Quiet

**Branden:** I'm usually not afraid to talk in front of people, unless it's a huge group of people, then I can be a little nervous. But, I'm a little bit of a quiet person. Um, not that much energy. Low energy.

## Conversation Question 2

▶ **What would you like to change about your personality?**

**Q1. Cassandra called her decision-making process 'scrambled.' Which of these is the best synonym for 'scrambled'?**

a) messy

b) simple

c) clear

**Q2. Which person in the group is a chronic procrastinator?**

a) Cassandra

b) Branden

c) JiYoung

**Q3. Which of these does Cassandra not do when she's making a decision?**

a) Make a pro and con list.

b) Ask her friends for advice.

c) Make a quick decision.

### Script

**Branden:** Alright, everyone. Welcome back. So, we're on to round two of our game, and so far, I'm winning. Yes! Ok, so the next question is, what would you like to change about your personality? What would you like to change about your personality? Ok? So, I'm going to set the timer for three minutes. And, let's get started. Is there something we don't like about ourselves? Ok?

**Cassandra:** You're looking directly at me.

**Branden:** I'll...no, don't, I'll start. I'll start. Um, I'm a chronic procrastinator. I always wait until the last minute to do things. That's one of my flaws, I think. Um...

**Cassandra:** I hear you, but is that really a flaw? Like, how's that hurt you in your daily life? Leaving things until the last minute?

Branden: Right, well if I leave too many things until the last minute, then I can't do everything I need to do.

Cassandra: Aha.

Branden: So, perhaps there may be some deadlines in my life, things I need to do by a certain time, and if there's like a dozen things I need to do, I don't have enough time to do it. So.

Cassandra: So, you're saying, you miss a deadline sometimes?

Branden: Yeah, yeah. It can cause me to be late. Not a good thing. Um, let's see, yeah, yeah.

Casandra: Let me jump in. On the other hand, maybe procrastination is a little bit of a good thing.

Branden: Oh!

Cassandra: Because I've heard about some studies that suggest that people who procrastinate also tend to have a very high IQ. Perhaps they could even be a genius.

Branden: Oh, really?

Cassandra: Really, I've heard that. So, how do you feel about that, Branden? Are you maybe a genius?

JiYoung: Oh! You are a genius?

Branden: I'm not, I'm not so, I'm not sure that's true. Even if I were a genius, I'm not saying that I am, but, if I were, if I'm still not able to do – accomplish my goals, then it doesn't matter, right? So.

Cassandra: Good point.

Branden: But, I think you may be on to something there. For future reference. Ok, so, what about you, Cassandra? Is there something you would like to change about yourself?

Cassandra: Oh, um, a lot of stuff? So, I don't know which one to pick.

Branden: Ok, choose one then.

Cassandra: Choose one. Uh, maybe the way that I make decisions.

Branden: Oh, ok, how so?

Cassandra: Uh, sometimes I take a really long time to make my decision. I write down the pros and cons. I think about it deeply. But then other times, I just choose something without thinking. So, my decision-making process is a little bit...strange. Kind of scrambled I think. Yeah.

Branden: Ok, so, on the other hand, on the other hand I've seen you in the office, Cassandra, and you never seem too indecisive there.

**Cassandra:** Oh, ok.

**Branden:** So, I think you're ok.

**Cassandra:** Really? Thank you, am I ok?

**Branden:** Yeah. I don't want you to be too hard on yourself.

**Cassandra:** Thanks. I know what you're saying. That's kind, but, in the office I try to be professional, but in my personal life, sometimes I'll just spontaneously make like a bad decision. Out of nowhere.

**JiYoung:** I get that, but, um, thinking a lot when you do something is very good. And then sometimes if you don't think and then choose something, it could be good too, right?

**Branden:** Yeah, perhaps, perhaps, but there has to be balance with whatever we're doing in our personality.

**Cassandra:** Oh! Well, we didn't hear from her.

**Branden:** Oh, oh no.

**JiYoung:** Oh, my gosh.

**Cassandra:** Extra time, please.

**Branden:** Extra time? Let's do, let's do twenty more seconds.

**JiYoung:** Ok, ok. I have a, I have a pretty same thing as Cassandra. Because when I do something or when I choose something, I'm thinking too much. So, I miss the chance or I miss the time, so. That's what I want to change in my character. So, I want to just directly, or just decide...

**Branden:** Well, JiYoung, I'm afraid I disagree. I've talked to some of your friends, and they say that you're very decisive.

**JiYoung:** Oh, really?

**Branden:** You always – you have a very strong mind.

**JiYoung:** Thank you.

**Branden:** Yeah, so just thought I'd throw that out there. Ok, guys, we are totally out of time. So, let's move on to the next round, but before we do so, what's our points? Who's winning?

**JiYoung:** Oh, my gosh, I have only one card.

**Branden:** Wa wa wa, I have four! I have four.

**Cassandra:** You snuck one in at the very last moment. I saw. I have three. Almost tie.

**JiYoung:** He is a genius.

**Branden:** Yeah.

**Cassandra:** That's why. Because he's a genius.

**Branden:** I am a genius. Ok, guys, moving on to round three.

[Answer]

**Q1. Cassandra called her decision-making process 'scrambled.' Which of these is the best synonym for 'scrambled'?**

a) messy

b) simple

c) clear

Cassandra: I take a really long time to make my decision. I write down the pros and cons. I think about it deeply. But then other times, I just choose something without thinking. So, my decision-making process is a little bit...strange. Kind of scrambled I think. Yeah.

**Q2. Which person in the group is a chronic procrastinator?**

a) Cassandra

b) Branden

c) JiYoung

Branden: I'll start. I'm a chronic procrastinator. I always wait until the last minute to do things. That's one of my flaws, I think. Um...

**Q3. Which of these does Cassandra not do when she's making a decision?**

a) Make a pro and con list.

b) Ask her friends for advice.

c) Make a quick decision.

Cassandra: I take a really long time to make my decision. I write down the pros and cons. I think about it deeply. But then other times, I just choose something without thinking.

## Conversation Question 3

▶ **What do you think about keeping animals in zoos or aquariums?**

**Q1. What trait does Branden not mention as important in a friend?**

a) pretty

b) rich

c) intelligent

**Q2. Who prefers to have friends that are straightforward?**

a) Cassandra

b) Branden

c) JiYoung

**Q3. Why doesn't Branden like to have funny friends?**

a) He hates jokes.

b) He prefers to be the center of attention.

c) He is afraid of clowns.

### Script

Branden: Alright, it is time for round three. So, so far I'm winning. I...

JiYoung: Aw.

Branden: I've won the first two rounds. But guys, don't worry, because this round is going to be special. Instead of one point, if you win you will get two points.

JiYoung: Ok.

Branden: So, at least you have a chance to tie me. Yeah, let's try. Ok, so, the next question: what personality traits do you consider important in a friend? Ok? What personality traits do you consider important in a friend? So, yeah, I have, I have lots of friends and, let me think, what do I like best about them? Well, what about, what about rich friends? Right?

JiYoung: Oh, rich friends?

Branden: Right? If your friends have a lot of money and you need some help...

**Cassandra:** I don't know about that.

**JiYoung:** Yeah, I don't know about that too.

**Branden:** Ok.

**Cassandra:** Um, ok, I get that.

**Branden:** But...

**Cassandra:** Of course, but I think that's not a prerequisite for friendship. I don't think the amount of money that you have in your bank determines if you can be a good friend or not.

**Branden:** On the other hand, it is beneficial.

**Cassandra:** You mean, they can pay for your stuff? Shopping?

**Branden:** Sure, yeah.

**JiYoung:** I get that. But, the rich friends, it has to be based on the faith or on the trust in each other.

**Branden:** Yeah, right.

**JiYoung:** That's going to be...yeah.

**Branden:** Ok, well what about pretty friends? So, when you take pictures together...come on, guys, hear me out, when you take pictures together, they make you look better, right?

**JiYoung:** I don't...

**Cassandra:** I'm afraid I disagree.

**JiYoung:** Yeah, I don't that's true.

**Branden:** Ok, I'm helping you guys out too much. Why do you disagree?

**JiYoung:** Um, I don't care how they look like, because they're my friend. So, yeah.

**Branden:** Oh, ok.

**Cassandra:** If anything, I don't agree because if I'm surrounded by very beautiful females, I will look like the ugliest girl in the group, so they're not helping me look any prettier. By comparison, I look the worst.

**Branden:** Well, that does make sense.

**JiYoung:** What about you? Some handsome friends?

**Branden:** Well...yeah. I think that it's...I think that it is good because, like I said, it's always...they make me look better.

**JiYoung:** Oh, really?

**Branden:** I don't know.

**Cassandra:** I hear you, but I don't understand.

**Branden:** You know what, I feel like everybody's disagreeing with me. Ok, what about JiYoung? What do you...?

**JiYoung:** Ok, I'm thinking about my best friends, but, I don't know if it's good or bad, but anyway, they are sometimes saying very directly to me, but it's very good for me, so...even though some people say a straightforward character's not good, but to me it was very good.

**Branden:** Perhaps, but if they are too straightforward it can be kind of rude, right?

**JiYoung:** Um, between friends, it's ok.

**Branden:** Oh yeah.

**Cassandra:** I know what you're saying, but I think over it's best to have someone who will tell you the truth. They will look you in the eye and tell you something that you need to know, maybe.

**JiYoung:** That's true.

**Cassandra:** It could be harsh, but it could be helpful, too.

**JiYoung:** Yeah, very helpful.

**Branden:** I hear you, but sometimes it's better off not knowing the truth. I don't want to know if it makes me feel bad.

**JiYoung:** Ok.

**Branden:** Alright, so.

**Cassandra:** I imagine Branden in this lovely world of handsome men all lying to each other.

**Jiyoung:** Oh, wow.

**Cassandra:** Sorry. Ok.

**Branden:** Alright. Any other ideas about that?

**Cassandra:** Oh, no, no. But, um, so my answer is like, of course, loyalty...

**Branden:** Loyalty.

**Cassandra:** Is important, but almost equally as important for me is a sense of humor. Like, somebody who's a good friend for me is somebody who can make me laugh and, yeah, have positive energy. Not always be complaining or talking about negative stuff.

**Branden:** I get that, but sometimes when people are too funny, they take the spotlight. They take all the attention away from you. Have you ever found that to be true?

**Cassandra:** Hmmm. On the other hand, I like when my friends take the attention off of me. It's better if they do all the talking and do all the joking, and I can just watch and enjoy.

**Branden:** Oh, ok. I'm afraid I disagree. I like to be the center of the show. I like getting all the attention. But, each to their own, right?

**Cassandra:** Fair enough.

**Branden:** Alright, guys, we are actually out of time. That's the end of round three. Uh, let's count our points.

**JiYoung:** Ah.

**Branden:** Oh, no!

**Cassandra:** Finally!

**Branden:** So, JiYoung? There's three right there.

**JiYoung:** I have three. I was trying, too. Oh, my god.

**Branden:** Good try.

**JiYoung:** Ok, thank you.

**Branden:** I have, I have five. And Cassandra?

**Cassandra:** I have somehow seven.

**JiYoung:** Wow.

**Cassandra:** Yay! Finally. Finally.

**Branden:** No, no. So, that means we're tied, ok? So, we can give ourselves a pat on the back right there. Guys, hopefully you enjoyed that and we're going to move on to the next part now.

**[Answer]**

**Q1. What trait does Branden not mention as important in a friend?**

a) pretty

b) rich

c) intelligent

**Branden:** what about rich friends? If your friends have a lot of money and you need some help...Well, what about pretty friends? So, when you take pictures together, they make you look better, right?

**Q2. Who prefers to have friends that are straightforward?**

a) Cassandra

b) Branden

c) JiYoung

**JiYoung:** I don't know if it's good or bad, but they are sometimes saying very directly to me, but it's very good for me, even though some people say a straightforward character's not good, but to me it was very good.

**Q3. Why doesn't Branden like to have funny friends?**

a) He hates jokes.

b) He prefers to be the center of attention.

c) He is afraid of clowns.

**Branden:** I get that, but sometimes when people are too funny, they take the spotlight. They take all the attention away from you. Have you ever found that to be true?

## Lecture 2

### Words in Action

**1. I don't agree.**

- to directly disagree

**Game3**

**Branden:** Ok, well what about pretty friends? So, when you take pictures together, they make you look better, right?

**Cassandra:** If anything, I don't agree because if I'm surrounded by very beautiful females, I will look like the ugliest girl in the group.

2. **I'm afraid I disagree**
- to directly disagree

**Game3**

JiYoung: Because when I do something or when I choose something, I'm thinking too much. So, I miss the chance or I miss the time, so. That's what I want to change in my character.

Branden: Well, JiYoung, I'm afraid I disagree. I've talked to some of your friends, and they say that you're very decisive.

3. **I hear you, but...**
- to indirectly disagree

**Game3**

Branden: Well...yeah. I think that it's...I think that it is good because, like I said, it's always...they make me look better.

Cassandra: I hear you, but I don't understand.

4. **On the other hand...**
- to indirectly disagree

**Game2**

Cassandra: I take a really long time to make my decision. I write down the pros and cons. I think about it deeply.

Branden: Ok, so, on the other hand, on the other hand I've seen you in the office, Cassandra, and you never seem too indecisive there.

5. **I know what you're saying, but...**
- to indirectly disagree

**Game3**

Branden: If they are too straightforward, it can be kind of rude, right?

Cassandra: I know what you're saying, but I think over it's best to have someone who will tell you the truth. They will look you in the eye and tell you something that you need to know, maybe.

**6. I get that, but...**

- to indirectly disagree

**Game1**

Cassandra: Is important, but almost equally as important for me is a sense of humor. Like, somebody who's a good friend for me is somebody who can make me laugh and, yeah, have positive energy. Not always be complaining or talking about negative stuff.

Branden: I get that, but sometimes when people are too funny, they take the spotlight. They take all the attention away from you. Have you ever found that to be true?

**7. Perhaps, but...**

- to indirectly disagree

**Game2**

JiYoung: I get that, but, thinking a lot when you do something is very good. And then sometimes if you don't think and then choose something, it could be good too, right?

Branden: Yeah, perhaps, but there has to be balance with whatever we're doing in our personality.

**8. I don't know about that.**

- to politely disagree

**Game3**

JiYoung: Oh, rich friends?

Branden: Right? If your friends have a lot of money and you need some help...

Cassandra: I don't know about that.

**9. I'm not sure that's true.**

- to indirectly disagree

> **Game2**
>
> JiYoung: Oh! You are a genius?
>
> Branden: I'm not sure that's true. Even if I were a genius, I'm not saying that I am, but, if I were, if I'm still not able to do – accomplish my goals, then it doesn't matter, right?

## Word Power

**1. optimistic**

- someone who tends to see the positive things in life; someone who has a positive outlook

> JiYoung: Oh, ok. My personality is, when I do something, when I meet someone, I'm thinking too much. What happens next, what's going on. So, I'm really worried about that. But, I'm trying to think positively a lot, too. So I think my personality is pretty positive.
>
> Branden: Ok, you're very optimistic.

**2. iffy**

- questionable; not sure; suspicious

> Cassandra: Oh! Time.
>
> Branden: Just like the time. So, anyway, we're going to stop there. That's round one. Let's see how many rejoinders...that last one was a little iffy, but I'll keep that one for myself. So, I have four.

**3. chronic**

- habitual; something you do routinely

> Branden: I'll start. Um, I'm a chronic procrastinator. I always wait until the last minute to do things. That's one of my flaws, I think. Um...

**4. be too hard on yourself**

- talk poorly about oneself; be mean to oneself

| | |
|---|---|
| Cassandra: | Really? Thank you, am I ok? |
| Branden: | Yeah. I don't want you to **be too hard on yourself**. |

**5. prerequisite**

- something that needs to happen before something else can happen

| | |
|---|---|
| Cassandra: | Of course, but I think that's not a **prerequisite** for friendship. I don't think the amount of money that you have in your bank determines if you can be a good friend or not. |
| Branden: | On the other hand, it is beneficial. |

**6. straightforward**

- direct; honest; clear

| | |
|---|---|
| JiYoung: | Ok, I'm thinking about my best friends, but, I don't know if it's good or bad, but anyway, they are sometimes saying very directly to me, but it's very good for me, so...even though some people say a **straightforward** character's not good, but to me it was very good. |

## Outro

### Dialogue

Branden: Oh, hello. Is something on your mind?

Cassandra: Hmm? Oh yeah. These days, I've been thinking about my future. What are my future goals? Where am I going to invest my savings? Things like that.

Branden: Oh, I see. Have you heard of cryptocurrencies? Their value is skyrocketing right now. I don't know, maybe that would be a worthwhile investment.

Cassandra: Hmm... **I don't agree.** You see, cryptocurrency isn't real money. We don't know if it will hold its value over time. Very risky, if you ask me.

**Branden:** Ok... I see what you mean. How about real estate? Many people think that real estate is a good investment.

**Cassandra:** Yeah, I see what you mean. But I'm not sure I agree. I think the bubble is about to pop, anytime now. Buying an overpriced apartment in the city is not my idea of a wise investment.

**Branden:** I'm afraid I disagree. People have been saying that for years. But historically, real estate in the big city has only increased in value. I can't see it slowing down anytime soon.

**Cassandra:** I don't know. Maybe I will just keep my extra cash in a savings account. At least it will be safe there.

**Branden:** I know what you're saying, but if you factor in the costs of inflation, you are actually losing money if you just keep it in the bank.

**Cassandra:** I get that, but it's better than losing it all when the market crashes!

**Branden:** On the other hand, what if it doesn't crash? You can't predict the future. I don't think it would hurt to invest if you have extra cash just laying around.

**Cassandra:** I see your point. I know! What if I just go back to school. I have always wanted to get my master's degree in philosophy.

**Branden:** I don't know about that. What kind of job are you going to get with a degree in philosophy? Let's be practical here.

**Cassandra:** I'm not sure that's true. Not everything in life is about making more money. What about leisure activities? Traveling? Things like that.

**Branden:** Perhaps, but I thought you were worried about saving money? Make up your mind dude! Do you want to enjoy life now or invest in your future. The choice is yours.

**Cassandra:** I hear you, but it's not easy to stay focused. Anyway, thanks for the talk. It's given me a lot to think about.

## Wrap-up

1. **I don't agree.**
   - to directly disagree

2. **I'm afraid I disagree.**
   - to directly disagree

3. **I'm not sure I agree.**
   - to directly disagree

4. **I hear you but...**
   - to indirectly disagree

5. **On the other hand..**
   - to indirectly disagree

6. **I know what you're saying, but...**
   - to indirectly disagree

7. **I get that, but...**
   - to indirectly disagree

8. **Perhaps, but...**
   - to indirectly disagree

9. **I don't know about that.**
   - to politely disagree

10. **I'm not sure that's true.**
    - to indirectly disagree

## Assignment

1. **Select the option that best completes the passage.**

> A: Look at this dress. I think it would look great on you.
> B: ____________ Pink isn't really my color.

1) I'm sure about it.
2) I can't help but agree.
3) I'm not sure I disagree.
4) I'm not sure I agree.

**2.** **Select the option that best completes the passage.**

> A: You don't need a car if you live in Seoul. The public transportation system is great.
> B: ______________ I like driving. It would be nice to have a car again.

1) I know what you're saying, but
2) I know what your saying, but
3) I know what you're saying, so
4) I know what you say, but

**3.** **Select the option that best completes the passage.**

> A: I don't think she likes him very much.
> B: ______________. If they didn't like each other, they wouldn't spend so much time together.

1) I'm afraid I agree.
2) I'm not sure that's true.
3) I'm sure that's true.
4) I'm sure about that.

**4.** **Select the option that best completes the passage.**

> A: I think it would be a good idea to go hiking in the afternoon.
> B: ______________ I heard it will rain today. Maybe it would be better to stay inside.

1) Perhaps, so
2) I hear it, but
3) I'm afraid I hear it, but
4) Perhaps, but

**5. Select the option that best completes the passage.**

A: I think Sally must be the tallest woman in the room.
B: ______________. She's wearing high heels that make her look taller than she really is.

1) I don't know what you said.
2) I'm sure that's it.
3) I don't know about that.
4) I'm scared that I disagree.

**6. Select the option that best completes the passage.**

A: I think getting a dog is a bad idea. They are a lot of work.
B: ______________ I would take care of it. You don't have to worry about that.

1) I get that, but
2) I hear that, but
3) You get me, but
4) I'm hearing that, but

**7. Select the option that best completes the passage.**

A: If you are tired, just drink more coffee.
B: ______________ I don't like the way coffee makes me feel. I get too jittery when I drink it.

1) I hear that, but
2) I get that, so
3) I hear you, so
4) I hear you, but

**8.** **Select the option that best completes the passage.**

A: These shoes look good.
B: __________ I think these fit my personal style better.

1) On the one hand,
2) On the alternate hand,
3) On the other hand,
4) On my hand,

**9.** **Select the option that best completes the passage.**

A: I like the American English pronunciation the most.
B: ______________ I think the British pronunciation sounds more sophisticated.

1) I disagree.
2) I agree.
3) On the other palm,
4) I'm afraid I agree.

**10.** **Select the option that best completes the passage.**

A: I love this singer. She is so talented.
B: __________. Most of her songs sound the same.

1) I'm afraid about it.
2) I'm afraid I disagree.
3) I disagree with her.
4) I heard it.

Week 10

# Mitigation

**Contents**

1. To soften with uncertainty
2. To soften with frankness
3. To soften with a general perspective
4. To soften with a personal perspective
5. To soften with an attention getter
6. To soften with a filler

**Objectives**

1. To understand 6 types of softening skills
2. To understand how 6 types of softening skills are used in real conversations
   1) Do we use different names for animals and people?
   2) Do surnames or family names have a special meaning in some cultures?
   3) Are there any names you strongly like or dislike?

## Intro

### Speaking Skills: Mitigation

**1. I guess...**

- to soften with uncertainty

Example

**A:** Do you lie the name Eva?

**B:** I guess it's alright.

**2. Maybe you should...**

- to soften with uncertainty

Example

A: I didn't get an interview at Samsung.

B: Maybe you should apply to some smaller companies.

3. **I just think that maybe...**
   - to soften with uncertainty

Example

A: Should I get this dress?

B: I just think maybe you should get pants instead

4. **To be honest...**
   - to soften with frankness

Example

A: Did you have a fun time last night?

B: To be honest, it was pretty boring.

5. **It just seems...**
   - to soften with a general perspective

Example

A: I can't believe I didn't get promoted! Don't you think I deserve a promotion?

B: I know you work hard, but it just seems that some other people work harder.

6. **...kind of...**
   - to soften with a personal perspective

Example

A: Do you want to take a walk in the park?

B : I kind of just want to stay home.

7. **Look...**
   - to soften with an attention getter

Example

A: Can I set you up on a date with my friend?

B: Look, I don't need a man to be happy.

**8. You see...**

- to soften with an attention getter

Example

A: I did not have a sound sleep last night. I am so tired.

B: You see, it's better to stop drinking coffee after 1p.m.

**9. You know...**

- to soften with a filler

Example

A: What did you think about the movie?

B: You know, I thought it was king of boring.

**10. Well...**

- to soften with a filler

Example

A: Can we go hiking in the afternoon?

B: Well, I'm not sure. The weather is pretty hot today.

## Lecture 1

### Conversation Question 1

▶ **Do we use different names for animals and people?**

**Q1. According to JiYoung, why don't Korean people give animals human names?**

a) Human names have meaning, so they are special.

b) Human names don't work well with animals.

c) She doesn't want to get confused between who is a human and who is an animal.

**Q2. Who thinks that naming an animal after a human would be insulting?**

a) Cassandra

b) Branden

c) JiYoung

**Q3. What is Cassandra's grandma's cat's name?**

a) Frederick

b) Freddie

c) Fred

Script

**Branden:** Hello, everyone. Welcome back. So, it's time for another game. My name is Branden, and I'm here with my colleagues, Cassandra and JiYoung. Welcome back.

**JiYoung:** Yes.

**Branden:** Alright, so, just like last time, the game will have three rounds, and each round will last for three minutes. I'll keep the time here. Whoever uses the most expressions for sharing our opinion will be the winner. Let's get started with the first question. Do we use different names for animals and people? Do we use different kinds of names for animals and people? Ok, so I guess I'll start off sharing my opinion. I guess this depends on our culture, right? I think that perhaps Korean culture, JiYoung you're Korean, right?

**JiYoung:** Yes, yes.

**Branden:** Might be different from Canadian, Canada or the US, where I'm from. So, uh, yeah, oh, sorry. Share your opinion with us.

**JiYoung:** Oh, yeah. We use the different names for animals and people. Because we don't give the human names to animals.

**Cassandra:** Never?

**JiYoung:** Never. I just saw one time, with my friend's cat's name. Truly, I didn't know she has a cat, but she kept saying the human's name, like oh, like JiYoung is sitting on the window. Like, JiYoung is – why is she sitting on the window? And then I realized that's the cat's name, so it's really weird, you know, feelings.

**Cassandra:** I guess that could be really confusing.

**JiYoung:** And, look, when I have a puppy and if I put the name, like, your names, hi Branden...

**Branden:** Yeah, it's kind of weird. But you never know, if you really don't like someone you could name them after an animal, right? Isn't it kind of insulting? To be honest, to be honest, I've considered naming a dog after somebody I really don't like as an insult. But, I don't know. What do you think?

**Cassandra:** Um, maybe you should reconsider that. Because if your animal is named after someone that you really detest, wouldn't those feelings transfer on to the innocent animal?

**Branden:** Yeah, I've thought about that, and that's the reason why I didn't do it. But, it was a thought.

**Cassandra:** Ok, ok, so, um...

**JiYoung:** I guess because, um, the reason why Korean people do not put the human's name on the animal is Koreans' names have a meaning. So, that's why people don't like to put the humans' names on the animals.

**Branden:** Right.

**Cassandra:** Ok.

**Branden:** Well, in the US, I'm from California, we name our animals just normal people names. Ok? So, I, my family's had dogs named Wilson, Jake, Jason, things like that. What about Canada?

**Cassandra:** Um, well, pretty much the same. So, we do both systems. Because I know animals that are named after like inanimate things or just cute words, like, my dog was named Sparky. That's not a human name, it's like a cute word. Sparky, Apple, I don't know, like Gruff. I don't know. Barky. Like, all these cute little like 'ee' names. But, we also name our animals after people like in the US, so. A quick anecdote is that my grandma lost her husband, my grandpa, but she ended up naming her cat after my deceased grandpa. So, my grandpa's name was Fred, Frederick, so she named the cat Fred, like Freddie, so Freddie is the cat, my dead grandpa is Fred.

**Branden:** Oh, wow.

**Cassandra:** It's a little weird sounding, but, I don't know, it's kind of cute in a way.

**Branden:** She, she liked her husband, right?

**Cassandra:** Of course, yeah, they had a good relationship.

**Branden:** Oh, oh.

**Cassandra:** She missed him, so...

**JiYoung:** Yeah, you know Korean people...

**Branden:** That's kind of cute.

**Cassandra:** Thank you.

**JiYoung:** Korean put the animals' name like Lucky or Happy, but not American name. Not Wilson, or, I don't know maybe Wilson can be.

**Branden:** Sure.

**Cassandra:** So, in Korea you could choose maybe like an English human name but not a human Korean name?

**JiYoung:** Ah, yeah.

**Cassandra:** Ok, that makes sense.

**Branden:** It's just that these days we consider animals to be like people. Like, part of our family. So, maybe one reason why people use human names, right?

**JiYoung:** I just think that maybe American names, English names, ok sorry.

**Cassandra:** No, it's ok.

**Branden:** No, continue, continue.

**JiYoung:** Sounds like cute and a little bit fancy, you know? So, that's why I choose the English name for the animal. Yeah.

**Branden:** Right, right, well they are definitely differences here. Alright, so, what kind of score do we have? So, JiYoung, you have...?

**JiYoung:** Five. I have five.

**Cassandra:** Oo, well done.

**Branden:** Five. Cassandra?

**Cassandra:** Three.

**Branden:** Three. And Branden, myself, has six.

**JiYoung:** Oh! One more.

**Branden:** So, yes, I'm the winner of round one. But, don't worry, you'll have another chance. We're going to go on to round two now. And, let's get ready for that.

**[Answer]**

**Q1. According to JiYoung, why don't Korean people give animals human names?**

a) Human names have meaning, so they are special.

b) Human names don't work well with animals.

c) She doesn't want to get confused between who is a human and who is an animal.

> **JiYoung:** I guess because the reason why Korean people do not put the human's name on the animal is Koreans' names have a meaning. So, that's why people don't like to put the humans' names on the animals.

**Q2. Who thinks that naming an animal after a human would be insulting?**

a) Cassandra

b) Branden

c) JiYoung

> **Branden:** Yeah, it's kind of weird. But you never know, if you really don't like someone you could name them after an animal, right? Isn't it kind of insulting?

**Q3. What is Cassandra's grandma's cat's name?**

a) Frederick

b) Freddie

c) Fred

> **Cassandra:** My grandma lost her husband, my grandpa, but she ended up naming her cat after my deceased grandpa. So, my grandpa's name was Fred, Frederick, so she named the cat Fred, like Freddie.

## Conversation Question 2

▶ **Do surnames or family names have a special meaning in some cultures?**

**Q1. Where does JiYoung's last name come from?**

a) Jeonju

b) Jindo

c) Jinju

**Q2. Whose last name comes from Ireland?**

a) Cassandra

b) Branden

c) JiYoung

**Q3. Cassandra's last name might come from Nike, the ancient god of what?**

a) Running shoes

b) War

c) Victory

### Script

**Branden:** Ok, it's time for round two. So, last time I was the winner, but don't worry guys, you have another chance. The next question: Do surnames, or family names, have special meaning in some cultures? No, I think we would all agree that surnames are in every culture, and they do have special meaning, but the meaning is different depending on where you're from. Ok? So, let's talk about this. I'll set the timer for three minutes. Right now. So, do surnames, or family names, have a special meaning in your culture?

**JiYoung:** Well, let me try first.

**Branden:** Sure. Go ahead, JiYoung.

**JiYoung:** Ok, well, we have a surnames or the family names. A surname's meaning has like, province, local meaning, right? My name is

Kang JiYoung, so Kang is my surname, so Kang is from the Jinju area.

Branden: Oh, ok.

JiYoung: And then JiYoung has the Chinese characters, so like 'Ji' has like the knowledge and 'Young' has a bright meaning. So, yeah. We have a special meaning.

Branden: Wow. I guess you're from Korea, right?

JiYoung: Yes.

Branden: I guess Koreans put a lot of thought into their names, right? It's really important.

JiYoung: Yes.

Cassandra: Ok, so, what you're saying is in terms of the surname, it mostly depends on your location, like your ancestor's location?

JiYoung: Yes.

Cassandra: Where they come from?

JiYoung: Yes, yes.

Cassandra: That's pretty cool. So, I think uh well, I can use one! Well, it's the same in the west, but we also have some other ways that you can get a family name, such as through your ancestors' occupation.

Branden: Sure, right.

Cassandra: So, like, a miller, a smith from like the occupation blacksmith, uh what else. Oh, like other things too, like if you're the son of somebody, like Jack's son. Your last name could be Jackson. So, I think that there are a variety of ways.

Branden: Yeah, you can get them from your ancestors' location or something like that.

Cassandra: Location, job, relationship.

Branden: Also from marriage, right? If you get married or if you have children, that's one way the names can be transferred over.

Cassandra: Yeah. Yeah, in Canada, actually, a lot of new last names are being created, so you take the father's last name, you hyphenate it, and you add the mother's or vice versa, so new names are being created.

Branden: Wow, that's interesting. To be honest, when I was growing up, most of the time when people got married, the wife would take the husband's last name, and her previous surname would be her new middle name. Does that happen in Canada, too?

**Cassandra:** Oh, interesting. Um, not to my knowledge, the middle name doesn't like...how can I say, the last name becomes the middle name um no...

**Branden:** But they become hyphenated.

**Cassandra:** They could be hyphenated or the woman still just takes the man's last name.

**JiYoung:** Oh, I see. Oh, we don't have a middle name.

**Branden:** Oh, you don't?

**JiYoung:** So, when you guys talk about a middle name, it's very strange.

**Cassandra:** Yeah. It is a strange thing, yeah.

**JiYoung:** So, when you're writing some documents, you write the middle name, too?

**Cassandra:** We have to.

**JiYoung:** Oh, really?

**Branden:** We do.

**JiYoung:** Oh.

**Cassandra:** Yeah, yeah. Um, I guess if we still have time could we talk about our own last names and what they mean?

**JiYoung:** Hm, the last name.

**Cassandra:** So, yours is the location?

**JiYoung:** Location.

**Cassandra:** Do you know about yours?

**Branden:** Not really. So, my name is from Ireland originally. And, it...Noland. My name is Branden Noland. So, I assume that means my ancestors had no land. Nykyforak. We're out of time but please continue.

**Cassandra:** Oh, it comes from maybe Nike? I think that's a Roman god of victory or something?

**Branden:** Sure, yeah.

**Cassandra:** So, yeah, it's from the Ukraine and old myths and stuff.

**Branden:** Wow.

**Cassandra:** Maybe.

**Branden:** How interesting.

**Cassandra:** This is not like an endorsement of the shoe company.

**Branden:** Nykyforak.

**Cassandra:** Like, Nike-forak. They pronounce it Nike-forak. That's where it comes from, yeah. Maybe.

**Branden:** Really? Interesting. Alright, so let's see what kind of points we have here. Oh, no! We're all tied.

**Cassandra:** We're all tied.

**Branden:** Two, two, two. Ok. So, I won the first round and then we are tied for round two. Let's see what the next round has in store for us.

**[Answer]**

**Q1. Where does JiYoung's last name come from?**

a) Jeonju

b) Jindo

c) Jinju

**JiYoung:** we have a surnames or the family names. A surname's meaning has like, province, local meaning, right? My name is Kang JiYoung, so Kang is my surname, so Kang is from the Jinju area.

**Q2. Whose last name comes from Ireland?**

a) Cassandra

b) Branden

c) JiYoung

**Branden:** My name is from Ireland originally. And, it...Noland. My name is Branden Noland. So, I assume that means my ancestors had no land. Nykyforak. We're out of time but please continue.

**Q3. Cassandra's last name might come from Nike, the ancient god of what?**

a) Running shoes

b) War

c) Victory

**Cassandra:** Oh, it comes from maybe Nike? I think that's a Roman god of victory or something?

## Conversation Question 3

▶ **Are there any names you strongly like or dislike?**

**Q1. Which of these boys were NOT mean to Cassandra in school?**

a) Alex

b) Branden

c) Jacob

**Q2. Who says that JiYoung's name is pretty?**

a) Cassandra

b) Branden

c) JiYoung

**Q3. According to Cassandra, older names aren't bad, they're just not.....**

a) Pretty

b) Important

c) Trendy

### Script

**Branden:** Alright, welcome back. We're on round three. So, so far I have two points, but you guys have one point, so there's still a chance you could tie me. Um, but I'll probably win, as is usual. Ok, so, our next question is: Are there any names you strongly like or dislike? Ok? So, it's kind of a broad topic, so let's see what we do. I'll set the timer now for three minutes. Ok. Names we strongly like or dislike. And I guess I will start us off. And, I guess names that are associated with bad people I don't like. Like, in history if there's somebody who did something really bad, I don't like that name. I associate the bad history with the name. I don't know. What about you?

**Cassandra:** Hm, you know, me too, and it also extends to my personal life. So, for example in my childhood, if for example some boy used to bother me in school, like I'm thinking of an Alex and a Jacob, those two boys bothered me a lot, so I don't like that name today.

Branden: I see.

Cassandra: I, I'm not very, what can I say, biased as an adult because I know why I feel that way, but if I just hear that name, I naturally feel a little uncomfortable, and then I have to remind myself they're not that person. They're a different version.

Branden: Alright, great.

JiYoung: Well, you know, my name is also a kind of old-fashioned name. And, you know, JiYoung, there's lots. You can hear everywhere that name if you have lots of Korean friends, so, yeah, I don't like my name.

Cassandra: I love your name, it's so pretty!

JiYoung: Thank you, I want to hear that. I like my name too.

Branden: You know, JiYoung doesn't seem like an old name. It seems very normal. Like you said, there are so many JiYoungs, so it does n't seem too old.

Cassandra: What's an example of like an old-fashioned name in Korea?

JiYoung: Um, a very long time ago, the woman's name like -Cha. Yeah, MalCha, SeunCha, yeah, it's like a country-style name.

Branden: Everything with Cha.

JiYoung: Yeah.

Cassandra: It's like that old feeling.

JiYoung: Very old.

Cassandra: Ah, ok.

Branden: What about in North America? Do we have any old names over there that we don't like?

Cassandra: Oh, definitely. And it's not that we don't like them, I just think...

Branden: We don't use them.

Cassandra: We don't use them that much. So, like, for example, if I were to name my daughter Betty...

Branden: Betty.

Cassandra: Hilda.

Branden: Doris.

Cassandra: Oh, Doris. Eva.

Branden: Bertha.

Cassandra: Bertha, yeah. There's so many, like, they're from my grandma's generation. They're not bad names, they're just not that trendy anymore. How about for males? Like, what's an untrendy male name?

**Branden:** That is an interesting point. It just seems like most of the untrendy names are actually female, right?

**Cassandra:** Maybe.

**Branden:** I'm having a hard time thinking of male names that aren't that trendy.

**Cassandra:** Maybe long ones like Alexander, like those kind of historical ones. But, even then...

**Branden:** You see, you see when people have long names, that's when they tend to shorten them. But good points.

**JiYoung:** But it seems like Alexander, something like that, is a very big name for us, I mean for like Koreans, like king's names.

**Cassandra:** Oh, so as a Korean that wouldn't be like a normal English name, really?

**Branden:** Because most of your names are two syllables, right?

**JiYoung:** Yes, yes. Or one.

**Branden:** Or one.

**Cassandra:** Interesting.

**Branden:** Alright, so let's see how we did. The time is up, guys. Um, what have you got, JiYoung?

**JiYoung:** Three.

**Branden:** Three? Ok, I have four! I have four here.

**Cassandra:** Two. Just two.

**Branden:** Two. Yes! So, I'm pleased to announce that Branden is the winner of rounds one, two, and three, and that's it, guys. Let's stay tuned for the next part.

[Answer]

**Q1. Which of these boys were NOT mean to Cassandra in school?**

a) Alex

b) Branden

c) Jacob

Cassandra: So, in my childhood, if, for example, some boy used to bother me in school, like I'm thinking of an Alex and a Jacob, those two boys bothered me a lot, so I don't like that name today.

**Q2. Who says that JiYoung's name is pretty?**

a) Cassandra

b) Branden

c) JiYoung

JiYoung: my name is also a kind of old-fashioned name. So, yeah, I don't like my name.

Cassandra: I love your name, it's so pretty!

**Q3. According to Cassandra, older names aren't bad, they're just not.....**

a) Pretty

b) Important

c) Trendy

Cassandra: Doris, Eva, Bertha, yeah. There's so many, like, they're from my grandma's generation. They're not bad names, they're just not that trendy anymore. How about for males? Like, what's an untrendy male name?

## Lecture 2

### Words in Action

**1. I guess...**
- to soften with uncertainty

**Game2**
Branden: I guess Koreans put a lot of thought into their names, right? It's really important.
JiYoung: Yes.

**2. Maybe you should...**
- to soften with uncertainty

**Game1**
Branden: To be honest, to be honest, I've considered naming a dog after somebody I really don't like as an insult. But, I don't know. What do you think?
Cassandra: Um, maybe you should reconsider that. Because if your animal is named after someone that you really detest, wouldn't those feelings transfer on to the innocent animal?

**3. I just think that maybe...**
- to soften with uncertainty

**Game1**
Branden: It's just that these days we consider animals to be like people. Like, part of our family. So, maybe one reason why people use human names, right?
JiYoung: I just think that maybe American names, English names, ok sorry.

**4.** **To be honest...**

- to soften with frankness

**Game1**

**Branden:** Yeah, it's kind of weird. But you never know, if you really don't like someone you could name them after an animal, right? Isn't it kind of insulting? To be honest, I've considered naming a dog after somebody I really don't like as an insult. But, I don't know. What do you think?

**5.** **It just seems...**

- to soften with a general perspective

**Game3**

**Cassandra:** Oh, Doris. Eva.

**Branden:** That is an interesting point. It just seems like most of the untrendy names are actually female, right?

**6.** **...kind of...**

- to soften with a personal perspective

**Game3**

**JiYoung:** Well, you know, my name is also a kind of old-fashioned name. And, you know, JiYoung, there's lots. You can hear everywhere that name if you have lots of Korean friends, so, yeah, I don't like my name.

**7.** **Look...**

- to soften with an attention getter

**Game1**

**JiYoung:** I didn't know she has a cat, but she kept saying the human's name, like JiYoung is sitting on the window. And then I realized that's the cat's name, so it's really weird, you know, feelings.

**Cassandra:** I guess that could be really confusing.

**JiYoung:** And, look, when I have a puppy and if I put the name, like, your names, hi Branden...

**8. You see...**

- to soften with an attention getter

**Game3**

**Branden:** I'm having a hard time thinking of male names that aren't that trendy.

**Cassandra:** Maybe long ones like Alexander, like those kind of historical ones.

**Branden:** You see, when people have long names, that's when they tend to shorten them. But good points.

**9. You know...**

- to soften with a filler

**Game1**

**Cassandra:** A quick anecdote is that my grandma lost her husband, my grandpa, but she ended up naming her cat after my deceased grandpa. So, my grandpa's name was Fred, Frederick, so she named the cat Fred, like Freddie.

**JiYoung:** You know, Korean people...put the animals' name like Lucky or Happy, but not American name. Not Wilson, or, I don't know maybe Wilson can be.

**10. Well...**

- to soften with a filler

**Game2**

**Branden:** Sure. Go ahead, JiYoung.

**JiYoung:** Well, we have a surnames or the family names. A surname's meaning has like, province, local meaning, right? My name is Kang JiYoung, so Kang is my surname, so Kang is from the Jinju area.

## Word Power

**1. insulting**

- something that hurts another's feelings; disrespectful

> **Branden:** Yeah, it's kind of weird. But you never know, if you really don't like someone you could name them after an animal, right? Isn't it kind of insulting? To be honest, I've considered naming a dog after somebody I really don't like as an insult. But, I don't know. What do you think?

**2. anecdote**

- personal story

> **Cassandra:** A quick anecdote is that my grandma lost her husband, my grandpa, but she ended up naming her cat after my deceased grandpa. So, my grandpa's name was Fred, Frederick, so she named the cat Fred, like Freddie, so Freddie is the cat, my dead grandpa is Fred.

**3. ancestors**

- the people in your family throughout history

> **Cassandra:** Ok, so, what you're saying is in terms of the surname, it mostly depends on your location, like your ancestor's location?

**4. hyphenate**

- to combine two words with a hyphen (-)

> **Cassandra:** Yeah, in Canada, actually, a lot of new last names are being created, so you take the father's last name, you hyphenate it, and you add the mother's or vice versa, so new names are being created.

**5. biased**

- unfairly prejudiced again someone or something

Cassandra: I'm not very can I say biased as an adult because I know why I feel that way, but if I just hear that name, I naturally feel a little uncomfortable, and then I have to remind myself they're not that person. They're a different version.

**6. old-fashioned**

- in an old style; not modern

JiYoung: Well, you know, my name is also a kind of old-fashioned name. And, you know, JiYoung, there's lots. You can hear everywhere that name if you have lots of Korean friends, so, yeah, I don't like my name.

## Outro

### Dialogue

Cassandra: I just think that maybe he's changed, that's all. You know when I first started working I wasn't that good at my job, either. I was going through a hard time in my personal life. I bet some of my ex-coworkers thought that I was rude, too! But now look at me? I'm a model employee! You see? People can change!

Branden: Well... you make a good point. Ok, I will give Jason another chance!

Cassandra: Hey, have you met the new employee, Jason? He's nice, isn't he?

Branden: Well... you don't know him like I do. I used to work with Jason at a different company...about 4 years ago.

Cassandra: What are you saying? Is there something wrong with him?

Branden: To be honest he didn't have a good reputation back then. I didn't work with him personally, but that's what other people told me. I guess he was kind of lazy, didn't do his work on time, stuff like that.

Cassandra: Whoa... that's kind of harsh. Maybe you should give him another chance. 4 years is a long time...maybe he's gotten better. It just seems like it's too early to make any judgments. He just started a few days ago.

Branden: Look... I know what your saying, but I'm not going to lie. He was rude and arrogant back then. Working with him was a nightmare. I don't have any reason to think that now's going be any different.

Cassandra: I just think that maybe he's changed, that's all. You know when I first started working I wasn't that good at my job, either. I was going through a hard time in my personal life. I bet some of my ex-coworkers thought that I was rude, too! But now look at me? I'm a model employee! You see, people can change!

Branden: Well... you make a good point. Ok, I will give Jason another chance!

## Wrap-up

1. **I guess...**
   - to soften with uncertainty

2. **Maybe you should...**
   - to soften with uncertainty

3. **I just think that maybe...**
   - to soften with uncertainty

4. **To be honest...**
   - to soften with frankness

5. **It just seems...**
   - to soften with a general perspective

6. **...kind of...**
   - to soften with a personal perspective

7. **Look...**
   - to soften with an attention getter

**8. You see...**

- to soften with an attention getter

**9. You know...**

- to soften with a filler

**10. Well...**

- to soften with a filler

## Assignment

**1. Select the option that best completes the passage.**

A: Do you think you would be able to let me borrow some money?
B: ______________ as a rule I don't loan money to people. I'm sorry.

1) See,
2) I see
3) Look,
4) I know

**2. Select the option that best completes the passage.**

A: Do you like your present?
B: ______________ it's ok.

1) I guess
2) I see,
3) It just looks
4) I guessed

**3. Select the option that best completes the passage.**

A: Do you think I should buy this stock?
B: ______________ you should choose a less risky investment.

1) I just think so perhaps
2) I just think that maybe
3) It is seeming
4) As honestly

**4. Select the option that best completes the passage.**

A: What's wrong? You look upset.
B: ______________ I have a presentation starting in 5 minutes, but my files somehow got corrupted.

1) They see,
2) He sees,
3) I see,
4) You see,

**5. Select the option that best completes the passage.**

A: What do you think about Jacob's bow tie?
B: ______________ I really don't like it.

1) You know,
2) I am knowing,
3) It's just seemingly
4) Wells,

**6.** **Select the option that best completes the passage.**

A: I don't know why everyone hates me at work.
B: I know you're a nice guy, but ______________ that other people don't appreciate your sense of humor.

1) It just seemingly
2) It's just honest
3) It just seems
4) It's seems

**7.** **Select the option that best completes the passage.**

A: Do you think this dress looks good on me?
B: ______________ I think it looks too tight.

1) To be honest,
2) With honesty,
3) To be me,
4) To be frankly,

**8.** **Select the option that best completes the passage.**

A: Can I buy a motorcycle?
B: ______________ I'll have to think about it.

1) I know,
2) Honest,
3) Kind of,
4) Well,

**9. Select the option that best completes the passage.**

A: I am thinking about majoring in history.
B: ______________ think about a more practical major.

1) Maybe you shall
2) Maybe it should
3) Maybe you should
4) Maybe you will

**10. Select the option that best completes the passage.**

A: Do you want to play a board game?
B: I ______________ want to go outside. The weather is fantastic?

1) Kind of
2) Kindly
3) Kind in
4) Kinder

Week 11

# Asking for Opinions and Information

**Contents**

1. To request a general opinion
2. To request general information
3. To request a personal opinion
4. To request a personal opinion before giving advice
5. To request a plan
6. To politely request an explanation or information
7. To request an official position
8. To summarize and clarify an opinion

**Objectives**

1. To understand 8 types of requesting skills
2. To understand how 8 types of requesting-skills are used in real conversations
   1) Do you like shopping for new clothes?
   2) What are some of the strangest fashions you have ever seen?
   3) Is your fashion sense the same in Korea as it is elsewhere?

## Intro

### Speaking Skills: Asking for Opinions and Information

**1. What do you think?**

- to request a general opinion

Example

A: What do you think about the current pandemic situation?

B: I think it's a real problem for the future. We should take action before it is too late.

**2. Talk to me about...**

- to request general information

Example

A: I loved my vacation last year in Japan.

B: Talk to me about the cuisine there.

**3. How do you feel about that?**

- to request a personal opinion

Example

A: What's your plan for dinner?

B: I think I'll make spaghetti tonight. How do you feel about that?

**4. How about you?**

- to request a personal opinion

Example

A: I heard you love going to saunas.

B: I do. How about you?

**5. I'm curious to know what you think.**

- to request a personal opinion

Example

A: My sister said it's a bad idea to have coffee before bed.

B: I'm curious to know what you think.

**6. What's your opinion?**

- to request a personal opinion before giving advice

Example

A: What do you think I should do with my son?

B: What's your opinion?

**7. What about you?**

- to request a plan

Example

A: What are you going to do tonight?

B: I'm not sure. What about you?

**8. I was hoping you could tell me...**

- to politely request an explanation or information

Example

A: I really dislike reading science fiction.

B: I've heard you say that many times. I was hoping you could tell me what it is you don't like about sci-fi books.

**9. I'd like to know your take...**

- to request an official position

Example

A: Did you hear the latest news about Donald Trump?

B: Yes, and I'd like to know your take on Trump.

**10. I hear you saying...**

- to summarize and clarify an opinion

Example

A: Women put too much effort into their appearance painting their nails, putting on make-up, and getting their hair dyed.

B: I hear you saying you prefer women who aren't obsessed with their appearance. Is that right?

## Lecture 1

### Conversation Question 1

▶ **Do you like shopping for new clothes?**

**Q1. What is JiYoung's favorite thing to buy?**

a) shoes

b) coats

c) suits

**Q2. Who says that they buy clothes no matter if they have the funds or not?**

a) Cassandra

b) Branden

c) JiYoung

**Q3. Which season is the best for clothes shopping, according to all three speakers?**

a) spring

b) fall

c) winter

Script

Branden: Hello, and welcome back. So, we're here for another game where we are going to practice the expressions that you learned in class. So, my name is Branden and I'm here with my colleagues, Cassandra and JiYoung, hello.

JiYoung: Yes, hi.

Branden: Good to have you here today. Ok, so, just like last time, we have three minutes per round, and whoever uses the most expressions will be the winner. Let's get started. The first question. Do you like shopping for new clothes? Ok, I'll set the timer here. Do you like shopping for new clothes? Let's get started. Ok.

JiYoung: How about you?

Branden: Well, in my opinion, if I have the money, I like shopping. If I have, if I know that I can buy stuff that I want. But, if I don't have the funds available, then it's not that fun. Personally.

Cassandra: Ok, so, I hear you saying it's a matter of disposable income, really. Or, just how much money you have to spend on clothes?

Branden: Yeah, yeah, if I don't have the money it makes me feel bad. Like, oh I want these clothes, but I can't get it.

Cassandra: Ah, I'm the opposite. I'll spend money on clothes no matter what.

Branden: Oh, yeah?

Cassandra: Yeah. I'm one of those people. I like – I like shopping for new clothes, yeah.

Branden: Sure, are you – do you buy expensive clothes?

Cassandra: No.

Branden: Like, how much money should you spend on clothes? What's your opinion? Just curious.

Cassandra: Oh, me? No, I just think it's whatever you have to...available, so if you want to save your money, maybe you shouldn't be spending it on clothes all of the time, but if you have a lot of money...

Branden: Right, right.

Cassandra: ...or you don't care about saving, then you can splurge on clothing. Yeah.

Branden: Yeah, I like buying clothes that I can use in different seasons. That are very versatile. That have many – be used in different situations. JiYoung, what do you think?

Cassandra: Yeah, how about you?

JiYoung: Yeah, as you know, Korea has four seasons. Like, spring, summer, fall, winter. So, I like to go shopping every season.

Branden: Oh, ok.

JiYoung: If I have a lot of money, more. Yeah.

Branden: I'm curious to know what season you like the most. Like, which season is the best for shopping?

JiYoung: Oh, personally I like to buy coats.

Branden: Coats, yeah.

Cassandra: Coats! They could be expensive, though.

JiYoung: Oh, it depends on the brand.

Cassandra: Yeah, yeah.

JiYoung: Yeah. How about you? What kind of seasons' clothes do you like?

Branden: I'm the same. I like winter.

JiYoung: Oh, yeah?

Branden: Yeah.

JiYoung: Why?

Branden: Well, like you, I like the coats. It makes me feel like I'm in a movie. Yeah, I have quite a few wool and cashmere coats that I wear. So, I do enjoy that.

Cassandra: Yeah, I know what you're talking about. He looks good in the winter. All his fancy coats, yeah.

Branden: Aw, yeah. Thank you.

Cassandra: I always like the winter. Not so much for the coats, just I don't like showing my body, so I don't like summer clothes because you tend to wear less in the summer. But in winter, yeah I like just like putting on a nice sweater. A sweater and a pair of jeans, that's kind of my comfort style.

**Branden:** I think that shopping or dressing in the summer is just less comfortable. Because you're sweating, it's hot.

**Cassandra:** Yeah.

**JiYoung:** Yeah, yeah, right.

**Branden:** What about you?

**Cassandra:** Oh, yeah I just, I don't really like summer at all. As a Canadian, I prefer cold weather.

**Branden:** Oh, it's really cold over there, right.

**Cassandra:** All the time, yes. Summers are hard for me, clothing-wise, hair-wise...my hair retains a lot of humidity, but that's a different subject.

**Branden:** Sure, sure.

**Cassandra:** So, we all agree. We all like shopping for new clothes?

**Branden:** Yeah, I think so.

**Cassandra:** Except for Branden a little bit?

**Branden:** No, I like it.

**Cassandra:** You like it? Ok, ok.

**Branden:** Speaking, oh! I was going to ask you – I'll ask you later about that. Alright, guys, so that's the end of round one. I have four points here. How did you guys do?

**Cassandra:** We're tied at two.

**JiYoung:** Two.

**Branden:** Two? Yes, I'm winning. I'm a winner. Ok, guys, we're going on to round two, let's get ready for that.

**[Answer]**

**Q1. What is JiYoung's favorite thing to buy?**

a) shoes

b) coats

c) suits

**JiYoung:** Yeah, as you know, Korea has four seasons. Like, spring, summer, fall, winter. So, I like to go shopping every season. If I have a lot of money, more. Yeah. Oh, personally I like to buy coats.

**Q2. Who says that they buy clothes no matter if they have the funds or not?**

a) Cassandra

b) Branden

c) JiYoung

| | |
|---|---|
| Branden: | Yeah, yeah, if I don't have the money it makes me feel bad. Like, oh I want these clothes, but I can't get it. |
| Cassandra: | Ah, I'm the opposite. I'll spend money on clothes no matter what. |

**Q3. Which season is the best for clothes shopping, according to all three speakers?**

a) spring

b) fall

c) winter

| | |
|---|---|
| JiYoung: | Yeah, as you know, Korea has four seasons. Like, spring, summer, fall, winter. So, I like to go shopping every season. |
| Branden: | I'm the same. I like winter. |
| Cassandra: | I always like the winter. |

## Conversation Question 2

▶ **What are some of the strangest fashions you have ever seen?**

**Q1. Where did JiYoung attend university in the states?**

a) Ohio

b) Idaho

c) Utah

**Q2. Who thinks that the gothic fashion is a little strange?**

a) Cassandra

b) Branden

c) JiYoung

**Q3. Why doesn't Branden like ripped jeans?**

a) They are too cool for him.

b) They look sloppy to him.

c) They look better on girls than boys.

Script

**Branden:** Alright, so it's time for round two. Let's get started with our next question. What are some of the strangest fashions you have ever seen? Ok? What are some of the strangest fashions you have ever seen? Let's start the timer here. Ok? Good. Alright, so, uh, talk to me about fashion in your country, you know, we all come from different countries, right?

**Cassandra:** I'd like to know everyone's take on North American fashion. Like, how do you feel about Americans, Canadians, how we dress? Do you think we dress well or not so trendy?

**Branden:** Well, I think this would be an excellent opportunity to get an outsider's perspective. Uh, you were actually going to school in Utah, didn't you?

**JiYoung:** Yes.

**Branden:** Ok, so, what do you, what do you think about the Utah fashion, from your experience?

**JiYoung:** Utah fashion, oh my gosh. Um, ok, um, they are students so they are wearing clothes freely, um I don't know how to say, oh my gosh, so hard!

**Cassandra:** Like, yoga pants? In my university...

**Branden:** It's hard.

**JiYoung:** Yeah, it's hard to describe the Utah fashion. Oh my gosh.

**Branden:** Because they don't have fashion, right?

**JiYoung:** Yeah, it so hard.

**Cassandra:** Yeah, student fashion is different from...

**JiYoung:** Yeah, student fashion.

**Branden:** Yeah, sure.

**Cassandra:** ...general public.

**JiYoung:** Sorry.

**Branden:** Well, there's a lot of strange fashions out there. Like, have you heard of the gothic fashion?

Cassandra: Oh, sure.

Branden: Where they wear, like, tights, black, leather, and they dye their hair black, and very white makeup.

Cassandra: I love that. What about you?

Branden: Yeah, it's kind of strange.

Cassandra: Oh, strange? Nah.

Branden: Well, I think everybody's...it's great that they can express themselves freely, but for me it's strange because I never thought about being like that.

Cassandra: Sure. Fair enough.

JiYoung: Ok, what about...what about wearing, like, what is it? Like...

Branden: Jeans?

JiYoung: Jeans, but it looks like a...

Branden: Skirts?

JiYoung: No. It's like...striped? I don't know.

Cassandra: Oh, ripped?

JiYoung: Yeah, ripped!

Cassandra: Like, holes and tears? Oh, like torn jeans.

JiYoung: Yeah!

Cassandra: Oh, that's an interesting one. They could look good on some people, but...

JiYoung: I really try...

Branden: Yeah, I don't like it.

JiYoung: Oh, you don't like it?

Branden: Yeah, I don't like it.

Cassandra: Why not?

JiYoung: Can I ask you why?

Branden: Why? Because it just seems sloppy, like if I want to have holes in my jeans, I can do it myself. I don't need to pay for it. You know? I don't know.

JiYoung: Yeah.

Cassandra: Ok, sure.

Branden: Also back in the day, they had this trend, maybe ten years ago, where some men would wear really baggy jeans, and the jeans would be hanging down and you could see their underwear. Do you remember that?

Cassandra: I do remember that. I want to erase that from my mind.

**JiYoung:** A big thing, yeah.

**Branden:** Ok.

**Cassandra:** That was a bad trend.

**Branden:** How do you feel about that?

**JiYoung:** Oh, it's cool, but strange. I don't know where the like...what's...I don't like that.

**Branden:** Very, very strange.

**Cassandra:** A thing that was a problem in Canada for awhile was some women were wearing yoga pants to their work. Like, not just to do exercise in. They wore like exercise pants to their workplace.

**Branden:** Right.

**Cassandra:** So, that caused some trouble in Canada. Whether or not that was an ok thing to do.

**Branden:** What's your opinion about that?

**Cassandra:** Oh, I think those pants aren't professional. But, for exercise, then, they're fine. Yeah. Did you have that trouble in America?

**Branden:** What – I was just going to say, yeah it's similar in America.

**Cassandra:** Similar, yeah.

**Branden:** We're very casual. That's one of the things I like about Korea, is people dress up a little bit over here, don't they?

**Cassandra:** Yeah, good style here.

**Branden:** I do like it. Alright, so that's all the time we have, and how many points do we have?

**JiYoung:** Two.

**Branden:** Two? I have – two? And I have four! So, once again, I am the winner, and yeah I'll pat myself on the back here. Let's move on to round three.

**[Answer]**

**Q1. Where did JiYoung attend university in the states?**

a) Ohio

b) Idaho

c) Utah

Branden: I think this would be an excellent opportunity to get an outsider's perspective. You were actually going to school in Utah, didn't you?

JiYoung: Yes.

**Q2. Who thinks that the gothic fashion is a little strange?**

a) Cassandra

b) Branden

c) JiYoung

Branden: Well, there's a lot of strange fashions out there. Like, have you heard of the gothic fashion?

Cassandra: I love that. What about you?

Branden: Yeah, it's kind of strange.

**Q3. Why doesn't Branden like ripped jeans?**

a) They are too cool for him.

b) They look sloppy to him.

c) They look better on girls than boys.

Cassandra: Like, holes and tears? Oh, like torn jeans.

Branden: Yeah, I don't like it. Because it just seems sloppy, like if I want to have holes in my jeans, I can do it myself. I don't need to pay for it. You know? I don't know.

## Conversation Question 3

**▶ Is your fashion sense the same in Korea as it is elsewhere?**

**Q1. What do Canadians dress for, according to Cassandra?**

a) The elements

b) Going to the club

c) Summertime

**Q2. Who once wore pajamas to their class at university?**

a) Cassandra

b) Branden

c) JiYoung

**Q3. Why did Branden feel like a foreigner in California?**

a) He dresses more formal than other Californians.

b) He dresses more casual than other Californians.

c) He wears gothic clothing.

### Script

**Branden:** Alright, welcome back to round three. So, this time, whoever wins will earn three points. So, you guys have a chance. Sound good?

**Cassandra:** Thank you.

**JiYoung:** Thank you, yeah.

**Branden:** Ok, I'm a nice guy. Question. Is your fashion sense the same in Korea as it is elsewhere? Is your fashion sense the same in Korea as it is elsewhere? So, let's get started. Starting the timer, now. Um, so, talk to me about fashion. What is your fashion like in Korea?

**Cassandra:** Much better.

**Branden:** Much better?

**JiYoung:** Oh, really?

**Cassandra:** Yeah. Because, in Canada, as I probably mentioned before, we dress more casually, comfortably, and kind of for the elements, we say. So, for the weather. So, in Canada, I really don't care about the way I look that much. I just want to be cozy. So, I wear kind of like exercise clothes more. A big sweater, oversized sweater, uh, like uh, I don't know what to call them, just like track pants is the word. Like, cozy pants and I put my hair up in a big messy bun. I don't really do my makeup. So, it's a little different than in Korea because I care more about my appearance in Korea.

**JiYoung:** Yeah, I agree.

**Branden:** Yeah, how do you feel about that? You have to care more, that's more effort. Don't you want to go back to Canada and be relaxed?

**Cassandra:** It's more effort, but I guess I look better because I put in the effort. So, maybe it's worth it. Yeah.

**Branden:** Oh, ok.

**Cassandra:** How about, how about for yourself?

**JiYoung:** Oh, yeah as you said, in Korea when you go somewhere we have to put makeup and put the dress on, and it's a little bit stressed, so. Yeah, I'm a little bit opposite you, I'm really...I think Canadian is more free to wear the clothes...I think that's good.

**Cassandra:** Sure, there's just a lot of different choices in Canada. You can dress really any way. No one will really look at you. Or..

**Branden:** Sure, sure.

**JiYoung:** It's good, right?

**Cassandra:** But Korea looks better. Koreans look so trendy.

**Branden:** So, so JiYoung, you, I may have mentioned before that you spent time in Utah, right, when you were going to school. I'd like to know your take on the fashion there. Was it different than what you're wearing now? How did you dress back then?

**JiYoung:** Oh, yeah, I was totally different. I remember when I was...it was like a...ok, when I woke up, I had pajamas on here, I'm a little bit late to class, I went there, the class, with the pajamas. So, no one cared. So, yeah, but in Korea, no, never can happen. So. Yeah, it's totally different, yeah.

**Cassandra:** What about for you?

**Branden:** Yeah, guys, I hear what you're saying. The fashion that I wear in Korea is slightly different than back home. Just like Canada, California is somewhat relaxed when it comes to fashion standards. So, when I went back to visit California, I was wearing, you know, a nice coat, a button up shirt, and people looked at me like I was a foreigner. They thought that I was from a different country. That I didn't...I didn't belong there. So, yeah, I didn't realize it until then, but my fashion has changed. I'm...I dress a little better. But, I like simple, I dress in jeans and a buttoned shirt. Works for me.

**Cassandra:** This was a hard round.

**Branden:** Sorry for not giving you guys a chance to talk, but I do like winning anyway.

**JiYoung:** Oh, my gosh.

**Branden:** Ok, so I have four points here.

**Cassandra:** One.

**Branden:** One.

**JiYoung:** I got zero.

**Branden:** But we enjoyed hearing your experience.

**JiYoung:** Yeah, oh my gosh.

**Branden:** Yeah, feel good about yourself. Ok, so that's it for today's game. Hopefully you enjoyed that. And now we're going to move on to the next part.

**[Answer]**

**Q1. What do Canadians dress for, according to Cassandra?**

a) The elements

b) Going to the club

c) Summertime

**Cassandra:** Yeah. Because, in Canada, as I probably mentioned before, we dress more casually, comfortably, and kind of for the elements, we say.

**Q2. Who once wore pajamas to their class at university?**

a) Cassandra

b) Branden

c) JiYoung

JiYoung: I remember when I woke up, I had pajamas on here, I'm a little bit late to class, I went there, the class, with the pajamas. So, no one cared. So, yeah, but in Korea, no, never can happen.

**Q3. Why did Branden feel like a foreigner in California?**

a) He dresses more formal than other Californians.

b) He dresses more casual than other Californians.

c) He wears gothic clothing.

Branden: The fashion that I wear in Korea is slightly different than back home. California is somewhat relaxed when it comes to fashion standards. So, when I went back to visit California, I was wearing, you know, a nice coat, a button up shirt, and people looked at me like I was a foreigner.

## Lecture 2

### Words in Action

**1. What do you think?**

- to request a general opinion

**Game2**

Branden: Ok, so, what do you think about the Utah fashion, from your experience?

JiYoung: Utah fashion, oh my gosh. Ok, um, they are students so they are wearing clothes freely, I don't know how to say, oh my gosh, so hard!

**2. Talk to me about...**

- to request general information

**Game2**

**Branden:** Good. Alright, talk to me about fashion in your country, you know, we all come from different countries, right?

**Cassandra:** I'd like to know everyone's take on North American fashion. Do you think we dress well or not so trendy?

**3. How do you feel about that?**

- to request a personal opinion

**Game2**

**Cassandra:** Like, how do you feel about Americans, Canadians, how we dress? Do you think we dress well or not so trendy?

**Branden:** Well, I think this would be an excellent opportunity to get an outsider's perspective.

**4. How about you?**

- to request a personal opinion

**Game1**

**Branden:** Do you like shopping for new clothes?

**JiYoung:** How about you?

**Branden:** Well, in my opinion, if I have the money, I like shopping. If I have, if I know that I can buy stuff that I want. But, if I don't have the funds available, then it's not that fun. Personally.

**5. I'm curious to know what you think.**

- to request a personal opinion

**Game1**

**Branden:** I'm curious to know what season you like the most. Like, which season is the best for shopping?

**JiYoung:** I like to go shopping every season. Oh, personally I like to buy coats.

**6. What's your opinion?**

- to request a personal opinion before giving advice

**Game2**

**Cassandra:** They wore like exercise pants to their workplace. So, that caused some trouble in Canada. Whether or not that was an ok thing to do.

**Branden:** What's your opinion about that?

**Cassandra:** Oh, I think those pants aren't professional. But, for exercise, then, they're fine.

**7. I'd like to know your take...**

- to request an official position

**Game3**

**Branden:** So, JiYoung, you, I may have mentioned before that you spent time in Utah, right, when you were going to school. I'd like to know your take on the fashion there.

**JiYoung:** Oh, yeah, I was totally different. I remember when I was...it was like a...ok, when I woke up, I had pajamas on here, I'm a little bit late to class, I went there, the class, with the pajamas. So, no one cared.

**8. I hear you saying...**

- to summarize and clarify an opinion

**Game1**

**Branden:** If I have the money, I like shopping. But, if I don't have the funds available, then it's not that fun. Personally.

**Cassandra:** Ok, so, I hear you saying it's a matter of disposable income, really.

## Word Power

1. **funds**

   - available money; budgeted money

> **Branden:** Well, in my opinion, if I have the money, I like shopping. If I have, if I know that I can buy stuff that I want. But, if I don't have the funds available, then it's not that fun. Personally.

2. **splurge**

   - spend more than your budget; spend for pleasure, not needs

> **Cassandra:** ...or you don't care about saving, then you can splurge on clothing. Yeah.

3. **sloppy**

   - messy; not put together

> **Branden:** Why? Because it just seems sloppy, like if I want to have holes in my jeans, I can do it myself. I don't need to pay for it. You know? I don't know.

4. **baggy**

   - souse; not fitting properly; too big

> **Branden:** Also back in the day, they had this trend, maybe ten years ago, where some men would wear really baggy jeans, and the jeans would be hanging down and you could see their underwear. Do you remember that?

5. **cozy**

   - warm and comfortable

> **Cassandra:** Yeah. Because, in Canada, as I probably mentioned before, we dress more casually, comfortably, and kind of for the elements, we say. So, for the weather. So, in Canada, I really don't care about the way I look that much. I just want to be cozy.

**6. effort**

- work

> **Branden:** Yeah, how do you feel about that? You have to care more, that's more effort. Don't you want to go back to Canada and be relaxed?

## Outro

### Dialogue

**Branden:** Hey, what are you doing?

**Cassandra:** Oh, I'm just looking at my friend's Instagram. She got married last weekend and just posted all of her wedding photos. Look at this. I'm curious to know what you think.

**Branden:** Oh wow. Cute. Good for her. Are you jealous?

**Cassandra:** Me? Not really. I don't think I want to get married. How do you feel about marriage?

**Branden:** Oh, I don't know. Maybe. I think marriage has it's advantages. You know, stability, family, all that. I do enjoy the single life though. How about you?

**Cassandra:** I like it too. Waking up in the morning and planning my day without having to care about anyone other than myself. You may think I'm selfish, but this is the good life.

**Branden:** Ok... I hear you saying you don't want to get married because you don't want to be accountable to other people. But the truth is we have to deal with other people all the time, such as at work, in social situations... What do you think?

**Cassandra:** Oh, that's true. Hmm... I just like having my own time. Talk to me about yourself. Are you a very social person?

**Branden:** Not really but I try to be. It's not healthy to stay inside the house all day. To be honest, I've been trying to find some social hobbies – you know, things you do with other people. I'd like to know your take on this. Do you have any suggestions?

Cassandra: Not really! I was hoping you could tell me!

Branden:: I thought about dancing lessons. That's something you can't do alone. What about you?

Cassandra:: I'm a terrible dancer! I would rather do something like, board games.

Branden:: Board games are great but most of the people we know don't play board games...

Cassandra:: Well, there's a first time for everything. I was thinking of inviting some of our coworkers over this weekend to play some board games. What's your opinion about that?

Branden:: Sure. Why not? I think I can make it. Let's ask the others during lunchtime to see what they think.

## Wrap-up

1. **What do you think?**
   - to request a general opinion

2. **Talk to me about...**
   - to request a general opinion

3. **How do you feel about that?**
   - to request a personal opinion

4. **How about you?**
   - to request a personal opinion

5. **I'm curious to know what you think.**
   - to request a personal opinion

6. **What's your opinion?**
   - to request a personal opinion before giving advice

7. **What about you?**
   - to request a plan

8. **I was hoping you could tell me...**
   - to politely request an explanation or information

9. **I'd like to know your take...**
   - to request an official position

10. **I hear you saying...**
   - to summarize and clarify an opinion

## Assignment

**1. Select the option that best completes the passage.**

> **A:** I had a really good experience travelling in South Korea.
> **B:** ______________ the famous places there.

1) How do I feel about
2) Talk to me about
3) I'm curious for
4) Talk about me

**2. Select the option that best completes the passage.**

> **A:** I heard you like hiking.
> **B:** I do. ______________

1) How do I feel about it?
2) Tell me it.
3) What are you?
4) How about you?

**3.** **Select the option that best completes the passage.**

A: People focus too much on material things. They can't enjoy life because they are too busy worrying about paying their mortgage, car payment, credit card bills, and the list goes on.
B: ______________ you prefer to live a simple life. Is that right?

1) So you tell
2) I hear you saying
3) I see you saying
4) How about that

**4.** **Select the option that best completes the passage.**

A: I don't think that is a good way to invest your savings.
B: ______________

1) How about me?
2) I'd like for your take on it.
3) What for you?
4) What's your opinion?

**5.** **Select the option that best completes the passage.**

A: Do you have any ideas about what we should do this weekend?
B: I'm thinking about going to Jeju. ______________

1) How do you feel about that?
2) What do I think about that?
3) What do you feel?
4) About you?

**6.** **Select the option that best completes the passage.**

> **A:** I really dislike social media.
> **B:** ________ what it is you don't like about social media?

1) I was hoping you could say me
2) I hoped for you that
3) I was hoping you could tell me
4) I was hoping you can explain me

**7.** **Select the option that best completes the passage.**

> **A:** Did you hear the latest news about the stock market?
> **B:** ________ on the stock market. Is now a good time to buy?

1) I'm curious seeing your take
2) What about you take
3) I'd like to explain your take
4) I'd like to know your take

**8.** **Select the option that best completes the passage.**

> **A:** What are you going to do tomorrow?
> **B:** I'm still thinking about it. ________

1) What about me?
2) How do you see it?
3) What for you?
4) What about you?

**9. Select the option that best completes the passage.**

A: My mom says it's a bad idea to go outside without a mask.
B: ____________

1) I would like to know what you see.
2) I'm curious to know what you think.
3) I'm curious about you.
4) I'm curious to know what I think.

**10. Select the option that best completes the passage.**

A: ____________ about the cost of higher education?
B: I think it's a real problem for the future. People are taking on too much student loan debt.

1) I'd like to know your think
2) I would like to think
3) I'm curious about you think
4) What do you think

Week
12

# Ending a Topic of Conversation

| | |
|---|---|
| **Contents** | 1. To delay answering to allow time before responding<br>2. To avoid answering by giving an indefinite response<br>3. To avoid answering by requesting a change in topic |
| **Objectives** | 1. To understand 3 types of delaying and avoiding skills<br>2. To understand how 3 types of delaying and avoiding skills are used in real conversations<br>1) Do you get along with your neighbors?<br>2) How do you keep your neighbors from complaining?<br>3) Have you ever called the police on your neighbors? |

## Intro

### Speaking Skills: Ending a Topic of Conversation

1. **That's a good question.**

- to delay answering to allow time before responding

Example

A: What do you think about the law to cap the gift price?
B: That's a good question.

2. **That's an interesting question.**

- to delay answering to allow time before responding

Example

A: The birth rate is decreasing these days as more women choose to enter the workforce or stay single. What do you think the government should do?
B: That's an interesting question.

**3. That's something to think about.**

- to delay answering to allow time before responding

Example

A: Maybe if I stop smoking, I could attract more women.

B: That's something to think about.

**4. I'd have to think about that.**

- to delay answering to allow time before responding

Example

A: How long should I wait to get a pay raise?

B: I'd have to think about that.

**5. I'd have to give that some thought.**

- to delay answering to allow time before responding

Example

A: Do you think that I should purchase a house?

B: I'd have to give that some thought.

**6. I'm not sure.**

- to avoid answering by giving an indefinite response

Example

A: Will you attend the colloquium this Saturday?

B: I'm not sure.

**7. I don't really know.**

- to avoid answering by giving an indefinite response

Example

A: Do you think I should take the subway or a taxi to get there faster?

B: I don't really know.

**8. I have no idea.**

- to avoid answering by giving an indefinite response

Example

A: Do you think I should break up with Gina?

B: I have no idea.

**9. I'd rather not say.**

- to avoid answering by giving an indefinite response

Example

A: Do you make more money than I do?

B: I'd rather not say.

**10. Maybe we should...**

- to avoid answering by requesting a change in topic

Example

A: My boss is driving me crazy! Do you know what he said to me today?

B: Maybe we should talk about something else during dinner.

## Lecture 1

### Conversation Question 1

▶ **Do you get along with your neighbors?**

**Q1. What happened to JiYoung one month ago?**

a) She moved in with her parents.

b) She moved into a new apartment.

c) She moved to Daejeon.

**Q2. Who got in trouble with a security guard for their bird?**

a) Cassandra

b) Branden

c) JiYoung

**Q3. Why didn't Cassandra like her previous neighbor?**

a) They would smoke in the shared hallway.

b) They would smoke in Cassandra's apartment.

c) Their smoke would creep into her bathroom.

### Script

**Branden:** Hello, everyone. Welcome back. I'm Branden and I'm here today with Cassandra and JiYoung. So, we're going to play a game using some of those expressions that you learned in class. Let's get started.

**JiYoung:** Yes.

**Branden:** The first question is: Do you get along with your neighbors? Do you get along with your neighbors? Ok? So, just like last time, I will start the timer for three minutes and whoever uses the most expressions will be the winner. Let's get started. Ok. Alright, so guys, neighbors. Do you like your neighbors? Do you get along with your neighbors? What do you think? Oh, ok, Cassandra.

**Cassandra:** Just...I have no idea, because I've never met my neighbors.

**JiYoung:** Oh, and this is a good question for me because I moved to a new house about one month ago, and actually I had a chance to say hello to my neighbors.

**Cassandra:** Congratulations.

**JiYoung:** With rice cake. Tradition...yeah, Korean traditional stuff, you know?

**Branden:** Wow, good for you. How were they? Do you like your neighbors?

**JiYoung:** Oh, yes I love them because when say hello, they say yeah so it was very nice.

**Branden:** Oh, it's always good to have a good relationship with your neighbors. So, good to hear that.

**JiYoung:** Yes, yes.

**Cassandra:** Right, right. I envy you.

**JiYoung:** Ah, really? Can you say...maybe you can say hello to first them.

**Cassandra:** Oh, it's a little bit uncomfortable for me. Um, just...I rarely see them and they don't seem very approachable. They seem like they just quickly want to open and close their door with keeping their head down. They look very shy. So, I don't want to embarrass them, so I don't speak with them. But, maybe if they speak with my first, I would be so happy. Yeah.

**Branden:** Oh, that's nice. Well, it is beneficial sometimes to have quiet neighbors. So...

**Cassandra:** True, true. I can't complain.

**Branden:** They'll stay out of your business.

**Cassandra:** And you?

**Branden:** Well, you know, I really don't know because just like you, I don't talk to my neighbors. I actually live on like the top story of my building, so I don't have any neighbors beside me, and to be honest, I am happy with that. I don't know. Uh, maybe we should move on to another topic because I don't want everybody to know how antisocial I am. No, let's think about our past, like I can think about the past. One time, you know, remember when I used to have that bird, that pet bird?

**Cassandra:** Yeah. I remember your bird.

**Branden:** Yeah, the bird was making too much sound, and my neighbors talked to the security guard, and the security guard knocked on my door. And, he was like 'hey, what's in there?'. So, that was one situation that kind of made me feel not good. I don't know. Do you guys have any bad experiences in the past with your neighbors? JiYoung, any?

**JiYoung:** Um, I don't really know because I have always had good neighbors. So, I'm so lucky, right?

**Branden:** Cassandra:

**Cassandra:** In my case, I'd rather not say because it brings back a bad memory.

**Branden:** Oh, come on, give it a shot.

**Cassandra:** Just, um, my, ok, real quick, just my previous neighbor, they enjoyed smoking in their...in their room. And the smell of their smoke would always creep into my bathroom. So, that was hard.

**Branden:** That happened to me before, too.

**Cassandra:** Oh, you too?

**Branden:** Yeah, I think it may be a common experience. Yeah.

**Cassandra:** Yeah.

**Branden:** Well, that's it for today's first question. Do you get along with your neighbors? Sometimes yes, sometimes no. Anyway, who has the most points?

**Cassandra:** Well...

**Branden:** Uh-oh! It looks like we are tied. We're all two, two, two. Ok, so, the next round, we'll see what happens.

**[Answer]**

**Q1. What happened to JiYoung one month ago?**

a) She moved in with her parents.

b) She moved into a new apartment.

c) She moved to Daejeon.

| | |
|---|---|
| Branden: | Do you like your neighbors? Do you get along with your neighbors? What do you think? |
| JiYoung: | This is a good question for me because I moved to a new house about one month ago, and actually I had a chance to say hello to my neighbors. |

**Q2. Who got in trouble with a security guard for their bird?**

a) Cassandra

b) Branden

c) JiYoung

| | |
|---|---|
| Branden: | Yeah, the bird was making too much sound, and my neighbors talked to the security guard, and the security guard knocked on my door. So, that was one situation that kind of made me feel not good. |

**Q3. Why didn't Cassandra like her previous neighbor?**

a) They would smoke in the shared hallway.

b) They would smoke in Cassandra's apartment.

c) Their smoke would creep into her bathroom.

| | |
|---|---|
| Cassandra: | My previous neighbor, they enjoyed smoking in their room. And the smell of their smoke would always creep into my bathroom. So, that was hard. |

## Conversation Question 2

▶ **How do you keep your neighbors from complaining?**

**Q1. Who makes a lot of noise in JiYoung's apartment?**

a) She makes the most noise.

b) Her husband makes the most noise.

c) Her son makes the most noise.

**Q2. What gift did Branden's neighbors give him when they asked him to walk more softly?**

a) rice cakes

b) a cake

c) fruit

**Q3. Which of these is the golden rule?**

a) Treat others how you would like to be treated.

b) Buy an apartment with thick walls.

c) Put mats on your floor so the neighbors can't hear you walk.

### Script

**Branden:** Ok, it's time for round number two. The next question: How do you keep your neighbors from complaining? I'll say it one more time. How do you keep your neighbors from complaining? Ok. So, any advice? Sometimes my neighbors complain about me, I'll be honest. It's happened in the past. Um, how can I prevent this? Let's start the timer now. Ok? There we go.

**JiYoung:** Ok, I have to think about that, because I have kids, a boy, and he is seven years and he's always running in the living room and bedroom, and every room he's running, so I'm always talking to him, stop running, stop running, walk, walk, always. But, it's really hard to control him. So, I spread the mat the whole rooms...so.

**Branden:** It sounds like there's some factors beyond your control, right?

**JiYoung:** Yes, yes.

**Branden:** What can you do? So, your neighbors complain sometimes about you?

**JiYoung:** Actually, one time. But it was from not directly, a maintenance officer called me, a little bit be quiet. Nicely he talked me to about that, so. Ok, sorry, and that's all.

**Branden:** You know, I have, I had a similar experience. I was apparently walking too hard on the floor. So, the neighbors, the neighbors heard my footsteps and they came to my house with a bag of fruit and told me, please, stop walking so hard on the floor. So, I don't know what to do about that, right? I can't stop – I can't stop walking, can I?

**Cassandra:** Yeah, that's a good question. I think in that case, it wouldn't be your fault. It's the fault of the construction of the apartment. Because, you can't stop walking. Right?

**Branden:** Yeah, I'm not sure. Like, maybe I have a habit of walking too hard. Maybe I should adjust my body movement, I guess?

**Cassandra:** Yeah, sure, sure, I'm on your side.

**JiYoung:** Yeah, that's a good question, because maybe you can buy some slippers with the cushion?

**Branden:** Oh, yeah?

**JiYoung:** Yeah.

**Branden:** So, there must be something I can do. Cassandra, do you have any advice to give us to stop our neighbors from complaining?

**Cassandra:** Uh, well, I don't know, maybe we should just focus on being a good neighbor? You know, not making too much noise. Um, if your children are really active, maybe bringing them outside to the park instead of running around inside. But, with kids, I know, it's hard. Kids will do what they want, and they have so much energy, yeah. But just the basics. Try to be respectful, that's my biggest piece of advice. Yeah, um, what else, what else.

**Branden:** Well, I don't know really. I suppose you can just move, right?

**Cassandra:** If you're the bad neighbor, you can remove yourself from it.

**Branden:** And then go somewhere else where the walls are thicker and the doors are thicker.

**Cassandra:** Sure.

**Branden:** That's another thing. Thick walls.

**Cassandra:** Thick walls.

**Branden:** Make sure you move into a place that has firm, solid construction.

**Cassandra:** Yup, best tip.

**Branden:** I don't know. I have no idea. But, I agree with Cassandra. Just, showing consideration due to others. Treat others how you would like to be treated. Yeah, that's, you can't go wrong with that advice. The golden rule.

**Cassandra:** That's something to think about.

**Branden:** Ok, so, the time's up. How many points do we have?

**JiYoung:** Oh, I got two.

**Branden:** Two? Three. And?

**Cassandra:** Three!

**Branden:** Ah, yes, so Cassandra and I are tied, ok? But don't worry, there may be another chance for you in the next round. Ok, let's move on to the next part.

**[Answer]**

**Q1. Who makes a lot of noise in JiYoung's apartment?**

a) She makes the most noise.

b) Her husband makes the most noise.

c) Her son makes the most noise.

**JiYoung:** I have kids, a boy, and he is seven years old and he's always running in the living room and bedroom, so I'm always talking to him, "Stop running." But, it's really hard to control him. So, I spread the mat the whole rooms.

**Q2. What gift did Branden's neighbors give him when they asked him to walk more softly?**

a) rice cakes

b) a cake

c) fruit

**Branden:** I was apparently walking too hard on the floor. So, the neighbors heard my footsteps and they came to my house with a bag of fruit and told me, "Please stop walking so hard on the floor."

**Q3. Which of these is the golden rule?**

a) Treat others how you would like to be treated.

b) Buy an apartment with thick walls.

c) Put mats on your floor so the neighbors can't hear you walk.

Branden: I have no idea. But, I agree with Cassandra. Just, showing consideration due to others. Treat others how you would like to be treated. Yeah, that's, you can't go wrong with that advice. The golden rule.

## Conversation Question 3

▶ **Have you ever called the police on your neighbors?**

**Q1. Why wouldn't JiYoung call the police about screaming?**

a) Because she knows who is screaming.

b) Because she isn't sure where the noise is coming from.

c) Because she loves to scream, so it may be her.

**Q2. Whose friend had their bike stolen from their house?**

a) Cassandra

b) Branden

c) JiYoung

**Q3. When you file a complaint with the police but don't give your name, it's....**

a) violent

b) anonymous

c) prevalent

### Script

**Branden:** Alright, it's time for round three. So, so far, Cassandra and I have two points, and JiYoung has one, right? Ok, so this round will be worth two points. You have a chance. Let's get started with the question. Have you ever called the police on your neighbors? Have you ever called the police on your neighbors? Hmm. Well, let's start the timer now. Ok, so this is an interesting question. I think it's very unusual to call the police on your neighbors. What are some reasons why we may do this? I don't know. Like, if I heard something violent happening, if somebody was being attacked at my neighbor's house, sure I think I would call the police. Hmm. Are there any other reasons that you can think of? What about Cassandra?

**Cassandra:** Off the top of my head, I have no idea because I've never experienced, you know, any trouble with the police or with my neighbors in my life, so like you said, obviously violence. Um, I don't know, like maybe if I heard extremely loud noises. Um, if I were in Canada and I heard extreme yelling and maybe some, maybe the sound of objects moving around and crashing...

**Branden:** Fighting?

**Cassandra:** Like fighting, yeah. Like a couple's fight. I'm not – I don't know if there's any violence there or not, but I assume, ah, this situation could become violent, I'd call the police.

**Branden:** Sure.

**Cassandra:** Yeah.

**Branden:** And in other countries, guns are more prevalent. So like if I hear gunfire that's a sure...

**Cassandra:** If you hear a gunshot, definitely call the police.

**Branden:** Sure, sure. In North America, we can have guns, so...

**Cassandra:** ...wherever you are.

**JiYoung:** Yeah, I have no idea because I haven't called the police before, so, it's very hard to say that. But, it's a very interesting question, I think. Because when I hear something, like screaming woman's yelling, I can call the police but I don't know where it comes from exactly so that's the hardest one why I cannot call the police.

**Branden:** Sure, sure. I have to think about it. I can think of one example where my friend had his bike stolen. So, he parked his bike in front of his house and one of the neighbors came by and took it.

So, he called the police and they looked at the CCTV and they saw the guy. It happened. But they never caught him.

**Cassandra:** Oh! Sad story.

**Branden:** Sure, sure. Uh, if you're...hmm. Let's see. I really don't have any idea. I have no idea, but perhaps if property was vandalized. If the neighbor was doing something to my house, like spray painting it or something, I'd call the police in that situation.

**Cassandra:** Of course.

**JiYoung:** I'm not sure. When you call the police, if police ask about your information, what about it? Can you – can you do that?

**Branden:** I think so.

**JiYoung:** Oh, really?

**Branden:** Why...well you mean you want to be private, right? You don't want the police to know your information.

**JiYoung:** Yeah.

**Branden:** Ah, I see.

**Cassandra:** Ah, like an anonymous complaint, anonymous tip.

**JiYoung:** Yeah.

**Branden:** Yeah, right.

**Cassandra:** I don't know how that works in Korea or in Canada, but I have no problem sharing my information.

**Branden:** I, I'd have to give that some thought. But, I have nothing to hide, so I think that it would be ok.

**Cassandra:** Alright.

**Branden:** Alright, so, ok, it looks like one point, three points, and three points.

**JiYoung:** Yeah.

**Branden:** So, what can I say? I'm the winner today. Alright, guys, that's it for this, these three rounds. We're going to move on to the next part now. Let's stay tuned for that.

**[Answer]**

**Q1. Why wouldn't JiYoung call the police about screaming?**

a) Because she knows who is screaming.

b) Because she isn't sure where the noise is coming from.

c) Because she loves to scream, so it may be her.

> JiYoung: When I hear something, like screaming woman's yelling, I can call the police, but I don't know where it comes from Exactly, so that's the hardest one why I cannot call the police.

**Q2. Whose friend had their bike stolen from their house?**

a) Cassandra

b) Branden

c) JiYoung

> Branden: I can think of one example where my friend had his bike stolen. So, he parked his bike in front of his house and one of the neighbors came by and took it. So, he called the police and they looked at the CCTV and they saw the guy. But they never caught him.

**Q3. When you file a complaint with the police but don't give your name, it's....**

a) violent

b) anonymous

c) prevalent

> JiYoung: I'm not sure. When you call the police, if police ask about your information, what about it? Can you do that?
>
> Branden: Well, you mean you want to be private, right? You don't want the police to know your information.
>
> Cassandra: Ah, like an anonymous complaint, anonymous tip.

## Lecture 2

### Words in Action

**1. That's a good question.**

- to delay answering to allow time before responding

**Game2**

Branden: So, the neighbors heard my footsteps, and they came to my house with a bag of fruit and told me, "please, stop walking so hard on the floor." So, I don't know what to do about that, right? I can't stop walking, can I?

Cassandra: Yeah, that's a good question. I think in that case, it wouldn't be your fault. It's the fault of the construction of the apartment. Because, you can't stop walking. Right?

**2. That's an interesting question.**

- to delay answering to allow time before responding

**Game3**

Branden: Have you ever called the police on your neighbors?

Cassandra: It's a very interesting question, I think. Because when I hear something, like screaming woman's yelling, I can call the police, but I don't know where it comes from exactly, so that's the hardest one why I cannot call the police.

**3. That's something to think about.**

- to delay answering to allow time before responding

**Game2**

Branden: Treat others how you would like to be treated. Yeah, that's, you can't go wrong with that advice. The golden rule.

Cassandra: That's something to think about.

**4. I'd have to think about that.**

- to delay answering to allow time before responding

**Game2**

**Branden:** How do you keep your neighbors from complaining?

**JiYoung:** Ok, I'd have to think about that, because I have kids, a boy, and he is seven years old and he's always running in the living room and bedroom, I'm always talking to him, "Stop running."

**5. I'd have to give that some thought.**

- to delay answering to allow time before responding

**Game3**

**Branden:** I don't know how that works in Korea or in Canada, but I have no problem sharing my information.

**JiYoung:** I'd have to give that some thought. But, I have nothing to hide, so I think that it would be ok.

**6. I'm not sure.**

- to avoid answering by giving an indefinite response

**Game3**

**Branden:** Let's see. I really don't have any idea. I have no idea, but perhaps if property was vandalized. If the neighbor was doing something to my house, like spray painting it or something, I'd call the police in that situation.

**JiYoung:** I'm not sure. When you call the police, if police ask about your information, what about it? Can you do that?

**7. I don't really know.**

- to avoid answering by giving an indefinite response

**Game3**

**Branden:** Do you guys have any bad experiences in the past with your neighbors?

**JiYoung:** I don't really know because I have always had good neighbors. So, I'm so lucky, right?

### 8. I have no idea.

- to avoid answering by giving an indefinite response

**Game3**

**Branden:** Like, if I heard something violent happening, if somebody was being attacked at my neighbor's house... sure, I think I would call the police. Are there any other reasons that you can think of?

**Cassandra:** Off the top of my head, I have no idea because I've never experienced, you know, any trouble with the police or with my neighbors in my life, so like you said, obviously violence.

### 9. I'd rather not say.

- to avoid answering by giving an indefinite response

**Game1**

**Branden:** Do you guys have any bad experiences in the past with your neighbors?

**Cassandra:** In my case, I'd rather not say because it brings back a bad memory.

**Branden:** Oh, come on, give it a shot.

### 10. Maybe we should...

- to avoid answering by requesting a change in topic

**Game1**

**Branden:** I actually live on the top story of my building, so I don't have any neighbors beside me. Uh, maybe we should move on to another topic because I don't want everybody to know how antisocial I am.

## Word Power

1. **approachable**
   - friendly; welcoming; easy to approach or meet

| | |
|---|---|
| Cassandra: | Oh, it's a little bit uncomfortable for me. Just...I rarely see them, and they don't seem very approachable. They seem like they just quickly want to open and close their door with keeping their head down. They look very shy. So, I don't want to embarrass them, so I don't speak with them. But, maybe if they speak with me first, I would be so happy. Yeah. |

2. **I can't complain.**
   - A saying that means even though some parts of a situation are negative, the situation as a whole is positive, so there's no real reason to complain.

| | |
|---|---|
| Branden: | Oh, that's nice. Well, it is beneficial sometimes to have quiet neighbors. So... |
| Cassandra: | True, true. I can't complain. |
| Branden: | They'll stay out of your business. |

3. **I'm on your side.**
   - I'm on your team.; I agree with you.

| | |
|---|---|
| Branden: | Yeah, I'm not sure. Like, maybe I have a habit of walking too hard. Maybe I should adjust my body movement, I guess? |
| Cassandra: | Yeah, sure, sure, I'm on your side. |

4. **tip**
   - a short, simple piece of advice

| | |
|---|---|
| Branden: | Make sure you move into a place that has firm, solid construction. |
| Cassandra: | Yup, best tip. |

**5. prevalent**

- popular; common; numerous

| | |
|---|---|
| Branden: | And in other countries, guns are more prevalent. So like if I hear gunfire that's a sure... |
| Cassandra: | If you hear a gunshot, definitely call the police. |

**6. vandalized**

- defaced; destroyed (as in property)

| | |
|---|---|
| Branden: | Sure, if you're...hmm. Let's see. I really don't have any idea. I have no idea, but perhaps if property was vandalized. If the neighbor was doing something to my house, like spray painting it or something, I'd call the police in that situation. |

## Outro

### Dialogue

Cassandra: Hey, you seem so tired lately. How are you doing? I mean, really. How are you?

Branden: Oh, I'd have to think about that. To be honest, there's a lot of stuff going on in my life...

Cassandra: What's wrong? Do you still miss your ex-girlfriend?

Branden: I'd rather not say. It's too hard to talk about Sharon.

Cassandra: Sorry for asking. Maybe we should talk about something else. Are you getting a healthy diet? Enough food and exercise?

Branden: Hmmmm.... I'm not sure. Do I look out of shape?

Cassandra: Haha, I have no idea about that. I think health is more about how you feel rather than how you look. How do you feel about yourself? Are you happy?

Branden: I'd have to give that some thought... hmmm.... What do you think it means to be happy?

Cassandra: Now that's something to think about! It's a really philosophical

| | |
|---|---|
| | question. A lot of people would say that if you are rich, then that makes you automatically happy. Do you think that money can buy happiness? |
| Branden: | That's an interesting question. I think happiness is subjective. It means different things to different people. It is up to everyone to find their own happiness in life. Wouldn't you agree? |
| Cassandra: | I don't really know... I guess I see your point. But in my experience most people around me seem to think That becoming rich and famous would make them happy. I wonder why that is... |
| Branden: | That's a good question. Perhaps it's time to start looking for more positive friends. |
| Cassandra: | Or richer friends! |

## Wrap-up

1. **That's a good question.**
   - to delay answering to allow time before responding

2. **That's an interesting question.**
   - to delay answering to allow time before responding

3. **That's something to think about.**
   - to delay answering to allow time before responding

4. **I'd have to think about that.**
   - to delay answering to allow time before responding

5. **I'd have to give that some thought.**
   - to delay answering to allow time before responding

6. **I'm not sure.**
   - to avoid answering by giving an indefinite response

7. **I don't really know.**
   - to avoid answering by giving an indefinite response

**8. I have no idea.**

- to avoid answering by giving an indefinite response

**9. I'd rather not say.**

- to avoid answering by giving an indefinite response

**10. Maybe we should...**

- to avoid answering by requesting a change in topic

## Assignment

**1. Select the option that best completes the passage.**

A: Will you go on the business trip next week?
B: ____________ I'll have to check my schedule.

1) I'm sure.
2) I'm for sure.
3) I'm not sure.
4) Absolutely.

**2. Select the option that best completes the passage.**

A: How many ex-girlfriends have you had?
B: ____________

1) I'd rather say.
2) I'd rather tell you.
3) I'd rather say no.
4) I'd rather not say.

**3.** **Select the option that best completes the passage.**

A: Who do you like better, Jason or Steven?
B: ____________

1) That's an interesting question.
2) Questioning interest.
3) That's a question of interest.
4) I'd have to question about that.

**4.** **Select the option that best completes the passage.**

A: Do you think I should quit my job?
B: ____________

1) I should have an idea.
2) I have no idea.
3) I have some idea.
4) I really have an idea.

**5.** **Select the option that best completes the passage.**

A: I had a very bad day.
B: Do you want to talk about it?
A: ____________ talk about something else until I cool down.

1) Maybe we should
2) Maybe we are
3) Should we really
4) Do I

**6. Select the option that best completes the passage.**

A: How long should I wait before selling my house?
B: ______________

1) I'd want to do it.
2) I'd have to give it some thinking.
3) I'd have to think about that.
4) I would know the answer.

**7. Select the option that best completes the passage.**

A: Do you think I should call in sick to work?
B: ______________

1) I'm really sick.
2) I really know.
3) I really don't do that.
4) I really don't know.

**8. Select the option that best completes the passage.**

A: Do you think this dress makes me look fat?
B: ______________

1) I'd have to give that a thought.
2) I'd have to give that some thought.
3) I am thinking about giving a thought.
4) I gave it a thought.

**9.** **Select the option that best completes the passage.**

A: Do you think we should say something about the new policies?
B: ______

1) That's a good question.
2) That's a good thinking.
3) I'd have to give that some questions.
4) That's what you think.

**10.** **Select the option that best completes the passage.**

A: Maybe I should start working out to lose my belly fat.
B: ______

1) There is something I am thinking about.
2) I think about that.
3) I'd have to think about something.
4) That's something to think about.

Week 13

# Initiating Conversation

| | |
|---|---|
| **Contents** | 1. To join a conversation you are not involved in<br>2. To join a conversation with a compliment<br>3. To join a conversation with someone you may know<br>4. To join a conversation by confirming a mutual friendship<br>5. To start a conversation with a question<br>6. To start a conversation with a stranger |
| **Objectives** | 1. To understand 6 types of initiating skills<br>2. To understand how 6 types of initiating skills are used in real conversations<br>1) How would we start a conversation at a college party?<br>2) How would we start a conversation at a wedding?<br>3) How would we start a conversation in a college class? |

## Intro

### Speaking Skills: Starting a Conversation with People You May Not Know

**1. I couldn't help but overhearing...**

- to join a conversation you are not involved in

Example

A: I couldn't help but overhearing you say something about a great spa. Can you tell me the name of that spa?

B: Yes, it is called Green Hills.

**2. Has anyone ever told you...**

- to join a conversation with a compliment

Example

A: Has anyone ever told you that you look just like Brad Pitt?

B: Actually, my girlfriend always says that.

3. **Anybody ever told you...**
   - to join a conversation with a compliment

Example

A: Anybody ever told you that you've got a great radio voice?

B: Wow, I should try to get a job as a DJ.

4. **Have we met before?**
   - to join a conversation with someone you may know

Example

A: Have we met before? Did you grow up in Kentucky?

B: I don't think so. I am actually from New York.

5. **You look so familiar.**
   - to join a conversation with someone you may know

Example

A: You look so familiar. Did you go to CUFS?

B: Yes, I graduated in 2014.

6. **Excuse me. I like your...**
   - to join a conversation with a compliment

Example

A: Excuse me. I like your scarf. Where'd you get that?

B: Oh, thanks. I bought it at the ABC store.

7. **Are you a friend of...?**
   - to join a conversation by confirming a mutual friendship

Example

A: Sorry to bother you, but are you a friend of Don's?

B: Oh, are you talking about Don Swanson?

**8. Can I ask you something?**

- to start a conversation with a question

Example

A: Can I ask you something?

B: Uh, yeah.

A: Do you know where the subway station is?

**9. Could I ask you something?**

- to start a conversation with a question

Example

A: Could I ask you something?

B: Sure.

A: What do you recommend ordering at this restaurant?

**10. Pardon me...**

- to start a conversation with a stranger

Example

A: Pardon me. You've got the most gorgeous eyes I've ever seen. I just had to tell you.

B: Oh, thank you. Actually, I have a boyfriend.

## Lecture 1

### Conversation Question 1

▶ **How would we start a conversation at a college party?**

**Q1. Why does Branden say to be careful when complimenting someone?**

a) Not everyone deserves compliments.

b) It could be misconstrued as flirting.

c) Some people hate being complimented.

**Q2. Who has great hair, according to Cassandra?**

a) Cassandra

b) JiYoung

c) Branden

**Q3. What's another way to ask: "Have we met before?"**

a) You look familiar.

b) I really like your earrings.

c) Has anyone ever told you that you have a great smile?

Script

**Branden:** Alright, welcome back everyone. It is time to practice some of those key expressions that you learned in class. Let's get started with the first question, ok? Question number one: Let's image we're all meeting each other for the first time at a college party. Ok? How would we start a conversation with each other? And, how convenient, we have expressions here for joining a conversation and participating in it. So, let's practice how we would use these expressions in a real conversation. Ok? Let's get started here. I'll set the timer for three minutes. Alright, so, uh, I will get started. How does that sound, everyone?

**Caoimhe:** Sounds good.

**Branden:** Ok. So, I have an expression here. Excuse me, I like your... Now, I would use this expression to start a conversation maybe to compliment someone. However, keep in mind that this could be misconstrued as flirting, right? So, like, Professor, I like your earrings, or I like your eyes, right? So, be...

**Caoimhe:** Are you flirting with me?

**Branden:** So be careful not to let the conversation get too awkward. Ok, excuse me, I like your...ok.

**Caoimhe:** Oh, thank you!

**Branden:** How would you respond to that?

**Caoimhe:** Um, I might, like, maybe if you say my earrings, I might tell you where they're from. But, you're a guy so you might not need to know that information. But, usually I would just say thanks and then maybe be like 'oh, where are you from?' or ask you a follow-up question.

**Branden:** Sure, talk about something else.

**Caoimhe:** Ok, yeah, so complimenting somebody is a good way. Um, so I often use this one. So, are you a friend of...? So, usually, the person who hosted the party so for example maybe this is Josh's college party and so I want to find out how somebody knows the host, so maybe I might say something like 'Oh, are you a friend of Josh?' Um, so I'd probably say that one.

**Cassandra:** Ok, I'll jump in with 'have we met before'?

**Branden:** Yeah.

**Caoimhe:** Mmhmm, yeah.

**Cassandra:** It's a great conversation starter, and, in this situation, we're all at Josh's party, so maybe we're all friends of Josh and maybe we actually have met each other before. We've seen each other passing by.

**Branden:** We probably go to the same university.

**Cassandra:** Yeah, yeah, so you can use that to start the conversation and to truly get that information. Have we met before?

**Branden:** I could say something like 'oh, yeah, you look familiar, I think I saw you in class that one time'.

**Cassandra:** Exactly.

**Caoimhe:** Yeah, I think it's often used as like 'you look familiar'. Like, have we met before?

**Branden:** Sure.

**Cassandra:** Yeah, this one too. You look familiar. Great.

**Branden:** Alright, I'll take the next one. Uh, pardon me. Pardon me. We would use this expression when we were perhaps interrupting someone's conversation. So, uh, pardon me, can I ask...can I ask you, uh, how do you know Josh? Or, can I ask you what's your major? Or, pardon me, where's the bathroom? Anything like that.

**Caoimhe:** Where's the bathroom would work well. Ok, yeah, that works well, so kind of similarly we could also ask 'could I ask you something?' or 'can I ask you something?' which is a little less formal, um, so, for example, can I ask you something? Do you know where I can get a drink around here? So, it's a college party, so there's probably beer. So, I might ask that if I'm looking for a drink.

Branden: Yeah, I could say yeah, sure, right over there.

Cassandra: Good. Ok, no, back to something we've kind of touched on already. Has anyone ever told you? So, it's a way of complimenting somebody. Has anyone ever told you, Branden, that you have great hair? Or...

Caoimhe: There's a lot of flirting here today.

Cassandra: I was going to move on to you next.

Branden: Well, now that you mention it, I think I need a haircut. Thanks for saying so. Yeah.

Cassandra: Again, it breaks the ice.

Branden: Right.

Caoimhe: Sure. Oh, time is up.

Branden: Ok, yeah so time is up. We managed to use some of these expressions. But don't worry, we're going to have more questions and more opportunities to use these. So, let's stay tuned for the next part.

**[Answer]**

**Q1. Why does Branden say to be careful when complimenting someone?**

a) Not everyone deserves compliments.

b) It could be misconstrued as flirting.

c) Some people hate being complimented.

Branden: Ok. So, I have an expression here. Excuse me, I like your... Now, I would use this expression to start a conversation maybe to compliment someone. However, keep in mind that this could be misconstrued as flirting, right?

**Q2. Who has great hair, according to Cassandra?**

a) Cassandra

b) JiYoung

c) Branden

**Cassandra:** Good. Ok, no, back to something we've kind of touched on already. Has anyone ever told you? So, it's a way of complimenting somebody. Has anyone ever told you, Branden, that you have great hair?

**Q3. What's another way to ask: "Have we met before?"**

a) You look familiar.

b) I really like your earrings.

c) Has anyone ever told you that you have a great smile?

**Caoimhe:** Yeah, I think it's often used as like, 'You look familiar'. Like, 'Have we met before?'

## Conversation Question 2

▶ **How would we start a conversation at a wedding?**

**Q1. Which of these is a good way to enter into someone else's conversation?**

a) a) I couldn't help but overhearing…

b) I like your bag!

c) Has anyone ever told you…?

**Q2. Who might flirt with someone by telling them they wear a suit well?**

a) Cassandra

b) Caoimhe

c) Branden

**Q3. What is the difference between 'pardon me' and 'excuse me'?**

a) There is no difference.

b) 'Excuse me' is more British.

c) 'Pardon me' is more British.

Script

**Branden:** Alright, it's time to consider some more of those expressions that we learned in class with the second question. Let's imagine we're all meeting each other for the first time at a wedding. I guess it could be Josh's wedding. We like to use him as an example. So, we're meeting each other at Josh's wedding. How would we start a conversation with each other? Ok? Let's use some of these expressions that we learned in class. Caoimhe, would you like to get us started?

**Caoimhe:** Yeah, sure, so at a wedding, I think I often ask 'are you a friend of...?' So, for example, are you a friend of the couple or are you a friend of the groom? Kind of like a way of finding out why you are at this wedding or why you're a guest, so it's a good kind of conversation starter, so for example, are you a friend of Josh?

**Branden:** Right, and I can say, 'oh, yeah, I used to work with him in the past, something like that.

**Cassandra:** Right.

**Caoimhe:** Exactly.

**Branden:** Very useful.

**Cassandra:** I'll jump in here with, 'I couldn't help but overhearing...' I really love this one because, um, especially at a wedding, there are different groups of people so, maybe, Josh's work friends, Josh's high school friends, so there's all these different tables of groups of people and if you're kind of walking by one of those groups and you want to join in to their conversation, you can say 'oh, I couldn't help but overhearing that...' and then repeat what they had said. And that's kind of a way to enter into a conversation.

**Branden:** Oh, very useful.

**Caoimhe:** Definitely.

**Branden:** Good, good. Alright, another useful one for a conversation 'you look so familiar'. So, chances are, we've all met Josh, it's his wedding after all, and we've probably run into each other in the past. So, if I've seen someone before but have not been formally introduced, I could use this expression. You look so familiar, have we met before? Perhaps.

**Caoimhe:** Yeah, that works well, yeah I think, at a wedding. Um, so we talked before about how we often give compliments in these situations. So, I think using, like, anybody or anyone ever told you...? which is a little bit more informal than 'has anyone ever told you...?' so I might use this. Um, I think at a wedding this would probably be used in a flirting way, more than making friends? But, like, has anyone ever told you you wear a suit really well?

**Branden:** So, it's sort of informal, like 'anybody ever told you that..."

**Caoimhe:** Yeah, yeah. I think that would work well, depending on your intentions.

**Cassandra:** Sure, sure. Oh, for sure.

**Branden:** I see what you mean, I see what you mean.

**Cassandra:** I would say that 'anybody ever tell you...' to a kid. Because it's kind of informal.

**Caoimhe:** Oh, yeah, yeah.

**Branden:** Good, good.

**Caoimhe:** I guess that would work well.

**Cassandra:** Also, of course, like, excuse me, I like your bag. I love your suit. I like your shoes.

**Branden:** Quite polite.

**Cassandra:** Everyone's dressed up in their best at the wedding, so, lots of opportunities to compliment.

**Branden:** Thank you so much. Alright, uh, going along with 'you look so familiar...', maybe met the person in the past but not been formally introduced, 'Have we met before? You look familiar.' So, uh, yeah, very common to use this in a social gathering where perhaps you've seen the person but you don't know their name or you haven't really talked to them before but you know the same person. Yeah.

**Caoimhe:** Yeah, so have we met before. And I think, yeah, we've used up almost all of them. Could I ask you something? Can I ask you something? Again, if we want to find like the bathroom or we want to know which table we're supposed to be seated at. Um, we often use this kind of question.

**Cassandra:** Right.

**Caoimhe:** At a wedding as well.

**Cassandra:** And pardon me. Don't forget your manners. Excuse me. Pardon me. I don't know, do you think pardon me sounds more formal than excuse me? Or do they sound the same to you?

**Branden:** It almost sounds, it almost sounds more British.

**Caoimhe:** Yeah, I think it is. Yeah.
**Cassandra:** It just sounds more British, that's the difference.
**Branden:** I would say excuse me far more often.
**Cassandra:** Right, right.
**Caoimhe:** I think it's a little bit more formal and more British.
**Branden:** Guys, you've all had some really good ideas here. Unfortunately, the time for this question is over. Uh, let's move on to the next question now.

**[Answer]**

**Q1. Which of these is a good way to enter into someone else's conversation?**

a) I couldn't help but overhearing···
b) I like your bag!
c) Has anyone ever told you···?

**Cassandra:** You can say 'oh, I couldn't help but overhearing that...' and then repeat what they had said. And that's kind of a way to enter into a conversation.

**Q2. Who might flirt with someone by telling them they wear a suit well?**

a) Cassandra
b) Caoimhe
c) Branden

**Caoimhe:** I might use this. Um, I think at a wedding this would probably be used in a flirting way, more than making friends? But, like, 'Has anyone ever told you you wear a suit really well?'

**Q3. What is the difference between 'pardon me' and 'excuse me'?**

a) There is no difference.

b) 'Excuse me' is more British.

c) 'Pardon me' is more British.

Cassandra: And pardon me. Don't forget your manners. Excuse me. Pardon me. I don't know, do you think 'pardon me' sounds more formal than 'excuse me'? Or do they sound the same to you?

Branden: It almost sounds, it almost sounds more British.

## Conversation Question 3

▶ **How would we start a conversation in a college class?**

**Q1. Why did Branden like Cassandra's pen?**

a) It was blue.

b) It looked new.

c) It looked expensive.

**Q2. Whose Korean is the best of the three?**

a) Cassandra

b) Caoimhe

c) Branden

**Q3. Why might you not compliment someone when you first meet them?**

a) It might sound cheesy.

b) Most people don't like to be complimented.

c) They might compliment you back.

## Script

**Branden:** Ok, so we're on to question number three. Previous, we explained how to use these expressions, now we're going to practice using these expressions in a real conversation and then maybe talk about some things we shouldn't do. Ok? Let's start with question number three. Let's imagine we're all meeting each other for the first time in a college class. Ok? Korean class?

**Caoimhe:** Ok.

**Cassandra:** Why not?

**Branden:** I think that's a good idea. Ok, we're meeting each other for Korean class. How would we start a conversation with each other? So, uh, yeah, let's just try to get this thing started. I'll set the timer now. Right here. Good.

**Caoimhe:** Ok, so do you want to start?

**Branden:** I will. Uh, so, uh, pardon me, um, is this the right textbook for the class? I'm not sure. Is it? What do you think?

**Caoimhe:** Yeah, that textbook's the one that was in the syllabus. I think that's...

**Branden:** Oh.

**Caoimhe:** Yeah, I think that's correct.

**Branden:** I'm so happy to hear that. Ok.

**Caoimhe:** Um, excuse me, can I ask you something? Could I please borrow a pen? I forgot my pencil case.

**Cassandra:** Oh! Certainly! Here you go.

**Caoimhe:** Ah, thank you so much.

**Branden:** Excuse me, I really like your pen. Is that...that looks expensive! Right?

**Cassandra:** Oh, I don't really know. It could be or it could not be.

**Branden:** Ok. I see.

**Cassandra:** It's my secret. Um, you know, you both look very familiar, so the two of you look familiar. Have we ever met before?

**Branden:** Um, I don't think so, but maybe in the last class? You know, we were in the same class but we didn't talk.

**Cassandra:** Probably, yeah, yeah.

**Branden:** That's probably it. I'm sure I've seen your face somewhere before in this building.

**Caoimhe:** Yeah, I also thought that you looked familiar. Are you a friend of Josh, by any chance?

**Cassandra:** Yeah!

**Caoimhe:** Ok.

**Cassandra:** How do you know Josh?

**Caoimhe:** Um, so, we actually studied together at a different academy, so yeah.

**Branden:** Oh, I see.

**Cassandra:** Oh, small world.

**Branden:** Can I ask you guys something? How do you know...I mean, you know Josh at the academy, but what kind of academy were you guys in?

**Caoimhe:** Ah, this was just like a Korean language academy. I think, yeah, when I was doing beginner level I met Josh that that time.

**Branden:** Sure.

**Caoimhe:** By the way, has anyone ever told you your Korean is really good?

**Cassandra:** Oh! You've heard my Korean? Oh, no, my Korean is not so good. But thanks for the compliment.

**Branden:** Well, we just heard it and it was pretty good. So, yeah.

**Cassandra:** Well.

**Branden:** I mean, could I ask you something? Would it be possible to like make a study group? I mean, she's really good at Korean. We're not. I think it might be a good match.

**Cassandra:** Oh, my gosh, why not?

**Caoimhe:** Sounds good. Let's exchange numbers. Let's do this.

**Branden:** Sure, very good. Alright, guys, I think that was a good demonstration and, very nice. What should we not do? Any ideas? It's always fun to talk about this.

**Cassandra:** The opposite, um...

**Branden:** No personal questions, right? Like, how old you are. How old are you?

**Cassandra:** You wouldn't enter in a conversation like that.

**Caoimhe:** I think just in general when we're like introducing ourselves after asking these questions we wouldn't really mention age, it's just not really so important in the West.

**Branden:** Yeah, and personally, I would avoid complimenting too much on someone's appearance because they might get the wrong idea. Like...anybody ever told you you have pretty eyes? I mean, it's weird. It's kind of cheesy. So, they're going to think you're flirting. So, be careful!

**Caoimhe:** Yeah, yeah, try not to be too complimentary.

**Cassandra:** Right, it might make someone feel uncomfortable.

**Branden:** Yeah. And then they're going to think that you're trying to get something from them or you have some ulterior motive and you don't want someone to think that.

**Cassandra:** Oh! Another one, like, the pen example, like kind of asking about money. Like, oh your bag is so expensive. Where did you buy it? Your bag looks expensive.

**Branden:** And you notice she tried to avoid the conversation because it was a little awkward.

**Cassandra:** Yeah, we don't really talk about money like when first meeting someone.

**Caoimhe:** Yeah. I think yeah there are a few kind of areas that yeah you should stay away from.

**Branden:** Of course, there are some cultural differences depending on where you're from. But, that's just our advice, so. Do with it as you will. Alright so that's all the time we have. Hopefully you enjoyed that and found it useful. Let's move on to the next part.

**[Answer]**

**Q1. Why did Branden like Cassandra's pen?**

a) It was blue.

b) It looked new.

c) It looked expensive.

**Branden:** Excuse me, I really like your pen. Is that...that looks expensive! Right?

**Cassandra:** Oh, I don't really know. It could be or it could not be.

**Q2. Whose Korean is the best of the three?**

a) Cassandra

b) Caoimhe

c) Branden

Caoimhe: By the way, has anyone ever told you your Korean is really good?
Cassandra: Oh! You've heard my Korean? Oh, no, my Korean is not so good. But thanks for the compliment.
Branden: Well, we just heard it and it was pretty good. So, yeah.

**Q3. Why might you not compliment someone when you first meet them?**

a) It might sound cheesy.

b) Most people don't like to be complimented.

c) They might compliment you back.

Branden: I would avoid complimenting too much on someone's appearance because they might get the wrong idea. Like...'Anybody ever told you have pretty eyes?' It's kind of cheesy. So, they're going to think you're flirting.

## Lecture 2

### Words in Action

**1. I couldn't help but overhearing...**

- to join a conversation you are not involved in

**Game2**

Cassandra: Especially at a wedding, there are different groups of people, maybe, Josh's work friends, Josh's high school friends, so there's all these different tables of groups of people and if you're kind of walking by one of those groups and you want to join in to their conversation, you can say 'oh, I couldn't help but overhearing that...' and then repeat what they had said. And that's kind of a way to enter into a conversation.

**2. Has anyone ever told you..**

- to join a conversation with a compliment

**Game2**

Caoimhe: I might use this. I think at a wedding this would probably be used in a flirting way, more than making friends? But, like, 'Has anyone ever told you you wear a suit really well?'

**3. Anybody ever told you...**

- to join a conversation with a compliment

**Game2**

Branden: Anybody ever told you you have pretty eyes? I mean, it's weird. It's kind of cheesy. So, they're going to think you're flirting. So, be careful!

**4. Have we met before?**

- to join a conversation with someone you may know

**Game3**

Cassandra: you know, you both look very familiar, so the two of you look familiar. Have we ever met before?

Branden: Um, I don't think so, but maybe in the last class? You know, we were in the same class but we didn't talk.

**5. You look so familiar.**

- to join a conversation with someone you may know

**Game3**

Branden: That's probably it. I'm sure I've seen your face somewhere before in this building.

Caoimhe: Yeah, I also thought that you looked familiar. Are you a friend of Josh, by any chance?

Cassandra: Yeah!

**6.** **Excuse me. I like your...**

- to join a conversation with a compliment

**Game3**

Branden: Excuse me, I really like your pen. That looks expensive! Right?

Cassandra: Oh, I don't really know. It could be or it could not be.

**7.** **Are you a friend of...?**

- to join a conversation by confirming a mutual friendship

**Game3**

Caoimhe: Kind of like a way of finding out why you are at this wedding or why you're a guest, so it's a good kind of conversation starter, so for example, 'Are you a friend of Josh?'

**8.** **Can I ask you something?**

- to start a conversation with a question

**Game1**

Caoimhe: Can I ask you something? Do you know where I can get a drink around here? So, it's a college party, so there's probably beer. So, I might ask that if I'm looking for a drink.

**9.** **Could I ask you something?**

- to start a conversation with a question

**Game2**

Caoimhe: Could I ask you something? Again, if we want to find like the bathroom or we want to know which table we're supposed to be seated at, we often use this kind of question.

**10. Pardon me...**

- to start a conversation with a stranger

> **Game3**
> Branden: Pardon me, is this the right textbook for the class? I'm not sure. Is it? What do you think?
> Caoimhe: Yeah, that textbook's the one that was in the syllabus. I think that's...

## Word Power

**1. follow-up question**

- a question that asks more details about a topic of discussion

> Caoimhe: Um, I might, like, maybe if you say my earrings, I might tell you where they're from. But, you're a guy so you might not need to know that information. But, usually I would just say thanks and then maybe be like 'oh, where are you from?' or ask you a follow-up question.

**2. break the ice**

- to do or say something that makes people feel more comfortable in a social situation

> Branden: Well, now that you mention it, I think I need a haircut. Thanks for saying so. Yeah.
> Cassandra: Again, it breaks the ice.

**3. formally introduced**

- to be introduced by name, especially by someone else

> Branden: So, if I've seen someone before but have not been formally introduced, I could use this expression. 'You look so familiar, have we met before?', perhaps.

**4. intentions**

- what you want to get out of something; goals

> **Caoimhe:** Yeah, yeah. I think that would work well, depending on your intentions.

**5. cheesy**

- unpleasant; weird; inauthentic

> **Branden:** Yeah, and personally, I would avoid complimenting too much on someone's appearance because they might get the wrong idea. Like...'Anybody ever told you you have pretty eyes?' I mean, it's weird. It's kind of cheesy. So, they're going to think you're flirting. So, be careful!

**6. ulterior motive**

- a hidden reason for doing something

> **Branden:** Yeah. And then they're going to think that you're trying to get something from them or you have some ulterior motive, and you don't want someone to think that.

## Outro

### Dialogue

**Cassandra:** Pardon me, I'm so sorry to interrupt, but I couldn't help but overhearing you talk about going to the hospital.

**Caoimhe:** It's okay. Yeah, we are making an appointment to get the vaccine. By the way, anybody ever told you that you look like that actress? What's her name?

**Cassandra:** Emma Stone? Yeah, I've heard that before, but I don't see it. Thank you, though! Has anyone told you that you could be a clone of...

| | |
|---|---|
| **Caoimhe:** | Jennifer Lawrence? Yes. I get that a lot, and I have no idea why! |
| **Cassandra:** | Again, I'm sorry to interrupt. I was just going to say that I went to Seoul National University Hospital for my shot, and it was super easy. But, now that I'm talking to you, I have to ask: Have we met before? |
| **Caoimhe:** | It's funny that you ask that because you look so familiar, too. |
| **Cassandra:** | Before I heard you talking, I thought about saying, "Excuse me, I like your tattoo." But then I started listening to you, and I felt like I had heard your voice before. |
| **Caoimhe:** | Let's see. Are you a friend of Sammie? |
| **Cassandra:** | That's where I know you from! Sammie's Halloween party last year! You were dressed as Black Widow. |
| **Caoimhe:** | And you were... |
| **Cassandra:** | ...Harley Quinn. |
| **Caoimhe:** | That's right. Oh my god, I drank too much that night. Can I ask you something? I'm new and don't have many friends here. Could we hang out sometime? |
| **Cassandra:** | Yeah, that would be awesome. Could I ask you something? Are you any good at taking photos? I'm trying to start a blog, and I feel like it would be great to take some pics together. |
| **Caoimhe:** | No way! I'd love to do that! Let's exchange Instas! |

## Wrap-up

1. **I couldn't help but overhearing...**
   - to join a conversation you are not involved in

2. **Has anyone ever told you..**
   - to join a conversation with a compliment

3. **Anybody ever told you...**
   - to join a conversation with a compliment

4. **Have we met before?**
   - to join a conversation with someone you may know

5. **You look so familiar.**
 - to join a conversation with someone you may know

6. **Excuse me. I like your...**
 - to join a conversation with a compliment

7. **Are you a friend of...?**
 - to join a conversation by confirming a mutual friendship

8. **Can I ask you something?**
 - to start a conversation with a question

9. **Could I ask you something?**
 - to start a conversation with a question

10. **Pardon me...**
 - to start a conversation with a stranger

## Assignment

**1. Select the option that best completes the passage.**

A: ____________ that you are selling your car. How much is it?
B: Yes. I am selling it for 3000 dollars.

1) I couldn't help for overhearing
2) I helped overhearing
3) I couldn't help but overhearing
4) I couldn't overhear

**2.** **Select the option that best completes the passage.**

> A: ______________. Do you live around here?
> B: Yes. I think we are neighbors.

1) You look so familiar
2) You are familiar
3) You aren't familiar
4) You have some familiarities

**3.** **Select the option that best completes the passage.**

> A: ______________? Aren't you in my class?
> B: I think you may have me confused with someone else. I don't go to this school.

1) Have we seen before
2) Have we been before
3) Have we been meeting before
4) Have we met before

**4.** **Select the option that best completes the passage.**

> A: ______________ style. Where do you buy your clothes?
> B: Oh, thanks. I actually make my own clothes. I am a fashion designer.

1) Excuse me. I liking
2) Excuse me. I like to
3) Excuse me. I like your
4) Excuse me. I like my

**5. Select the option that best completes the passage.**

A: ________

B: Sure.

A: Do you know how to get to the station from here?

1) Could I get you something?
2) Could I answer you something?
3) Could I give you something?
4) Could I ask you something?

**6. Select the option that best completes the passage.**

A: I know you! ________ Richard Ambrose?

B: That's right. We went to high school together.

1) Are you a friend of
2) Are you friends for
3) Are you friendly to
4) Are you a friend by

**7. Select the option that best completes the passage.**

A: ________ that you are beautiful?

B: Yes, I am a model. People tell me that all the time.

1) Has anyone ever shown you
2) Has anyone ever told you
3) Has anyone ever demonstrated
4) Has anyone ever told me

**8. Select the option that best completes the passage.**

> **A:** ____________ that you could be a model?
> **B:** No. I don't think I am tall enough to be a model.

1) Anybody ever told you
2) Anybody ever told you something
3) Anybody never told you
4) You ever told me

**9. Select the option that best completes the passage.**

> **A:** ____________ You look like you aren't from around here.
> **B:** That's right. I am visiting from out of town.

1) Pardon you.
2) Pardon yourself.
3) Pardon somebody.
4) Pardon me.

**10. Select the option that best completes the passage.**

> **A:** ____________?
> **B:** Uh, yeah.
> **A:** Do you know of a good place to get something to eat around here?

1) Can I ask you a thing
2) Can I borrow something
3) Can I ask you something
4) Can I do something

Week 14

# Review

**Contents**

W1. What are your hopes?
W2. Follow-up questions
W3. Asking for clarification
W4. Interrupting
W5. Accepting a question or interruption
W6. Expressing opinions
W7. Agreeing
W9. Disagreeing
W10. Mitigation
W11. Asking for Opinions and Information
W12. Ending a Topic of Conversation
W13. Initiating Conversation
W14. Review

**Objectives**

1. To review the target expressions and vocabulary from weeks 1-7
2. To review the target expressions and vocabulary from weeks 9-13
3. To prepare for the final exam

## Review: Weeks 1-7

### Week 1

**Q1. Which of these phrases is not a way to show surprise or disbelief?**

a) Really?
b) Seriously?
c) That's right.

**Q2.** **What activity did Cassandra want to try?**

a) Swimming
b) Karate
c) Boxing

**Q3.** **Which of these is not a rejoinder to express agreement?**

a) Seriously?
b) Yeah.
c) That's right.

**Q4.** **Which of these is a great way to show sympathy?**

a) I'm sorry to hear that.
b) Really?
c) That's cool.

## Week 2

**Q5.** **Cassandra tried to dye her hair blonde at a salon once. What color did her hair end up being?**

a) red
b) blue
c) green

**Q6.** **Which of these is a good synonym for 'rearrange', as in 'rearrange the furniture'?**

a) reposition
b) renovate
c) request

**Q7.** **Which of these phrases is not a way to ask for clarification?**

a) Is that…?
b) When…?
c) Do you mean…?

**Q8. Which of these is not a way to ask a follow-up question?**

a) Oh, when did that happen?
b) Really? Why?
c) So, when I was a kid.

## Week 3

**Q9. Which of these phrases is used when you want to ask for clarification and show disbelief?**

a) Wait. What?
b) What do you mean?
c) I thought…

**Q10. Which professor was accused of having expensive tastes?**

a) Cassandra
b) Caoimhe
c) Branden

**Q11. Which of these would not be a lowkey birthday celebration?**

a) A dinner with friends
b) A trip to Las Vegas
c) A night at the movies

**Q12. Which of these was not how people in Ireland celebrate their birthdays?**

a) By wearing green.
b) By having a birthday party.
c) By eating cake and playing games.

## Week 4

**Q13. Which interruption is a yes/no question instead of an imperative sentence?**

a) Excuse me.
b) Hold up.
c) Can I ask something?

**Q14. Caoimhe said that in Ireland they believe if you eat a certain food, you will have strange dreams. What was that food?**

a) steak
b) cheese
c) potatoes

**Q15. Which of these is not a strong way to interrupt someone?**

a) Let me interrupt you.
b) Ok, so···
c) Excuse me.

## Week 5

**Q16. What greeting has replaced shaking hands in the West during COVID-19?**

a) Elbow bumping
b) Bowing
c) High-fiving

**Q17. If you want to 'butt in' to a conversation, what do you want to do?**

a) Start a conversation with your butt.
b) Interrupt a conversation
c) Finish a conversation

**Q18. Which one of these does not accept the question?**

a) No problem.
b) Ask away.
c) You don't agree?

**Q19. Which of these is a good response to 'Can I ask you something?'**

a) You don't agree?
b) Ask away.
c) Let me interrupt you there.

## Week 6

**Q20. Branden mentions his favorite style of art. What type of art is it?**

a) Modern art
b) Renaissance art
c) Performance art

**Q21. Which of these can be used to express unexpected news?**

a) You know what?
b) As far as I can tell…
c) If you ask me…

**Q22. Which museum did Cassandra visit on a date?**

a) The currency museum
b) The art museum
c) The war museum

**Q23. Which of these is a great word to describe people who are interested in history?**

a) History rockers
b) History buffs
c) History haters

## Week 7

**Q24. If you list the 'pros and cons' of something, what are you listing?**

a) The professionals and the amateurs
b) The good points and the bad points
c) The summary and the purpose

**Q25. Which of these is a way to show that you share the exact same opinion with someone?**

a) As far as I can tell...
b) I guess so.
c) I'm totally with you.

**Q26. What animal does Cassandra have a phobia of?**

a) cockroaches
b) spiders
c) snakes

**Q27. Which of these phrases is the most informal way to agree with someone?**

a) That's a good point.
b) Yeah.
c) I totally agree.

## Answer: Weeks 1-7

**Q1.** c) That's right.
**Q2.** c) Boxing
**Q3.** a) Seriously?
**Q4.** a) I'm sorry to hear that.
**Q5.** b) blue
**Q6.** a) reposition
**Q7.** b) When......
**Q8.** c) So, when I was a kid.
**Q9.** a) Wait. What?
**Q10.** c) Branden
**Q11.** b) A trip to Las Vegas
**Q12.** a) By wearing green.
**Q13.** c) Can I ask something?
**Q14.** b) cheese

**Q15.** b) Ok, so...
**Q16.** a) Elbow bumping
**Q17.** b) Interrupt a conversation
**Q18.** c) You don't agree?
**Q19.** b) Ask away.
**Q20.** b) Renaissance art
**Q21.** a) You know what?
**Q22.** c) The war museum
**Q23.** b) History buffs
**Q24.** b) The good points and the bad points
**Q25.** c) I'm totally with you.
**Q26.** a) Cockroaches
**Q27.** b) Yeah.

## Review: Weeks 9-13

### Week 9

**Q1. Which of these is an indirect way to disagree with someone?**

a) I'm not sure I agree.
b) I totally disagree.
c) I'm afraid I disagree.

**Q2. What does Branden not like about himself?**

a) He's too tall.
b) He's a chronic procrastinator.
c) He takes on too many tasks.

**Q3. Which of these is a great synonym for 'scrambled', as in Cassandra's decision-making process?**

a) Clear.
b) Direct.
c) Messy.

**Q4. Branden says that Cassandra shouldn't 'be too hard on [herself]'. What did he mean?**

a) She should not be so critical of herself.
b) She should be more critical of herself.
c) She should focus more on others and not focus on herself.

**Q5. Which of these is the most direct way to disagree with someone?**

a) I'm not sure I agree.
b) I'm afraid I disagree.
c) I know what you're saying, but…

## Week 10

**Q6. Which of these is not a way to soften with an attention getter?**

a) Look…
b) You see…
c) To be honest…

**Q7. Cassandra tells an anecdote about her grandmother. What's an anecdote?**

a) A long story
b) A personal story
c) A fake story

**Q8. Which of these softeners is also a filler word?**

a) Well…
b) It just seems…
c) I guess…

**Q9. Which of these is a way to soften a statement with uncertainty?**

a) Look, I think…
b) I just think that maybe…
c) To be honest…

**Q10. Which of these words means to spend more than your budget on something?**

a) Splurge
b) Save
c) Fund

**Q11. Which of these is not a way to ask for a personal opinion?**

a) I'm curious to know what you think.
b) How do you feel about that?
c) I hear you saying…

**Q12. Why doesn't Branden like ripped jeans in fashion?**

a) They are too cool for him.
b) He thinks they look sloppy.
c) He thinks they are for students, not professionals.

**Q13. Which of these words means 'available money'?**

a) Scholarships.
b) Paycheck.
c) Funds.

**Q14. Which of these is a way to summarize what someone has said?**

a) I hear you saying…
b) What's your opinion?
c) I'm curious to know what you think.

## Week 12

**Q15. Which of these is a way to end a conversation by changing the subject?**

a) Maybe we should…

b) I'm not sure.

c) I have to think about that.

**Q16. Which of these is a way to delay answering to allow time to think?**

a) That's a good question.

b) I'm not sure.

c) I have no idea.

**Q17. Which of these described a small piece of advice?**

a) A demand.

b) A tip.

c) A proposal.

**Q18. Branden's neighbors complained about him for doing what?**

a) Smoking

b) Walking too loudly

c) Watching TV too loudly

**Q19. Which of these is a good way to avoid answering a question?**

a) I'd rather not say.

b) That's a good question.

c) I have to think about that.

**Q20. Which of these is not a good way to start a conversation with someone?**

a) Saying 'pardon me'
b) Complimenting them
c) Flirting with them

**Q21. Which of these is another way to ask 'Do I know you?'**

a) You look familiar.
b) Can I borrow your pen?
c) Excuse me…

**Q22. What does it mean to be 'formally introduced'?**

a) To be introduced by age.
b) To be introduced by name.
c) To be introduced by how you know another person.

**Q23. Which of these means to think fondly about the past?**

a) Reminisce.
b) Ponder.
c) Consider.

**Q24. Who is the person that they all know?**

They go to his college party, they attend his wedding, and they take Korean classes with him.

a) Robert
b) Ben
c) Josh

## Answer: Weeks 9-13

Q1. a) I'm not sure I agree.
Q2. b) He's a chronic procrastinator.
Q3. c) Messy.
Q4. a) She should not be so critical of herself.
Q5. b) I'm afraid I disagree.
Q6. c) To be honest......
Q7. b) A personal story
Q8. a) Well......
Q9. b) I just think that maybe......
Q10. a) Splurge
Q11. c) I hear you saying......
Q12. b) He thinks they look sloppy.
Q13. c) Funds.
Q14. a) I hear you saying......
Q15. a) Maybe we should......
Q16. a) That's a good question.
Q17. b) A tip.
Q18. b) Walking too loudly
Q19. a) I'd rather not say.
Q20. c) Flirting with them
Q21. a) You look familiar.
Q22. b) To be introduced by name.
Q23. a) Reminisce.
Q24. c) Josh

## Outro

### Wrap-up

1. **Study the key expressions from weeks 1-13.**

2. **Review the weekly vocabulary from weeks 1-13.**

3. **Good luck on your final exam!**

## Assignment

**1. Select the option that best completes the passage.**

A: I have to go to the hospital. My friend got hit by a car while he was walking his dog.
B: ______________ I am so sorry to hear that.

1) Oh, so.
2) That's cool.
3) That's nice.
4) Oh, no!

**2. Select the option that best completes the passage.**

A: Would you mind if I took a few days off work? I am getting married next week.
B: ______________ Take all the time you need.

1) I'm sorry to hear that.
2) That's great.
3) Yes, I mind.
4) That's effective.

**3. Select the option that best completes the passage.**

A: ______________ you know John was promoted to manager yesterday?
B: That is not surprising. He is always good worker!

1) Who
2) What
3) Did
4) When

**4. Select the option that best completes the passage.**

> A: What do you think we should eat for dinner?
> B: ________ Vietnamese food? For some reason spring rolls sound really good right now.

1) What about
2) Is that
3) Why
4) How for

**5. Select the option that best completes the passage.**

> A: I didn't order food this last year to save money.
> B: ________ you didn't even order one pizza?
> A: Yes, that is right.
> B: Good for you. But I couldn't do that. I love pizza.

1) I thought
2) You're telling me
3) What are you trying to say
4) You thought

**6. Select the option that best completes the passage.**

> A: I think watching T.V. is such a waste of time.
> B: ________ I watch T.V. too much?
> A: Well, now that you mention it. It may be a good idea to reduce the amount of time you spend watching T.V.

1) You think
2) How about
3) I thought
4) Is that

**7. Select the option that best completes the passage.**

A: My parents said that I couldn't stay out after midnight.
B: ________ You still live with your parents?

1) Hold up.
2) Hold this.
3) May speak something?
4) Can I tell something?

**8. Select the option that best completes the passage.**

A: I don't know why I can't find a girlfriend.
B: ________ Maybe you need to do something about your body odor.
A: Are you saying that I smell?
B: Just saying some deodorant couldn't hurt.

1) Can I tell something?
2) Could I say something?
3) Let me interrupt someone.
4) Sorry to wait.

**9. Select the option that best completes the passage.**

A: Can I ask you something?
B: ________

1) Whatever you do.
2) Yes, where is it?
3) Ask for me.
4) Yes, what is it?

**10.** **Select the option that best completes the passage.**

> A: I have some questions about the new company policy.
> B: ____________

1) You're fired.
2) Fire away!
3) Get it over!
4) Get over it.

**11.** **Select the option that best completes the passage.**

> A: I don't know why my grades suck so much.
> B: ______________ that you always wait until the last minute to do your assignments. You need to work on your time-management skills.

1) It seems as far
2) I tell
3) It seems to me
4) It feel as

**12.** **Select the option that best completes the passage.**

> A: Engineering is too difficult. I'm thinking about changing my major to Art History.
> B: ____________ I think you should keep your major. You will probably make more money after you graduate.

1) I say you
2) I tell
3) As far as I want
4) I have to say

**13.** **Select the option that best completes the passage.**

A: It's too hot to play soccer.
B: ______________ Let's go swimming instead.

1) That's what I tell.
2) I'm totally agreeable.
3) That's what I've been saying.
4) That's what I rectified.

**14.** **Select the option that best completes the passage.**

A: If we are going hiking, we should buy some more water bottles at the convenience store. It is important to stay hydrated.
B: ______________

1) That's a good thinking.
2) I'm knowing it.
3) I see him.
4) That's a good point.

**15.** **Select the option that best completes the passage.**

A: You don't need to exercise to lose weight. Just go on a diet!
B: ______________ I like exercising. It feels good to be outside moving my body.

1) I know what you're saying, but
2) I know what your saying, but
3) I know what you're saying, so
4) I know what you say, but

**16. Select the option that best completes the passage.**

A: I am always tired at work.
B: Maybe you shouldn't stay up all night playing computer games.
A: ____________

1) So I seem.
2) That's a point.
3) Yes, so concur.
4) I guess so.

**17. Select the option that best completes the passage.**

A: Are you ready to go outside?
B: I ____________ want to watch a movie instead. The weather's a little too hot for me.

1) kind of
2) kinder
3) kind in
4) kinder

**18. Select the option that best completes the passage.**

A: What do you think Jason's new car?
B: ____________ I really don't like the color. Who thought it was a good idea to paint a car orange?

1) You know.
2) I am knowing.
3) It's just seemingly.
4) Wells,

**19.** **Select the option that best completes the passage.**

> **A:** What are you going to do during the summer vacation?
> **B:** I think I am going to go to Busan. ______________

1) What about me?
2) How do you see it?
3) What about you?
4) What for you?

**20.** **Select the option that best completes the passage.**

> **A:** I heard you like to play board games.
> **B:** I do. ______________

1) Tell me it.
2) How about you?
3) What is good for you?
4) How do I feel about it?

**21.** **Select the option that best completes the passage.**

> **A:** Do you think I should get a part-time job?
> **B:** ______________

1) I'd have to give that a thought.
2) I'd have to give that some thought.
3) I'm thinking about giving a thought.
4) I gave it a thought.

**22.** **Select the option that best completes the passage.**

> **A:** I heard your cat died. Are you ok?
> **B:** Not really. I'm kind of upset.
> **A:** ________ get a new cat. It might help you feel better.

1) Maybe you should
2) Maybe we are
3) Should we really
4) Do I

**23.** **Select the option that best completes the passage.**

> **A:** ________ ?
> **B:** Sure.
> **A:** Do you know how I can get to the post office from here?

1) Can I ask you a thing
2) Can I borrow something
3) Can I ask you something
4) Can I do something

**24.** **Select the option that best completes the passage.**

> **A:** ________ . Have we met before?
> **B:** Yes. I think we work at the same company.

1) You look so familiar
2) You are my familiarity
3) You aren't familiar
4) You have some familiarities

Week
15
# Final Exam

### 1-2. Listen to the conversation and choose the best answers. (Week 9)

| | |
|---|---|
| Woman: | Many people think that real estate is a good investment. |
| Man: | **I'm not sure I agree.** I think the bubble is about to pop, anytime now. Buying an overpriced apartment in the city is not my idea of a wise investment. |
| Woman: | **I'm afraid I disagree.** People have been saying that for years. But historically, real estate in the big city has only increased in value. I can't see it slowing down anytime soon. |
| Man: | I don't know. Maybe I will just keep my extra cash in a savings account. At least it will be safe there. |
| Woman: | **I know what you're saying, but** if you factor in the costs of inflation, you are actually losing money if you just keep it in the bank. |

**1. What does the man think about the real estate market?**

1) It is a wise investment.
2) The prices will continue to increase.
3) He has always wanted an apartment in the city.
4) The prices will decrease in the near future.

**2. According to the passage, which statement is true?**

1) The man doesn't want to invest his money.
2) Overall, the value of real estate decreases over time.
3) Overall, the value of cash increases over time.
4) You can make money by saving it in the bank.

## 3-4. Listen to the conversation and choose the best answers. (Week 10)

| | |
|---|---|
| Man: | Hey, have you met the new employee, Jason? He's nice, isn't he? |
| Woman: | **Well...** you don't know him like I do. I used to work with Jason at a different company. |
| Man: | Is there something wrong with him? |
| Woman: | **To be honest** he didn't have a good reputation back then. I didn't work with him personally, but that's what other people told me. **I guess** he was kind of lazy, didn't do his work on time, stuff like that. |
| Man: | **Maybe** he's changed. **You know**, when I first started working I wasn't that good at my job, either. I was going through a hard time in my personal life. But now look at me? I'm a model employee! **You see?** People can change! |

**3. According to the passage, which option is true?**

1) The man used to work with Jason.
2) Jason has always been a model employee.
3) Jason and the speakers work for the same company now.
4) Jason has always been a punctual person.

**4. A ccording to the passage, how has the male speaker changed over time?**

1) He used to be lazy, but now he is punctual.
2) He used to be good at his job, but now he performs poorly.
3) He used to be a model employee, but now he is like Jason.
4) He used to be bad at his job, but now he does well at work.

## 5-6. Listen to the conversation and choose the best answers. (Week 11)

| | |
|---|---|
| Woman: | My friend got married last weekend. |
| Man: | Oh wow. Good for her. Are you jealous? |
| Woman: | Me? Not really. I don't think I want to get married. **How do you feel about marriage?** |
| Man: | Oh, I don't know. Maybe. I think it has some advantages. You know, stability, family, all that. **What do you think?** |
| Woman: | I like being single. Waking up in the morning and planning my day without having to care about anyone other than myself. You may think I'm selfish, but this is the good life. |
| Man: | Ok... **I hear you saying** you don't want to be accountable to other people. **Is that it?** |

**5. According to the passage, which option is true?**

1) The woman doesn't want to be responsible for other people.
2) The woman is jealous of her friend.
3) The man thinks getting married has too many disadvantages.
4) The woman's friend got married last month.

**6. Which topic is the woman most likely to talk about next?**

1) her friend's wedding
2) how she feels about accountability to others
3) dinner plans
4) advantages of marriage

## 7-8. Listen to the conversation and choose the best answers. (Week 11)

| | |
|---|---|
| Woman: | Are you a very social person? |
| Man: | Not really but I try to be. It's not healthy to stay inside the house all day. I've been trying to find some social hobbies – you know, things you do with other people. Do you have any suggestions? |
| Woman: | Not really! **I was hoping you could tell me!** |
| Man: | I thought about dancing lessons. That's something you can't do alone. |
| Woman: | I'm a terrible dancer! I would rather do something indoors like.... board games. |
| Man: | Board games are great but most of the people we know don't play board games... |
| Woman: | Well, there's a first time for everything. |

**7. According to the passage, which option is true?**

1) The man wants to find hobbies he can do alone.
2) The woman is a very talented dancer.
3) The speakers have mutual friends.
4) The man has a lot of social hobbies.

**8. According to the passage, which option is NOT true?**

1) It's possible that they will play a board game in the future.
2) Dancing is a social hobby.
3) The man thinks solo hobbies are healthier than social hobbies.
4) The man wants to be a social person.

## 9-10. Listen to the conversation and choose the best answers. (Week 12)

| | |
|---|---|
| Woman: | Do you still miss your ex-girlfriend? |
| Man: | I'd rather not say. It's too hard to talk about Sharon. |
| Woman: | Sorry for asking. **Maybe we should** talk about something else. Are you getting a healthy diet? Enough food and exercise? |
| Man: | Hmmmm.... **I'm not sure.** Do I look out of shape? |
| Woman: | **I have no idea** about that. I think health is more about how you feel rather than how you look. How do you feel about yourself? Are you happy? |
| Man: | I think happiness is subjective. It means different things to different people. It is up to everyone to find their own happiness in life. Wouldn't you agree? |
| Woman: | haha I think you are avoiding my question. |

**9. What is the main reason the woman changes the topic during the conversation?**

1) She is not interested in the man's love life.
2) The man doesn't want to talk about his ex-girlfriend.
3) The man would rather talk about diet and health.
4) The man looks out of shape.

**10. Which option most closely matches the man's idea about happiness?**

1) What it means to be happy depends on who you ask.
2) Happiness depends on the state of your health.
3) Love is essential for happiness.
4) He was happy when he was with Sharon.

## 11-13. Listen to the conversation and choose the best answers. (Week 13)

| | |
|---|---|
| Man: | **Are you a friend of** Sammie? |
| Woman: | That's where I know you from! Sammie's Halloween party last year! You were dressed as Thor. |
| Man: | And you were... |
| Woman: | ...Harley Quinn. |
| Man: | That's right. Oh my god, I drank too much that night. **Can I ask you something?** I'm new and don't have many friends here. Could we hang out sometime? |
| Woman: | Yeah, that would be awesome. **Could I ask you something?** Are you any good at taking photos? I'm trying to start a blog, and I feel like it would be great to take some pics together. |

**11. Where did the speakers first see each other?**

1) at a club.
2) at a birthday party.
3) at a Christmas party
4) at a Halloween party

**12. According to the passage, which option is NOT necessarily true?**

1) Both of the speakers know Sammie.
2) The man wants to make new friends.
3) Sammie introduced the speakers to each other.
4) The woman is trying to start a new blog.

**13. Which of these is an indirect way to disagree with someone?**

1) I'm not sure I agree.
2) I'm afraid I disagree.
3) I totally disagree.
4) That's not right.

**14.** **What does it mean to be "too hard on yourself?" (Week 9)**

1) to work hard even though you are tired
2) to focus on others rather than yourself
3) to increase your stress
4) to be too critical of yourself

**15.** **Which of these is a way to soften with an attention getter? (Week 10)**

1) Look…
2) To be honest…
3) It just seems…
4) Well…

**16.** **What is an anecdote? (Week 10)**

1) a long story
2) a fake story
3) a touching story
4) a personal story

**17.** **Which of these words means to spend more than your budget on something? (Week 11)**

1) borrow
2) spend
3) splurge
4) fund

**18.** **Which of these words means "available money"? (Week 11)**

1) scholarships
2) paycheck
3) extras
4) funds

**19. Which of these is a way to summarize what someone has said? (Week 11)**

1) I hear you saying…
2) I'm curious to know what you think.
3) I'd like to know your take…
4) Do you think that…

**20. Which of these is a way to delay answering to allow time to think? (Week 12)**

1) I'm not sure.
2) I have no idea.
3) Yes, I agree.
4) That's a good question.

**21. Which of these is another way to ask "do I know you?"? (Week 13)**

1) You're not from around here, are you?
2) You look familiar.
3) Excuse me…
4) Would you like to hang out sometime?

**22. What does it mean to be formally introduced? (Week 13)**

1) To be introduced by age.
2) To be introduced by how you know the other person.
3) To be introduced by name.
4) To see each other for the first time.

**23. Select the option that best completes the passage. (Week 9)**

A: I love learning foreign languages. I think it is so interesting to be able to communicate with people around the world.
B: ________________. Learning a new language is so time-consuming and tedious!

1) I'm afraid about it.
2) I've heard it.
3) I agree with it.
4) I'm afraid I disagree.

**24. Select the option that best completes the passage. (Week 9)**

A: I think John must be the richest guy in our class.
B: ____________. Just because he's wearing an expensive watch doesn't mean he's rich.

1) I don't know what you said.
2) I'm sure about it.
3) I don't know about that.
4) I agree with you.

**25. Select the option that best completes the passage. (Week 10)**

A: Do you think you would be able let me copy your homework?
B: ____________ as a rule I never cheat on assignments and I can't help you cheat, either. I'm sorry.

1) Look,
2) I see
3) See,
4) I know

**26. Select the option that best completes the passage. (Week 10)**

A: I don't know why it's so difficult for me to make new friends.
B: I know you're a nice guy, but ____________ that you have trouble talking to strangers.

1) seemingly
2) it's just honest
3) it just seems
4) it's seems

**27. Select the option that best completes the passage. (Week 11)**

A: Last weekend I visited Jeju island for the first time.
B: ________________ the famous places there.

1) How do I feel about
2) Talk to me about
3) I'm curious for
4) Talk about me

**28. Select the option that best completes the passage. (Week 11)**

A: I heard you like playing online games.
B: I do. ________________

1) How about you?
2) Tell me it.
3) What are you?
4) How do I feel about it?

**29.** **Select the option that best completes the passage. (Week 12)**

A: How old are you?
B: ________________

1) I'd rather say.
2) I'd rather tell you.
3) I'd rather not say.
4) I'd rather say no.

**30.** **Select the option that best completes the passage. (Week 13)**

A: ________________ that you are selling your car. How much is it?
B: Yes. I am selling it for 3000 dollars.

1) I couldn't help for overhearing
2) I couldn't help but overhearing
3) I helped overhearing
4) I couldn't overhear

31-40. Fill in the blanks by using one of the words on the list. Choose the BEST answer for each one. (Week 9~13)

| tip | ulterior |
|---|---|
| biased | spotlight |
| sloppy | iffy |
| cheesy | prevalent |
| chronic | trendy |

31. Perms are very __________ these days. Everyone has one.

32. A recommendation letter written by a family member could be _________.

33. When you're on stage I just have one _______ to give you. Don't forget to smile!

34. This paper looks a little __________ . There is a chance that the student cheated.

35. If you don't want to look _________ you should tuck in your shirt, shave your beard and comb your hair.

36. Attractive people are always the center of attention. They can't help but take the _________ wherever they go.

37. Janice compliments me too much. Do you think she has an _____________ motive?

38. If you flirt in an obvious way it could be seen as somewhat ____________.

39. We found out that the disease is _________ . It's not going away any time soon.

40. The occurrence of tuberculosis is more _______ in Korea than in Canada.

## Answer: Final Exam

| | | | | | | | |
|---|---|---|---|---|---|---|---|
| 1 | ④ | 2 | ① | 3 | ③ | 4 | ④ |
| 5 | ① | 6 | ② | 7 | ③ | 8 | ③ |
| 9 | ② | 10 | ① | 11 | ④ | 12 | ③ |
| 13 | ① | 14 | ④ | 15 | ① | 16 | ④ |
| 17 | ③ | 18 | ④ | 19 | ① | 20 | ④ |
| 21 | ② | 22 | ③ | 23 | ④ | 24 | ③ |
| 25 | ① | 26 | ③ | 27 | ② | 28 | ① |
| 29 | ③ | 30 | ② | | | | |

| | | | |
|---|---|---|---|
| 31 | trendy | 32 | biased |
| 33 | tip | 34 | iffy |
| 35 | sloppy | 36 | spotlight |
| 37 | ulterior | 38 | cheesy |
| 39 | chronic | 40 | prevalent |

# Assignment answer

## Week 1

1. ④ Yeah.
2. ① Oh, no!
3. ③ Wow.
4. ④ Oh!
5. ③ Seriously?
6. ① I'm sorry to hear that.
7. ① Really?
8. ① That's cool.
9. ③ That's great.
10. ④ That's right.

## Week 2

1. ③ What about
2. ① How
3. ② Why
4. ④ Do you
5. ② Where
6. ④ Do you mean
7. ③ Is that
8. ① Did you
9. ② What
10. ② When
11. ④ who

## Week 3

1. ① What do you mean
2. ④ What are you trying to say
3. ③ It sounds like
4. ② Okay, so
5. ④ You think
6. ① What kind of
7. ② I thought
8. ④ You're telling me
9. ① Wait. What?
10. ④ Is that it?

## Week 4

1. ③ Wait. I'm sorry.
2. ② Let me interrupt you.
3. ① May I say something?
4. ③ Hold up.
5. ④ Wait a second.
6. ① Can I ask something?
7. ② Sorry to interrupt, but
8. ④ Excuse me.
9. ① But
10. ③ Could I say something?

## Week 5

1. ③ Ask away.
2. ① Be my guest.
3. ② Sure.
4. ④ You don't agree?
5. ① Fire away!
6. ④ Go ahead.
7. ④ Yes?
8. ③ No, problem.
9. ① Yes.
10. ③ Yes, what is it?

## Week 6

1. ④ I have to say
2. ① You know what?
3. ② I feel
4. ③ If you ask me
5. ④ I think
6. ① In my opinion
7. ④ I do think
8. ② as for me
9. ② As far as I can tell
10. ③ It seems to me

## Week 7

1. ② I totally agree.
2. ④ I guess so.
3. ② I concur.
4. ③ That's what I've been saying.
5. ④ That's true.
6. ① I'm totally with you.
7. ② Yeah, I know.
8. ④ That's a good point.
9. ① Yeah.
10. ③ Of course.

## Week 8 - Midterm Exam

## Week 9

1. ④ I'm not sure I agree.
2. ① I know what you're saying, but
3. ② I'm not sure that's true.
4. ④ Perhaps, but
5. ③ I don't know about that.
6. ① I get that, but
7. ④ I hear you, but
8. ③ On the other hand,
9. ① I disagree.
10. ② I'm afraid I disagree.

## Week 10

1. ③ Look,
2. ① I guess
3. ② I just think that maybe
4. ④ You see,
5. ① You know,
6. ③ it just seems
7. ① To be honest,
8. ① I know,
9. ③ Maybe you should
10. ① kind of

## Week 11

1. ② Talk to me about
2. ④ How about you?
3. ② I hear you saying
4. ④ What's your opinion?
5. ① How do you feel about that?
6. ③ I was hoping you could tell me
7. ④ I'd like to know your take
8. ④ What about you?
9. ② I'm curious to know what you think.
10. ④ What do you think

## Week 12

1. ③ I'm not sure.
2. ④ I'd rather not say.
3. ① That's an interesting question.
4. ② I have no idea.
5. ① Maybe we should
6. ③ I'd have to think about that.
7. ④ I really don't know.
8. ② I'd have to give that some thought
9. ① That's a good question.
10. ④ That's something to think about.

## Week 13

1. ③ I couldn't help but overhearing
2. ① You look so familiar
3. ④ Have we met before
4. ③ Excuse me. I like your
5. ④ Could I ask you something?
6. ① Are you a friend of
7. ② Has anyone ever told you
8. ① Anybody ever told you
9. ④ Pardon me.
10. ③ Can I ask you something

## Week 14 ··············································· Week 15 - Final Exam

1. ④ Oh, no!
2. ② That's great.
3. ③ Did
4. ① What about
5. ② You're telling me
6. ① You think
7. ① Hold up.
8. ② Could I say something?
9. ④ Yes, what is it?
10. ② Fire away!
11. ③ It seems to me
12. ④ I have to say
13. ③ That's what I've been saying.
14. ④ That's a good point.
15. ① I know what you're saying, but
16. ④ I guess so.
17. ① Kind of
18. ① You know,
19. ③ What about you?
20. ② How about you?
21. ② I'd have to give that some thought.
22. ① Maybe you should
23. ③ Can I ask you something
24. ① You look so familiar

# 게임으로 배우는 영어 회화


| | |
|---|---|
| **초판 인쇄** | 2022년 8월 26일 |
| **초판 발행** | 2022년 8월 31일 |
| **지은이** | 조기석 |
| **발행인** | 고윤성 **Director, University Knowledge Press** |
| **편집장** | 신선호 **Executive Knowledge Contents Creator** |
| **도서편집** | 장혜정 **Contents Creator** |
| | 노재은 **Contents Creator** |
| **디자인** | 김대욱 **Designer** |
| | 최선아 **Designer** |
| **인사행정** | 이근영 **Managing Creator** |
| **재무관리** | 조아라 **Managing Creator** |
| | 정예찬 **Managing Creator** |
| | 김문규 **Managing Creator** |
| **사전·앱북** | 장지혜 **Contents Creator** |
| **캐릭터** | 정정은 **Contents Creator** |
| **발행처** | 한국외국어대학교 지식출판콘텐츠원 |
| | 02450 서울특별시 동대문구 이문로 107 |
| | 전화 02)2173-2493-7 |
| | FAX 02)2173-3363 |
| | 홈페이지 http://press.hufs.ac.kr |
| | 전자우편 press@hufs.ac.kr |
| | 출판등록 제6-6호(1969. 4. 30) |
| **인쇄·제본** | (주)케이랩 053)583-6885 |

ISBN 979-11-5901-909-8 [13740]　　정가 18,000원

* 잘못된 책은 교환하여 드립니다.




---


HU:iNE 은 한국외국어대학교출판부의 어학도서, 사회과학도서, 지역학 도서 Sub Brand이다. 한국외대의 영문명인 HUFS, 현명한 국제전문가 양성(International+Intelligent)의 의미를 담고 있으며, 휴인(携引)의 뜻인 '이끌다, 끌고 나가다'라는 의미처럼 출판계를 이끄는 리더로서, 혁신의 이미지를 담고 있다.


이 책의 음원(mp3)은 한국외국어대학교 지식출판콘텐츠원 홈페이지(press.hufs.ac.kr) 게시판-자료실에서 다운받아 사용하시기 바랍니다.